KILLER POKER ONLINE / 2

KILLER POKER ONLINE / 2

Advanced Strategies for Crushing the Internet Game

John Vorhaus

LYLE
STUART

Kensington Publishing Corp.
www.kensingtonbooks.com

LYLE STUART BOOKS are published by

Kensington Publishing Corp.
850 Third Avenue
New York, NY 10022

All Kensington titles, imprints, and distributed lines are available at special quantity discounts for bulk purchases for sales promotions, premiums, fund-raising, educational, or institutional use. Special book excerpts or customized printings can also be created to fit specific needs. For details, write or phone the office of the Kensington special sales manager: Kensington Publishing Corp., 850 Third Avenue, New York, NY 10022, attn: Special Sales Department; phone 1-800-221-2647.

First printing: September 2006

10 9 8 7 6 5 4

Printed in the United States of America

ISBN 0-8184-0661-5

To everyone who says these books have helped.
Thank you for thanking me.

Contents

The Foreword
by Wil Wheaton

I pulled my cell phone from my pocket and hit "2" to speed
dial my wife. The call connected, but went straight to voice
mail. "Hi, this is Anne," my wife's recorded voice said. "I'm
sorry I missed your call, but—"

I hit the pound key and spoke after the beep: "Hey, it's me.
I busted out. Call me when you get the message."

After two days at the 2005 World Poker Tour Championship at Bellagio, two days spent playing the best poker of my
life against the toughest field of professional players I've ever
seen in one place, I'd taken a terrible beat at the hands of an
internet player, and two hands later, took another one at the
hands of Annie Duke. I went from seventh in chips to staring
into Lake Bellagio in a matter of minutes. Such is the reality of
no limit tournament poker.

I closed my phone, shoved it deep into my pocket, and
stared into the lake. A few minutes later, a fellow poker player
gave me a Newcastle Brown Ale. "You look like you could use
it," she said.

I thanked her, put the bottle to my lips, and drank. I leaned
on the rail and resumed staring into the lake. Suddenly, *Con Te*

Partiro boomed and the Bellagio fountains came to life. While they danced, a hand gently tapped me on the shoulder.

I turned around. "Yes?"

The hand belonged to a kind-faced woman who said, "I just saw you bust out. I'm so sorry."

I shrugged my shoulders. Wallowing in misery is every poker player's privilege, as long as we keep the details of our bad beats to ourselves.

"Thanks."

"Would you be willing to talk to John Vorhaus?"

John Vorhaus, I thought, *where have I heard that name before?*

"John's a journalist and the author of *Killer Poker.*"

I wondered if she was just continuing her thought, or if I had a big, fat tell that let her right into my mind.

Of course! I thought. *Ryan gave me* Killer Poker *for my birthday last year.*

"Sure," I said. "But give me a few minutes to compose myself, okay?"

"Of course," she said. "We'll be inside when you're ready."

She walked back into the Fontana Room, and I looked at the lake, the fountains, the Eiffel Tower across The Strip . . . anything to remove the image of two hideous queens hitting the flop from my mind.

A few minutes (and a couple more Newcastles) later, I walked back into the room. I glanced at my chips, neatly stacked in front of Mr. Bust Wil's Kings, and found the kind-faced woman. She stood next to an equally kind-faced man. He wore wire-rimmed glasses and a khaki vest. He made notes as Phil Ivey and Greg Raymer raised and reraised each other preflop. If he hadn't been wearing an UltimateBet cap, I never would have pegged him for a poker writer. He looked more like a war correspondent from Vietnam or El Salvador.

"Ivey's been beating up this table for hours," he whispered to her. "Raymer just came over the top of him for about 30,000."

Raymer put on his trademark "Fossilman" glasses and

rested his chin on his hand. Ivey thought for a long time, before he tapped the felt and mucked his cards with an almost imperceptible nod to Greg.

After a lifetime in the entertainment industry, it's very difficult for me to get star struck, but as I stood there, in the Fontana Room at Bellagio, and watched the 2004 World Series of Poker champion lock horns with one of the game's rising stars, goosebumps rose on my arms. Imagine standing on the field during the Super Bowl or sitting on the bench during the NBA finals (or, if you've bought this book, standing in the Fontana Room at Bellagio during the WPT Championship) and you'll have an approximation of how I felt.

The hand having ended, the man in khaki turned to me and extended his hand.

"Hi, I'm John Vorhaus," he said.

We shook hands.

"You've met my wife, Maxx Duffy," he said, with a nod to the kind-faced woman.

"Yes," I said, as the first genuine smile in hours spread across my face. Somewhere in the back of my mind, in that place I describe as "The Monkey Brain," I knew that I'd just met two kindred spirits who were going to become lifelong friends.

"I'm blogging this for UltimateBet," John said. "Would you mind talking to me about the tournament?"

"I'd be happy to," I said.

We walked back outside, and I told John my bad beat story. He listened and took notes, and I'll never forget how we ended the conversation: "Hey, I would have played both those hands exactly the same way."

"Really?" I said.

"Oh yeah, but sometimes you do everything right and the other guy still catches a four-outer to crush you," he said. "That's poker."

Later that night, I had dinner with John and Maxx. The following day, we traded hand histories and chip counts as we covered the tournament; he for UltimateBet, and me for what I hope will ultimately become my version of *Positively Fifth Street* or *Big Deal*. Over the next five days, as we cemented our friendship, John took me under his wing and willingly answered every question I asked, no matter how stupid, about poker, journalism, poker journalism, and anything else that came into my fragile, eggshell mind. I came to realize that John Vorhaus is the living embodiment of chapter 81 of the *Tao Te Ching*, which says in part:

> *The sage never tries to store things up.*
> *The more he does for others, the more he has.*
> *The more he gives to others, the greater his abundance.*

When you're done with this book, I'm sure you'll agree that John never stores anything up. Within its pages (and its companion *Killer Poker* volumes), John will be to you what he has become to me: teacher, mentor, critic, and friend.

Okay, so now you know what I know: John is a great guy . . . but before I get out of your way and let you get to the actual book you've paid to read, I would like to give an example of what a great teacher he is.

I am a member of Team PokerStars, a group of poker players that includes Greg Raymer, Chris Moneymaker, Isabelle Mercier, Evelyn Ng, and Tom McEvoy. (I, like you, also marvel at how I managed to sneak my way into this incredible company. Maybe when you finish this book, you'll come and replace me.)

Once a week, Tom faces off in a heads up match with the PokerStars player who has accumulated the most points on the PokerStars Tournament Leader Board. From time to time, Tom can't play, and another member of Team PokerStars gets the call to play in his place.

Where do you think this is going?

>>

(When you get to the fourth page of the introduction, that's going to be really, really funny. I promise.)

Ding! I got called off the bench . . . to play against infamous tournament sensation and 2005 European Poker Tour Champion Noah *"Exclusive"* Boeken. I was terrified.

Ring . . . ring . . . ring . . .

"Come on, John, pick up! Pick up!"

Rin—"Hey, Cowboy Wil!"

"Hey, JV."

I dispensed with the usual friendly chatter about the things we both love: baseball, our dogs, movies, and our wives. I got right to the point.

". . . so I accepted the opportunity to play, and then I found out that I'm playing against *Exclusive*."

There was an uncharacteristic silence while John thought.

Finally, he said, "Noah Boeken?"

"Yes. Do you think you could help prepare me for the match?"

John immediately replied, "Of course. I'll email you the chapter on heads up play from *Killer Poker Online/2* right now. Call me when you're done and we'll go from there."

A weight lifted from my shoulders. "Thank you! I owe you several beers."

John laughed and hung up. A few minutes later, I printed out chapter 8, sat beneath a giant Chinese elm tree in my backyard, and began to study.

A few hours later, I was in John's office. We talked for an hour or so, and just as he did at Bellagio, John patiently answered all the questions I had, even when his answers gently indicated that I'd asked the dumbest questions in the history of the world.

"So," John said to me while I scratched his dog Ranger's ears, "how about if we log onto UltimateBet, and you can sweat me while I play a match? Then, we can log onto PokerStars, and I'll sweat you while you play a match?"

I agreed and got to watch John put his *Killer Poker Online* into action. He talked me through each hand, discussed why he made the moves he did, and built a nice chip lead against his opponent. Then, just when victory seemed ensured, he took a horrible, horrible, horrible beat that crippled him. Two or three hands later, he was busted.

Just like me, way back when we met at Bellagio.

"Dude! That was so weak!" I said.

John shrugged his shoulders. "No," he said, calmly, "that's poker. Now you play."

So I did. John never told me what to do, but critiqued each play I made, gently and not so gently . . . I felt like a quarterback getting a private lesson from Joe Montana or a baseball player learning from Ted Williams.

And so it was, with John standing at my back, that *mordred_88* called my all in bet and caught runner-runner to make a straight and bust my A-K.

"This isn't exactly filling me with confidence," I said. "Maybe I should just offer *Exclusive* a chop on the second hand."

We laughed together.

"Okay," said John, "now let's play against each other."

"What a world we live in," I said. "Here we are, sitting not four feet from each other, surrounded by poker chips and cards, and we're going to play online."

He offered, "If you'd rather, we can play a more traditional game."

"Are you kidding me?" I said. "Screw that! Let the computer handle all the heavy lifting!"

Ten minutes later, *Wil_Wheaton* faced off against *JVorhaus* in a $5+.50 online grudge match.

As we played, I used the techniques, psychology, and philosophy John had taught me. I felt confident, in control, and powerful.

John, of course, used the same techniques, psychology, and philosophy, and twenty minutes later, we were still nearly even in chips. Imagine a football game, played entirely between the forty yard lines, if you need a visual.

"It's like I'm playing a me-bot," John said.

"This will be the longest heads up match in the history of online poker," I said.

We continued to fight it out, and eventually I won.

I typed *gg* into the chat box.

"You did not just type into the chat box, when we're in the same room," he said.

I typed *yes i did. lol* into the chat box.

"Okay, let's play again," he said.

We started a new match, and I used John's techniques, psychology, and philosophy to defeat him again. My confidence climbed up one more notch. *Maybe I can give* Exclusive *a run for his money after all,* I thought.

We ended up playing two more times and split them.

Then, "Mister Cowboy Wil," John said graciously, "I have to let you go."

It was the proudest moment of my life.

"I feel like I came to the feet of the master and snatched the pebble from your hand," I said.

John just smiled, and I instantly felt terrible and stupid. Terrible, if I had actually out-played him and now I was gloating; stupid if he'd taken it easy on me to increase my confidence when it mattered.

"I'm really happy that I could help you," he said. "Play as much as you can between now and Sunday, and call me the moment you win."

"Or when I'm knocked out," I said.

"No," John said. "Call me the moment *you win.*"

I smiled. "Okay, I will."

Over the next few days, emboldened by my success in our matches, and using the techniques, psychology, and philosophy John taught me, I went 9-3 in heads up matches online. When I sat down to play Noah Boeken the following Sunday, I expected to feel terrified, hesitant, and outmatched. Instead,

I felt confident, in control, and powerful. Noah and I battled back and forth for 190 hands. I used John's techniques, psychology, and philosophy—the same things you're going to learn in this book—and though I was seriously on the ropes a couple of times, I battled back . . . and won.

Yeah, you read that correctly. I beat the 2005 EPT champion in a heads up match online . . . and if I haven't made it clear by now, it wouldn't have happened without John Vorhaus.

Shortly after the *Congratulations! You finished the tournament in 1st place! Thank you for playing* message popped up on my screen, I did three things:

1. I screamed out, "Holy shit! Anne! I won! Ohmygod Iactuallywonohmygodohmygodohmygod! Holy fucking shit ass shit shit shit!"
2. I called my mom and told her the same thing, but with 25 percent less inappropriate language.
3. I printed out the tournament results, just to make sure it was real.

Then, I called John. "I won!" I said.

"That's fantastic," he said. His voice was remarkably calm, which, I have come to learn, is a big part of who John is. "I'm not surprised at all. Way to go, Cowboy Wil."

I should probably break away from my narrative for a moment to fill in some blanks for you, dear reader: John calls me "Cowboy Wil" for the same reason all my other poker friends call me "Hamlet": that for reasons man was not meant to know, my pocket kings always get killed. That tournament at Bellagio, where John and I met? I had kings twice in three hands. Both times I got all my money in as a big favorite before the flop, and both times I took horrible beats to lose. But that's poker.

And why do I keep saying "that's poker"? Because a huge part of this book is philosophy. And while it's useful to know what hands you should and shouldn't play under certain conditions, poker is a game of imperfect choices and incomplete information. Students of John's books learn that no two hands are the same, and having a good foundation in the philosophy of the game will put more money in your pocket than all the hand charts in the world. When you finish this book, you will know much more than what the correct play is in a certain situation. You will know *why* you do or don't make it.

And remember when I described "the internet player" who made a terrible call to cripple me at Bellagio? I made that distinction because you're going to see a lot of plays online that you simply won't see in a brick-and-mortar casino: people will make insane plays, clever plays, hyper-aggressive plays, and countless fundamental mistakes that always seem to crack your pocket kings. When you finish this book, you won't make those plays, and you'll know how to crush the fools who do.

Remember the tells I wondered about Maxx picking up from me? I mentioned that because physical tells are meaningless online. In fact, one online poker site has made that the cornerstone of their advertising campaign ... but there are certain tells you *can* pick up on (mostly in betting patterns), and when you finish this book, you'll know how to avoid giving them yourself, how to use notes to pick out and record them, and how to use that information to punish your opponents.

Okay, one final thought before I go:

Why play online? Isn't it more "real" to play in a casino?

Well, I live within twenty minutes of Commerce and The Bike in LA, and Las Vegas is a $50, fifty-minute flight (or four-hour drive) away. I have not willingly played in a "real" casino since the World Series of Poker in July 2005. And why should I? Online games are faster, more convenient, and positively swimming with inexperienced players who think poker is just like the final tables on ESPN and WPT and play accordingly. I never have to wait more than a minute or two for a sit and go tournament to start, and if I'm feeling particularly randy, I can play up to four games at once (a fool's errand that I don't recommend, but it's certainly easier to multi-table online than it is in a "real" casino). But the best thing about online? If I get a huge win, or take a terrible loss, and I'm ready to walk away, getting back to my family is as simple as logging off and walking into the living room.

You're going to love this book, and I think you're going to have the same esteem for John as I do when you're finished. And if you'd like to put your newly discovered skills to the test, come over to PokerStars.com and play with me . . . it's been a while since I got to play an official John Vorhaus me-bot.

Always play smart, and may the river be kind.

Namaste.

WIL WHEATON is author of *Just a Geek, Dancing Barefoot,* and *Do You Want Kids with That?* and future World Series of Poker champion.

Acknowledgments

"Writing a book," said Winston Churchill,

is an adventure. To begin with, it is a toy and an amusement; then it becomes a mistress, and then it becomes a master, and then a tyrant. The last phase is that just as you are about to be reconciled to your servitude, you kill the monster, and fling him out to the public.

Writing this book was an adventure of a homebound, sedentary sort, involving long forays into internet poker, quick darts back to my word processor, investigation of online resources, then back to the game, back to the text, back to the game, back to the text, until I could no longer tell whether I was taking breaks from writing to play poker or breaks from poker to write.

My job was, as always, made easier by the unstinting support of my wife, Maxx Duffy, who, with the patience of several saints, would often stick her head in my office, find me playing yet another sitngo and, smiling, say, "Hard at work, I see." My job is also made easier by the support of my parents, who take bemused pride in their prodigal boy. My dad has Alzheimer's disease now and no longer quite knows what I'm up to, but that never stops him from saying, "Keep doing what you're doing."

I owe a huge debt to everyone associated with UltimateBet .com, too numerous to mention, but not too numerous to thank. As UB's news ambassador and blogger-without-portfolio, I have had the opportunity to extend and expand my "weird cult following," and even parlay it into a TV poker gig on Fox Sports Net. Props to all UBers, players and staff alike. You guys rule cyberspace, IMHO.

Tony Guerrera rules numbers in a way I never could, and here's a big shout out to him for his worthy contribution here. Thanks to Cowboy Wil Wheaton for chipping in with the foreword, and thanks also to Greg Dinkin and Frank Scatoni of Venture Literary Agency, whose instincts are unerring and efforts unrelenting. In the words of my dad, "Keep doing what you're doing."

Last, a humble and heartfelt thanks to you, the reader of these words. You make my life rise.

Introduction:
THE BLESSING AND THE
CURSE

I had a long layover in London's Heathrow Airport last night. With hours to kill and a laptop computer as my weapon of choice, I went looking for some wireless internet access so I could log on to my UltimateBet account and beguile the time with a little online poker. This being the budding 21st century and not the dark dial-up days of 1999, I had no difficulty finding a hotspot in a pub just off the main departure lounge, nearby Clarke's Shoes, Boots the Chemist, and Glorious Britain, purveyors of fine English trinkets including plastic bobby helmets at 2 pounds 30 pence each.

Booting up and logging on were a snap, and though the connection was pricey, north of three bobby helmets an hour, I figured to cover the cost with my usual stellar style of online play: selective, aggressive, and viper-quick to exploit the flaws of others. It seemed like a foolproof plan, and would have been but for the inopportune involvement of a certain fool: me. See, I had just flown overnight from Los Angeles, an eleven-hour grind during which I had watched three bad movies, eaten two horrific meals, finished one *New York Times* crossword puzzle, and slept not at all. Worse, I was now in an

English pub, where indulging my taste for British beer seemed like the logical thing to do. "Think globally, drink locally," right?

Well, it's a toxic combination, sleep debt and strong ale, and it rendered my normally solid online poker in exactly the sense that one renders fat: removing the meat and muscle and leaving just soft, squishy goo. By the time they called my flight to Rome, I had managed to piss away two weeks' worth of hard-earned online profit. I hope that *mokey23*, the main beneficiary of my largess, appreciated the gift.

And that's internet poker in a nutshell in these budding days of the 21st century: It takes long-term steady play and steely concentration to win any kind of serious coin online, but it takes only a momentary lapse of reason to lose it all back again. The blessing and the curse of online poker is that it's available to us 24 hours a day, 7 days a week, 365 days a year, and, increasingly these days, through 360 degrees of global longitude, too. (Comes the day we can log on at 30,000 feet we'll run the real risk of defunding entire travel budgets before the plane even lands.) With easy, immediate access to the game we love, it's no wonder we enter play in almost every conceivable state of mind: sleepy, grumpy, dopey, and several other flavors of dwarf.

I'm not telling you anything you don't know, I know. If you've played even a small amount of internet poker, you've no doubt already encountered its common pitfalls. You know what it's like to seduce yourself into playing the wrong game at the wrong time. You've seen your bankroll in catastrophic freefall. You've suffered through a string of bad beats so improbable that, logic and common sense notwithstanding, you've allowed yourself to believe that the online game is fixed, frozen solid, with the virtual deck stacked against you and you alone. You've staggered away from the computer feeling like the victim of alien possession, which alien's nefarious agenda was to piss away as fast as possible all of your money to *mokey23*. You have learned, in other words, the fundamental truth of online play, a truth that countless players have learned in the scant years of internet poker's existence:

IT'S EASIER TO LOSE FAST
THAN TO WIN FAST

Why might this be true? For one thing, winning fast relies on the harmonic convergence of many good cards and many bad players, a convergence that's relatively rare. Losing fast, though, requires only *your* bad play, and if you're playing badly, you're *always* there, hand after hand after miserable, execrable, disastrous hand. I can think of some other reasons for explosive bankroll decompression, and I'll list them in a moment, but I'd like you to think of some, too. This book, like all my books, is intended to be interactive. You'll only get out of it what you put into it, and what I specifically want you to put in is your own original thought, for reading a book is one thing, but participating in it is something altogether else. So I encourage you to embrace the idea of doing the mental exercises presented in these pages. You don't have to do them all, and you don't have to do them particularly well. No one will be looking over your shoulder grading your effort. But if you're determined to get your money's worth from this book's cover price of seven bobby helmets (at current rates of exchange), you'll make the effort not just to read the thing, but to engage it, involve yourself in it, make it your own. That's how one's practice of poker grows.

So let's think together, shall we, about why and how we find it easy to lose fast online. Here are some ways my bankroll bleeds:

I play when I'm tired, when my judgment is soft. I play angry, or keep playing when I've been made angry. I distract myself with television, telephone or radio. I play in tough environments like pubs in British airports. I play in games too big for my bankroll. I play too many games at once. I play when I

just don't care. Once I played in a post-operative, Vicodin-
addled haze, and man was that a crash-and-burn.

And now here are some ways yours does:
>>

You'll note that I've left you some jotting space on the pages, and any time you see the >> symbol, it means *your thoughts here*. Or you can keep a notebook, or open a computer file. It really doesn't matter how you record your thoughts, so long as you *do* record your thoughts. As I said, that's how the practice of poker grows.

And it's growing your practice of poker that really interests me. Whether you play online for fun or for profit, you naturally want to do the best you can. You naturally want to improve. So it's reasonable to set the goal of *improvement* over even the goal of winning. Presumably if improvement happens, winning will follow. Of course, improvement requires tools, techniques, strategy, tactics, and deep understanding . . . all of which I confidently hope to bring you in this book. But improvement also requires the right state of mind: a state of mind that acknowledges setbacks and takes them in stride, that recognizes errors and moves to correct them and that notes without rancor past pitfalls and determines to avoid them in the future.

This is not just a matter of saying, "I will play poker with discipline." It's fine to be disciplined—necessary, in fact—but discipline only squelches the urge, it doesn't address the underlying cause. You might have the willpower to not smoke a cigarette all day, all week, or all month, but until you've actually *quit smoking,* you haven't changed your state of mind. I might be "disciplined" enough not to play poker next time I'm killing time in Heathrow (or I might not) but until I confront my underlying cockiness, all I have is a fundamentally flawed state of mind that says, *I can beat this game anywhere, any time, even at Heathrow, even under the influence of sleep debt and strong ale.* From that p(o)int forward, it doesn't matter if I play specific hands with discipline or not. I've already made the mistake of indiscipline, and disaster is the predictable result.

The right state of mind for an online poker player, then, is *attentive humility.* Being attentive means simply bringing all of your concentration and focus to bear when you settle in for an online session. Humility means never imagining that you've got the game licked. You haven't. I haven't. The top pros haven't. Nobody has. All any of us can do is strive to keep closing the gap between the players we are and the players we want to be. And that's the "blessing" part of internet poker's blessing-and-curse construction. While it's possible to lose fast, it's also possible to learn fast—faster than previous generations of poker players could ever have imagined. There are so many different sites offering so many different games, structures, limits, satellites, and tournaments (and speeds—regular, turbo, even ultra turbo) that excellence in poker is an achievable goal for he or she who has a mind to put his or her mind to it.

While I'm stumbling through this thicket of awkward pronouns, let me take a moment to address the issue of awkward pronouns. In a perfect world, there would be a gender-neutral third person singular pronoun that we could use instead of his/her, he/she, or they. So far, this gift of language has not been bestowed upon English, nor is it likely to crop up between now and when I finish this book. Should I then use a stilted construction, nod to political correctness and use *she,* or bow to convenience and use *he?*

I'm gonna go with convenience. Though women are entering poker in record numbers (and, from Annie Duke and Jennifer Harmon to anonymous distaff winners of cash games and tournaments worldwide, proving themselves capable of waxing any man's keister), the fact yet remains that the vast majority of poker players, both online and in the realworld realm, are male. It's changing, but it has a long way to go. With that in mind, then, I'm going to use *he* as the default personal pronoun in this book, and take it as given that, whether you pee standing up or sitting down, you'll cut me some slack.

Further to the subject of cutting slack, I hope you won't mind if you find in this text one or two things borrowed from my earlier *Killer Poker* books. If this is your first visit to Killer Poker Land, I urge you to spend some time in your local bookstore skimming some of the other titles and bringing yourself up to speed, for much of what we talk about here will be based on, and built from, much of what we talked about there. Or skip all that and just absorb the core Killer Poker philosophy, "Go big or go home." In any case, there's bound to be a certain amount of repetition, and that's by design. It's not that I can't count on you to remember having read it, or that I can't count on me to remember having written it. It's just that some points bear repeating, and I won't be shy about repeating them as necessary.

One big difference between those books and this: the form of poker under consideration here is exclusively no limit Texas hold'em. Since I wrote the first *Killer Poker* book (or even since I wrote the last one), no limit hold'em (NLHE) has taken over, both online and in the realworld. Other types of poker endure, for sure, but NLHE is the 800-pound gorilla in poker's living room right now. You can't ignore it and you can't avoid it, so you might as well invite it to sit on the sofa and offer it a banana. The situations I will speak to in this book, then, are those of NLHE. If you favor Omaha, seven-card stud, or one-up, two-up high-low strawberry, I hope you can extract some relevance from my examples. If not, what can I say? I know that most of you play no limit hold'em, so no limit hold'em is what we'll discuss.

Per this discussion, consider the wannabe rounder living in North Platte or South Bend, circa 1996. Apart from his (or her; okay, his) home games, he might only get to play real poker against real foes a couple of times a year, during infrequent forays to Las Vegas or distant riverboats, there to cram in as many hours of poker as his brief stints allow. In the name of improving his play, he could very well have it in mind to investigate different approaches to playing a hold'em hand like K-Q suited under the gun (UTG). Trouble is, he may encounter that hand only once or twice during his stay; a mere handful of times during his whole poker playing year. It's tough to go to school on a subject when meaningful lessons are so few and far between.

Now fast forward ten years to the brave new world of internet poker, where if you want to put in twenty or thirty hours at the table, you need only unplug the phone and lay in a healthy supply of Red Bull. Given the accelerated pace of play online, with hands coming at you fast and furious (2x fast and 2x furious if you're playing more than one game at a time) it's reasonable to expect to see that same UTG K-Q suited a couple of times an hour, giving you ample opportunity to analyze and strategize, refining your approach to playing that hand while your last experience of it is still fresh in your mind.

The impact of this supercharged learning curve cannot be understated. From internet qualifier Chris Moneymaker's win at the main event of the 2003 World Series of Poker forward, we have seen poker players weaned on internet play crossing over to triumph in large tournaments and live cash games. Why do you suppose this is? What advantages do you imagine an internet player has over someone who has only played in realworld games?

>>

Here's one I can think of: An internet player, accustomed as he is to the blistering pace of online play, may find live games to be luxuriously slow. Relative to what he's used to, live play offers ample time to analyze situations, weigh factors, and come to conclusions. Adjusting to the brick-and-mortar (b&m) realm, he actually gears down to a much slower speed, not unlike a runner who has trained with ankle weights but removes them before a big race. Nor do individual decisions vex him, for he has practiced making poker choices by the thousands or tens of thousands in the privacy of his own home (or office when the boss wasn't looking) for the last seventeen months straight, for hours at a time. He has seen a lifetime's worth of hands and crammed a lifetime's worth of learning into his short poker sojourn.

Here's another edge I can think of: We outnumber them. Five years ago, the internet player in a realworld tournament was an oddity, a rarity. Leather-assed cardroom veterans viewed us as dead money, test tube babies with no clue and no chance. Moneymaker alone did not change all that. He just waved the flag of the future. Now, every realworld poker tournament, large or small, features a field filled with savvy and schooled internet players. Some tournaments, like the Party Poker Million and UltimateBet's Ultimate Poker Classic in Aruba, were created specifically to give online players a realworld target, if you will, to shoot for. Online players have crossed over to b&m cash play in force as well, and while the snide old guard may still regard us individually as dead money, collectively we define the field. Not to put too fine a point on it, if you want victory in realworld poker these days, you're gonna have to go through internet players to get it.

Of course, the internet player does not have every edge. Many online players making the transition to realworld play have no experience in picking off tells, for instance, or guarding against giving off their own. You can often recognize an internet player in a b&m game by the fact of his folding (or tipping his intention to fold) before the action gets to him. He's used to clicking the *fold in turn* button on his computer, and not aware of the need to wait to act. Internet players can also be quite impatient. Used to playing a souped-up version of the game, they can find the practical considerations of real-world play—the pushing of pots, the shuffling of cards—make b&m games annoyingly, even agonizingly, slow. Impatience, of course, can lead to the loosening of starting standards and other reckless adventures. Can you think of additional ways that internet players cede advantage in a realworld game?

>>

In any event, the distinction between internet player and b&m player is getting fuzzier and fuzzier with each passing day. Just a few years ago, online players occupied a sort of ghetto; you felt sorry for them because they didn't live in a place where cardroom poker was available and they had to make do with that sorry substitute, the online game. Many—most?—realworld players had at the same time a certain hidebound resistance to online play. It wasn't the game they grew up with, and they viewed it with disdain. They couldn't imagine sitting down to a computer screen if b&m games were available to them. Today's serious poker player has no such prejudice. He knows that online poker is no less "real" than realworld poker and considers it his mission to master both. He has learned what those in the vanguard knew to be true from the start: Online poker is no better nor worse than realworld play; it's just different, that's all.

It's odd to think of "a few years ago" as ancient history, yet, in the swiftly evolving world of internet poker, that's exactly what it is. A few years ago, you could count the number of viable internet poker sites on one hand. Now, you can't even keep track; new sites spring up every day. (*Naming* online poker sites is a growth industry; so far as I know, shoemoney tonight.org, floptopset.net, and pokerbeatsworking.com remain unclaimed.) Not only has online poker evolved but also a whole support industry has sprung into being, with data mining "sniffer" programs like Poker Tracker, online poker news and strategy sites, poker schools, discussion boards, blogs, bulletin boards and forums, ad nauseum. Furthermore, online sites have become a mainstay of realworld tournaments, funneling players by the hundreds or thousands to such prestigious televised tournaments as the World Series of Poker and those of the World Poker Tour.

It's worth talking about television for a minute, for if internet poker is a forge for new players, then televised poker is the fuel that fires it. Thanks to the invention of the lipstick cam, allowing us at last to see what all those lying liars actually hold, poker on television has gone from the functional equivalent of watching snow melt to some of the most compelling reality TV on the air today. In turn, the ready availability of internet poker means that anyone who watches Pro Poker Throwdown or whatever can instantly scratch the inevitable itch to play.

The fact that "ordinary guys" are winning on TV merely enhances the appeal of televised poker and in fact creates a delicious vicious circle. People see people winning millions in televised tournaments. They're inspired to play online; they do so, and some of them satellite their way into the televised tournaments. There, their sheer weight of numbers ensures another win, or at least a high finish, for another average Joe. People see said Joe bringing home the cheese, and the cycle begins again.

In the meantime, the internet poker player base continues to expand, and those who have been around for a while—or those who learn fast—continue to profit. This, too, goes against the conventional wisdom of, say, 2002, when it was glibly predicted that anyone who wanted to make money playing internet poker had sure as hell better do it fast before all the fish were caught, skinned, filleted, pan fried, and digested with a greedy and self-satisfied burp. Now we know otherwise. Sure, losing players go broke and quit online poker every day. They hazard 100 or 200 bucks, and when their bankroll's gone they decide that their time is better spent on other leisure activities like philately or quoits. But others come along to take their place, and this will continue so long as televised poker—poker porn, if you will—keeps whipping newbies into a frenzy of poker excitement.

Sure, the bubble may burst. Governments might crack down. Global economies could collapse, and leave none of us with two virtual nickels to rub together. The polar icecaps might melt and flood us all. Certainly the media, with its notoriously short attention span, will eventually turn its shining spotlight elsewhere. But even when that happens, we'll still have a poker playing population that has increased geometrically in recent years. The waters will continue to teem with fish.

Does this mean that internet poker is an ongoing gold rush? Of that I'm not so sure. Undoubtedly, hundreds or thousands of players have won hundreds or thousands of dollars playing poker on the internet. Have they held onto their winnings? They'll tell you they have, but you can't necessarily trust their assertions, for poker players, like all bettors, may suffer from gamnesia, the tendency to forget last week's losses and remember only the wins. Plus, as we know, it's easier to lose fast than to win fast online. Many is the healthy bankroll that has suddenly suffered and died.

Worse, as many successful online poker players have discovered, it's a challenge to move money out of the virtual realm and into our realworld wallets. I'm not talking about the mechanics of moving money around; that problem has long since been solved. Nor am I talking about shady sites bogarting your dough, though that has happened and can happen, and it pays to play only at sites you trust. Rather, I'm talking about the need to maintain a large bankroll to keep generating large profit. Cut significantly into your bankroll (to pay the rent, say) and you have to drop down to lower levels, and potentially less profitable games, to protect your bankroll from a big negative swing that could kill it.

So there is, I think, a certain mythos surrounding internet poker. Many people see it as an opportunity to Get Rich Quick in Your Bathrobe. While some have, most don't. As with any gold rush, it's the efforts of the many that fund the fortunes of the few. Will this book make you one of the few? I wish I could say for sure that it will, but that would neither be truthful nor, I think, doing you a service. After all, it's in the nature of the few to be, well, few. While diligent and dedicated players are not in short supply online, even the diligent and dedicated may lack the smarts, confidence, drive, talent, time, discipline, home life, mindset, and skill set to win big online.

Plus, you could always get unlucky.

Thus, we have internet poker as it presents itself to us in the budding days of the 21st century. It's not the money tree that many of us hoped it would be. It's not the road to ruin that many of us (or maybe many of our spouses, pets, or clergy) feared it would be. At the end of the day, it's "a powerful force that can only be used for good or for evil." How we use it has always been, and continues to be, pretty much up to us.

Sigh.

I shoulda bought the bobby helmets instead.

Rome, March 2005

PART I

♣♠♦♥

THE MIND GAME

♧♤♢♡

1
♣ ♠ ♦ ♥
WHO ARE YOU?

♧ ♤ ♢ ♡

I can read minds, sort of.

No, I can't guess your favorite color or think of your number from one to ten, but I can make a reasonably good stab at what's in most people's heads most of the time. The art came easily to me once I understood that 90 percent of everything everybody thinks is pretty much the same as everybody else. I discovered this skill in a poker game, waiting for a guy to bet or not bet into a really scary board of A♣-Q♣-J♣. I held just 8♥-7♦ and I remember being afraid the guy would bet, for I would have to credit him with a piece of that flop, and fold. And then it hit me with the force of revelation: If I'm afraid of the board, *so is he!* Looking at him, I could almost see the little thought balloon floating over his head:

Please don't bet!

When he checked, I bet and won the pot. Thus did my mind reading career begin.

I have since learned that mind reading is a useful skill across a wide range of my activities. As a writer trying to figure out how characters in stories think, I start by asking myself: *What do I think?* From this I can extrapolate what's going on in my characters' minds. As an editor working with writers, it's easy for me to know what my writers are afraid of—hard censure, hard notes, and hard work—because when I'm a writer working with an editor, I'm afraid of these things, too. Negotiating has also become easier for me since I learned not just to see things from the other fellow's point of view, but really to inhabit and own his perspective.

The trick of mind reading, then, turns out to be simple. To read other people's minds, start by reading your own. If you're open enough and honest enough to tell yourself what you really, truly think and feel and hope and fear, you'll pretty much have the measure of everyone around you. If you tell yourself these things in a vague and approximate way, you end up with a vague and approximate notion of others' thoughts. But if you analyze yourself with precision and in detail, you get a precise and detailed look into other people's heads.

Do you think I'm wrong? Try it. In fact, try it on me. I'll bet you can easily list five things I'm thinking right now. Start by asking yourself what you think of my claim to be able to read minds, and what you would be thinking if you were me, trying to sell that claim to you.

>>

Here are some of the things I'm thinking:

- *I don't think they'll buy it; it's such an outlandish claim.*
- *But it really works, and it works on so many levels.*
- *They're probably wondering what this has to do with poker.*
- *Speaking of poker, I'd rather be playing right now than writing.*
- *I wonder if I've gotten any new email in the last five minutes.*
- *They're gonna think I'm crazy, starting a poker book with a rant about mind reading.*

- *Maybe I am crazy, starting a poker book with a rant about mind reading.*
- *But we all know that simple self-awareness is the golden key to success in poker, and even if we can't read others' minds, there's no end of benefit to being willing and able to read our own.*
- *Or maybe we don't all know that. Maybe just I believe it.*
- *Gosh, maybe I'm on the wrong track.*
- *In fact, what gives me the authority to write this book in the first place?*
- *You're a fraud, JV. Soon everyone will know.*
- *No new email. Just spam.*

Did you get me right? Half right? Even a little bit right? What did you learn about me? (And, oh, by the way, what did you learn about *you?*) As you can see, you don't even need to be in the immediate company of the person whose mind you're trying to read. Is this not useful in online poker, where our foes are scattered all over the planet, and all we have available to decipher them is the scant information they make available to us through their screen names, points of origin, bets and raises, checks and calls, buy ins, rebuys, and very occasional lines of chat?

Now let me explore what I think I know about you. I don't expect to get you completely, but check me if some of this doesn't apply. First, as mentioned earlier, I think you're probably male. That's not mind reading, though, just demographics. From home games, to Duffy's Card Shack, to online play, to the main event at the World Series of Poker, men comprise the thick majority of the poker playing community. Online, of course, any he-man can hide behind a screen name like *CurlyShirley*, so it doesn't pay to make too many spurious gender judgments. That said, I'll assume that most of my readers are male; you should assume that most of your online opponents are, too.

You're young, I surmise, for the bulk of the online playing population is, as are most poker book buyers and readers.

You're young enough and eager enough not only to invest your time and energy in online play but also to invest your time and energy in *improving* your play. As we grow older—as you'll discover if you're yet young—it gets harder and harder to keep the flame of learning burning. It can be done, of course, but that adage about old dogs and new tricks is not without merit. If I'm wrong, by the way, if you're not young, then more power to you for staying alive in your mind long after most of your peers have sunk into the know-it-all complacency that antecedes stuffy nostalgia, long naps on the davenport, and death.

You probably live in the United States. Whether it's that our culture and technology create a favorable environment for the online player, or that the rest of the world simply hasn't caught up or caught on, I can't say. It's worth noting that while most players are U.S. citizens, not a single online poker site has its corporate home or computer servers on U.S. soil. This is for legal reasons, of course, but it amuses me to think that I live in a place where it's legal to play online but not legal to host the game. (Now I'm being disingenuous. It's *not* legal to play online; it's just that there are so many of us that the powers-that-be are powerless to impose their will on us. Thus is it always. When law enforcement battles technology, technology wins.) Though you live in the United States, you enjoy playing against people from Australia, Sweden, Burkina Faso, and Nagorno-Karabakh. It brings a touch of the exotic to your life.

Talking of young and talking of legal, there's a fairly good chance that you're below legal gambling age. You have discovered in online poker a way to play poker for real even though technically you're not allowed. At this point I should issue a disclaimer: If you're not street legal where you live, please use the information in this book on play money sites only, will you? Thanks. Glad we got that out of the way.

You may be in college; so many online players are. If you're not there now, you most likely were, for internet poker requires smarts across a broad range of subjects—math, computers, psychology—plus, people who buy and read books of any kind are much more likely to be higher educated than, you know, not. You and your friends might consider it the height of good fun to spend a Friday or Saturday evening immersed in the online poker experience. I could tell you and your friends that you need to get a life, but I'm not your dorm mother, so no.

If cardroom poker is not readily available in your neck of the weeds, you consider online poker to be a godsend. Even if casinos are legion and close, you spend a hunk of your budgeted poker time online because it's just so damn convenient. No traffic, no parking problems, no boho with bad breath sitting next to you. You probably play at least a little online poker every day. You find the puzzle of poker to be endlessly fascinating and utterly compelling. You've tried various sites, but over time you've made one or two your home. Likewise, you've experimented with a wide variety of cash games, sitngos (sit and go tournaments), and scheduled tournaments, and have settled on your favorites. Though you mix it up from time to time, you play what you play—mostly, as noted, no limit hold'em. Furthermore, you play within a "comfort zone" of limits and/or buy ins, unless the tidal ebb or flow of your bankroll dictates a shift down or up.

You have experienced the pitfalls of online poker, including unexpected disconnects, untimely interruptions, sites going south (and taking your money with them), and unbelievable suckouts. Despite all that talk of collusion, you haven't seen any, nor have you seen any evidence of bots, either independent or site sponsored. It crosses your mind that you might not know the difference, but even viewed through the narrow prism of an avatar or a screen name, all of your online foes strike you as all too human. Besides, if they're bots, they're not all that good, so who cares?

You've met your share of angerbots, though: people who lose their temper online and use the protective anonymity of a screen name to launch testosterone- and rage-fueled chat-box screeds:

> How could you call with that sh*t?
> You're the worst player ever!
> aaaaasssssshhhhhooooollllleeeee!!!!!

Perhaps you've even lost your temper in this way, though you know enough, one hopes, not to let such sentiment bleed out your chat window, or, indeed, affect your play. One hopes. Still, you know what it's like to be pissed off online. Maybe it pisses you off that people get pissed off. Certainly, there's *something* that pisses you off about online poker. Probably several somethings. These include . . .

>>

In writing that list, you discovered one or two things you didn't even know bugged you that much. Such is the power of the list.

In sum, then: You're no newbie. You've played enough on-line poker to be well past questions of site functionality and game mechanics. You've got basic strategy down pat. You don't know all your odds inside out, but you know enough not to draw slim into a small pot, and you know not to play crap hands (even if sometimes you do). You've read many poker books, and you've learned at least a little something from all of them. You have high hopes for this book. You'd like to take your internet game to the next level, or at least get your money's worth in terms of tools for profit on the virtual felt. I have high hopes, too, and feel safe in promising that you'll learn enough at least to cover the cover price. But check back with me in about 85,000 words and we'll both know.

Now, let's get started, shall we? We've got a lot of work to do.

2

♣ ♠ ♦ ♥

SHARPS AND FLATS

♧ ♤ ♢ ♡

On my worst days of online poker, I willfully distract myself to a ridiculous degree. I might be playing in a scheduled tournament, a sitngo, and a cash game, all at the same time. The radio is on, or maybe a podcast. I've got the TV showing a baseball game with the sound down, and I'm scratching my dog behind his ears because my dog insists. I'm also answering emails, taking phone calls, and beating my head against the word processor—and it's still not enough to occupy my restless mind. As you can imagine, this is not the best way to play internet poker, letting it engage so small a sliver of my interest. And guess what? I know it, too. Not that this stops me from doing it . . . nor ruing it when, inevitably, the telephone, the television, or my own purple prose causes me to miss critical information on the poker screen or hit *raise* when I meant to hit *fold*.

On my best days of online poker, I turn off everything: all the music, sound, and pictures. I close Word and Outlook Express. I close the door, which can annoy the dog, but I explain it to him in terms he can understand: Daddy's winning kibble money now. I lay a single game screen against my computer desktop—a soothing picture of poppies—and give a single cash game or tournament table my full and undivided attention. I may or may not be taking notes, but I'm certainly taking everything in. *Seat one likes to reraise from the small blind. Seat three will bet the turn if no one bets the flop. Seat six likes to drag (slow play) his big hands.* I am acquiring, as I described it in *The Killer Poker Hold'em Handbook,* the clear gestalt of the game. I'm in tune with what's going on, because I'm fully focused. As Mrs. Malaprop might put it, I'm dilated in.

Then again I have this friend, screen name *WiggleTooth,* on whose monstrously large LCD monitor he plays four games at once. He plays big, too, $500 buy in NLHE x 4, for hour after hour, and insists that playing four games at once not only maximizes his hourly win rate but keeps him from playing too loose through impatience or boredom, because with so much going on onscreen, he has no time to be impatient or bored. This guy keeps meticulous records, and I've seen them. Literally, the only time he doesn't perform well is when he's playing just one game: His mind wanders, his play degrades, and he loses money. Incredibly enough, single dipping is a gaping hole in his game.

All of which is to say that everyone has a best and a worst way to play online. I used to think that double dipping—playing even so much as two games at once—was a recipe for sure disaster. Having seen evidence to the contrary, from *WiggleTooth* and others, I'm now prepared only to say that I know one person who should never double dip, and that's, well, me.

Every time we sit down to play online, we're faced with variables, choices not just of game type and betting limit, or tournament versus cash play, but also of environment: music or no music; phone or no phone; rats gnawing at our feet or no rats gnawing at our feet. How you sort and select these variables is up to you, but one thing you *must* do is sort and select. To play online consistently effectively, you have to give some thought to, and honest inspection of, when and how you play poorly or well. More to the point, you have to figure out what's going on when you don't play well, and then see to it that *it never happens again.*

I'm trusting that you have enough experience of online

play, and enough personal frankness, to address this question in a meaningful way. Do you drink when you play online? How does that work out for you? Do you go for that one extra cash game rebuy or that one last sitngo when things haven't been going your way? Do things continue not to go your way? Do you play when you're tired? This one's particularly insidious, because we poker players get tired and wired at the same time. We're so wound up from playing poker that the only thing we imagine winding us down is, hey, more poker. However, since we're also tired, we can't really play effectively. Also, being tired degrades our ability, among other things, to perceive being tired.

There are a couple of approaches you can take to really get to the heart of how you inhabit your online poker space. One is to spend frequent moments in quiet contemplation of the question, remembering that the point of the exercise is not to recriminate but just to ruminate, and that open, honest acceptance of all your aspects is the true path of the poker warrior. Another is to keep a notebook by your computer, or a computer file labeled "State of Mind" and in it just record in passing all your observations about the way you think and the choices you make. I divide my notes into "Sharps"—ways I play better—and "Flats"—ways I play worse. Here are a few of each I have noticed, and noted, in my play:

SHARPS
Heads up play
Playing in the morning
Not afraid to lose
Confident (even arrogant)
Fresh hot coffee
After a good day's work
Sufficiently funded for the game
Happy
By myself

FLATS
Double dipping
Alcohol
Playing tired
Angry at the world
When I stop caring
Taking phone calls
Trying for a hit-and-run win
Avoiding work
Feeling guilty about avoiding work

Thinking about your own online playing experience now, fill in some blanks if you will.

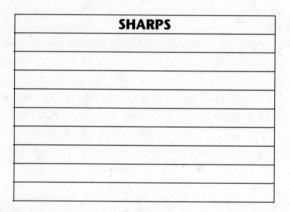

SHARPS

FLATS

There are many other ways to think about how you inhabit the situation of online poker. It's a question that never gets fully answered. Nor should it, for there's always room for improvement. What I want to stress—what I can't stress enough—is the need to be sensitive to your mindset. Be open and articulate with yourself about what works and doesn't work for you. From time to time your ego may take a beating. Mine certainly does when, for instance, I call a big bet when I *just know* I'm beat, and then have to face the sad fact of my own stupid stupidity. But ego is not the issue. *Money* is the issue, and it's axiomatic that the more frequently you bring your *sharp* mind to the table instead of your *flat* one, the more money you'll make playing poker. Only you can know whether you've got the sharp or the flat mind in play, and you will only know if you're frank. Let your ego take its lumps. Your bankroll will thank you in the end.

Be aware also of how quickly you can shift from sharp to flat. It only takes a hand or two to send you spinning down . . .

You're in the middle of a multi-table tournament, and you've got it going on, with a reasonable stack, a decent image, and a nice, crisp mind. Then you pick up pocket aces on the button. It's folded around to you. You raise and get a loose call from someone who (a) has no business being in the hand, (b) sticks around for a ridiculous draw, (c) gets there, and (d) takes all your chips.

Check your state of mind right now. What emotions are you feeling? Anger? Rage? Despair? Resentment? Is any of these emotions conducive to perfect poker? Asked and answered, counselor, asked and answered.

Now you compound the problem. Instead of saying, "Well, that happens," and retiring from play for the day, you immediately jump into a sitngo, desperate to purge the bitter taste from your mouth. So desperate, in fact, that you come out storming, trying to run the table through the sheer force of your bully behavior. And your strategy—no, I won't call it a strategy, I'll call it an attitude—works for a while because your opponents (sensible people not currently suffering from psychic lockjaw) are taking the time to size you up. While you're doing your thing, they're going to school on you. *Well,* they're thinking, *he's the straw that stirs the drink. Or anyway so he thinks.* After that, it's a simple matter for them to lay out, play passively, and let you hoist yourself on the petard of your own uncontrollable wrath.

Trying to make J-T look like A-A, you get out ahead of a hand.

Someone plays back at you.

You're not ready to relinquish your table captain's hat, so you raise back.

Somehow all the money gets in the middle.

And you're on the wrong side of pocket aces.

You bust out most heinously.

And you instantly jump into another sitngo. Now you're really ticked! *I'll show me!* you silently shout as you whack off your nose to spite your face. Understand that from this point forward you have no hope of playing well. While it's easy to slip from sharp to flat, it's almost impossible to go the other direction. Ghosts of recent mistakes will haunt you. Rage and remorse will degrade your play. There's only one thing to do now. *Tear yourself away from the table!* Leave. Go for a walk. Go for a beer. Go for a *schvitz.* Just get away from your computer before you make a bad situation worse, much worse. The damaged state of mind I'm describing here is one of the leading causes of superheated online loss.

You know what? If the situation I've just described has never happened to you, that's great. If it's happened to you and you can admit it, that's bad but not a disaster. If it's happened to you and you know it's happened, *and you still won't admit it,* then you've got a problem you need to address right now. If it helps, the situation I've just described hasn't happened to me since, oh, well, yesterday. *And I'm the guy who writes the books!* Does it undermine my credibility to tell you this? I don't think so. I think I'm just modeling honesty. I've learned to accept my mistakes. But I've also learned to get away from the game.

So go easy on yourself, but be hard on yourself, too. Accept that you'll have these flare ups. Accept that your emotions will get the better of you. Just don't accept sticking around when it happens.

Without going all new age on your ass, I think the critical component of sharp play online is actually, oddly, *good spirit*. So many weird bad things happen to us online . . . we get trapped, we get unlucky, we get disconnected, we get sucked out on . . . the list goes on and on. If online poker is to be part of our daily experience, it needs to be something we can embrace with joy, even when weird bad things happen. Otherwise, over time, the screen becomes our enemy, and though we like to play, want to play (need to play?) we don't have fun when we play. We start expecting weird bad things to happen to us, and when they do, partly because we bring them down on ourselves through weird bad play, we just sink deeper and deeper into the glower.

Lighten up! Remember the words of the sage:

YOU'RE BORN BROKE, YOU DIE BROKE, EVERYTHING ELSE IS JUST FLUCTUATION.

But if your fluctuation is negative because your state of mind needs tending, then you'll just end up pouring more and more money into your online experience, and I can't see *that* making you happy, can you? So, let's boil it down to the simplest of terms we can:

1. If you're sharp, keep playing.
2. If you're flat, don't.
3. See yourself as you are.
4. Have fun.

Moving on . . .

3

♣ ♠ ♦ ♥

HANDLES

♧ ♤ ♢ ♡

When you first start playing online, the information available to you seems so scant you almost feel like you're flying blind. All the old familiar clues and cues of the cardroom or casino environment are missing. You can't look your foes in the eye, pick off physical tells, overhear their conversations, or watch for the telltale lapses in concentration that show when they're losing their sharp. You've got nothing to go on but a thin trickle of deductions gleaned from screen names, avatar choices, buy in amounts, and how they seem to be running. It's not much and it's not nearly enough, so you just default to your straight up tight-aggressive style of play and hope your hands hold up. Over time, though, you become aware of online poker's peculiar brand of tells: uncharacteristic hesitation from a consistently instant bettor; the odd size of a bet tipping a trap or a bluff; or a line of chat betraying ignorance, arrogance, or some other exploitable mental state. Over time, you've discovered some other online information giveaways, and these include:

>>

Some of these tells are so subtle you almost don't know they're there—and you'd certainly miss them if you weren't

28

tuned in. Say your opponent pauses before he bets. Is it real
hesitation derived from indecision, or is he sitting on a monster and trying to suck you in with a hoover bet? Your answer
to this question lies in the sum of your past experience with
this foe, in what you've come to understand as his norm, in
prior evidence of deceptive play, or just in "a rift in the fabric
of space" that makes you feel like he's lying. Does that sound
too hokey? I mean, seriously, *a rift in the fabric of space?* Yet,
every online player with any sensitivity sooner or later experiences this phenomenon and can distinguish with some certainty the hesitation of indecision from the stall of a slowplay.
Though online poker seems to give us slim intelligence to
work with, there's actually plenty of information out there allowing us to make our reads. And as we gain experience in online play, we come to trust our reads as solidly as we would in
any realworld game.

In a sense, we can be even more certain of our online reads
because aside from the odd false stall there's not much our
foes can show us by way of fake tells. Plus, since we're seeing
so many hands in so short a space of time, it takes less time for
our opponents' patterns of play to emerge. It's these patterns
we become attuned to, and these patterns that give us real insight into their game. If they're smart enough to mix up their
play, well, that tells us something, too. But most online foes
(like most poker players in the realworld) are remarkably consistent in their actions. You need only see someone check-fold
a few times to be able to identify him as weak or cautious and
to trust that assessment until he gives you reason to believe
otherwise. Yes, he could feign weakness a few times to lull you
into an underestimation, but what he *can't* do is try to deceive
you with his eyes, face, body, or breathing. If you disable his
chat, he can't even deceive you with his words. He's reduced
to his patterns, and his patterns will give him away.

Viewed through a certain filter, then, online poker is a
code-breaking exercise. The sum of our opponents' patterns of
betting, raising, calling, and folding amounts to the code they're
transmitting. Sure, they can transmit false code—smart players

do—but most people try to play mostly correctly according to their understanding of what correct play is. It's this effort to play correctly that gives you your rock-solid reads. Consider these cases:

- In a ten handed ring game, you notice that player *Mudhead* routinely raises from the button or the cutoff seat. The first time he makes this move, you might credit him with a hand, but by the third or fourth iteration you can surmise that he's a fan of the *real estate raise*, the pure position steal. This tells you several things about him. First, you know that he's capable of raising without a terribly strong hand (because he raises too frequently to be strong every time). Second, you know he's sufficiently schooled to go for the real estate raise. Third . . . well, you tell me third.

  >>

- You're playing heads up against one *Porgy Tirebiter*, who seems to be a loose, passive player. A flop comes two-suited or two-straighted. You bet into it. He calls. The turn is a blank. You bet. He folds. Probably, he was on a draw. At first you can't be sure, but if it happens again and again, you *can* be sure, and the information not only guides you tactically through this particular situation but also it fully lays bare your opponent's strategic thinking, or lack thereof. You now know that he'll take draws when the pot odds don't justify. You also know he's more interested in trapping than bluffing, since he'll willingly surrender hands he doesn't hit. You further know . . .

  >>

- The player to your right, *More_Science*, seems to be playing his small blind correctly, according to his conservative mindset. He rarely calls raises from that position, nor will he even complete an unraised blind unless a bunch of limpers give him odds for his call. Suddenly from out of nowhere he makes a big preflop bet out of the small blind into a large field. What hand, or range of hands, would you put him on? What can you deduce from this action about his approach to the game?

>>

I'm feeling a little self-consciously schoolmarmish right now, telling you things you no doubt already know. *More_Science*, for example, clearly holds A-A, K-K, or Q-Q; we'd be shocked to see him turn over anything else. He has given us no reason to believe that he's capable of a frisky out-of-position bluff, and every reason to believe that he's playing a real hand in a real way. But it's worth going through the analysis just the same, and not just for the sake of playing your hand correctly (folding in almost all cases). You also move closer to acquiring a clear sense of this player's profile, a reliable yardstick with which you can measure future actions against past behavior. Profiling, then—deducing an online poker player's mindset and capabilities from his actions—is something we should routinely do if we want to make money at this game.

Profiling your foes gives you the further benefit of keeping your focus fixed on the game. If you're like me, the sort of player who's pretty much bored by every pot he's not in, profiling will give you something interesting and challenging to do when you're out of the hand. You could even keep score, using your knowledge of your enemies' patterns to predict what they hold, and awarding yourself points when you're right. It sounds silly, I know, but it's better than letting your mind wander, for a wandering mind is a reliable crippler of online play.

With the warp-speed pace of internet poker play, it becomes important not just to profile your foes but to do so quickly and efficiently, so that you know how to respond to them in the moment. This is not so much about storing long-term information on an enemy (though you can do that, and it's helpful) but about observing a player's patterns, assigning those patterns a label, and then using the label to clarify what kind of player you're dealing with right here and right now. Players will switch gears, of course—and when they do, you amend your label. But your first order of business is to assign a label, so that you can derive a probability of someone playing a certain way.

Yes, you're making a number of assumptions, and no, those assumptions are not backed by massive statistical support. Yet, I contend that a player who has demonstrated the ability to check-raise bluff deserves a different designation—even if it's a tentative, speculative one—from a player who has shown strong tendencies to call and fold. So I watch the patterns to crack the codes, and then sum up my sense of my foes by labeling them and typing their labels in the text box that every site now routinely provides for our note taking pleasure.

Many online players disparage this effort. They so rarely see a given foe more than once that they see no point in *making book* (taking notes) on him just on the off chance that they'll play together again later. *But you're playing together now, aren't you?* So why not record salient information as it becomes available to you? To name a thing is to own a thing. Just ask Adam and Eve, to whom God gave dominion over all living things, plus naming rights. Once you've distilled a foe's patterns down to a definable handle, you know, well, how to handle him. Even if your assessment is only 50 percent right, that's better than blundering lunkenly into an unlabeled opponent. Especially when it's so easy to apply the tag.

What follows are some of the handles I routinely assign to the profiles of the players I face, along with associated characteristics and characteristic plays. Take a moment to amplify my definitions. Guess, in other words, what you would expect to encounter from a player with a certain label. Note how much information about a player is implied from just his handle and not much more. Don't be afraid to be wrong in your assessments. It's learning to make assessments that's important—and more than most players bother with. If to name a thing is to own a thing, then to define an opponent, and to extend and expand your definition, is to own the deed to his house.

KOSHER. A kosher player is simply simple. Straightforward and honest, he plays his own hand and doesn't think much about yours. Offering little or nothing in the way of deception, he bets, calls, raises, or folds according to the real strength of his holding. Take his actions at face value. About the trickiest play in his repertoire is the check-raise; a check-raise bluff is beyond him.
>>

TIMMY. Short for timid Timmy, this player is weak, passive, and unlikely to make any sudden moves for fear of startling himself. Timmies don't play to win, they play not to lose. Therefore, you find them liberally inhabiting the middle stages of tournaments, but rarely making the final table. Aggressively attack uncontested flops against a Timmy. He won't play back unless he has a real hand.
>>

SPEEDER. A speeder is a dangerous player. He plays fast in every sense of the word, and part of his motivation for playing fast is to get *you* to play fast, too. If he's better able than you to analyze and act on the fly, he can make money on the margin, so he attempts to increase the pace of play not just through swift choices but through promiscuous raises and reraises. Take your time against a speeder. Pause to consider your decisions. This will not only ensure that you're thinking things through but also frustrate him by breaking his rhythm.
>>

WALLY. A Wally (short for cally Wally) is a weak-loose player. Wallies call too much, fold and raise too little, and chase all sorts of draws without regard to, or indeed knowledge of, pot odds. They'll routinely call preflop raises with inferior values but, paradoxically, only raise preflop with premium hands. Like their kosher cousins, they're more interested in trapping than bluffing. On the one hand, you can bet for value forever against a Wally because he'll never bluff-raise into you. On the other hand, you can't bluff a Wally because his calls-with-bottom-pair will wear you out.

>>

FRISKY. A frisky player is fearless, creative, difficult to gauge, and difficult to put on a hand. He'll raise with anything or nothing, and can trap, bluff, and drag. He can play strong hands strongly or weakly; he can play weak hands weakly or strongly. Frisky players play a lot of hands and play them well, but they can be beaten through trapping because their own friskiness will often get them out ahead of their hands.

>>

FEELIE. Feelie describes a broad class of players who are more interested in feeling good at the table than in playing proper poker. Recognize them by the pride with which they show you their successful bluffs and good laydowns. Feelies have ego problems. They need constant external validation, and this need will make them reveal far too much about their play. Do everything in your power to reinforce their sense of smug superiority. Make them feel good enough and they'll stick around to lose all their money to you.

>>

ANGERBOT. Angerbots are a variation on the feelie theme. They want to feel good about their play, and they get there largely by telling you how bad yours is. While it's remotely possible that their enraged chatbox rants are all an act, it's much more likely that they're emotionally out of control. We should not be surprised at this, for the online community is full of players—young men especially—who haven't yet learned to tamp their Vesuvian tempers.

>>

BOOKBOT. A bookbot tries to play correctly according to the starting hand requirements and strategies he's absorbed from his studies. He has technical precision, but lacks "feel." He'll play predictably and miss opportunities that other, more creative, players would seize. He won't hurt himself too badly in any game—but he probably won't hurt you either.

>>

There are, of course, melds or hybrids of these handles. You can have a kosher-Timmy or a frisky-speeder or a bookbot-angerbot (who will play correctly until he loses his cool). It really doesn't matter what definition you give to a player, and it doesn't pay to become too obsessed with fitting players into types. After all, if you try to squish everything into a pigeon-hole, all you end up with is a bunch of squished pigeons. But the effort to assign handles to your foes pays dividends no matter what words you use, and even no matter how accurate you are, because it gets you into the habit of actively thinking about how your opponents think and of correlating the patterns of their play to types or patterns you have encountered before. So the next time you play, make an effort to analyze your foes and assign some handles of your own. If nothing else, it will give you a sense of confidence, the confidence that comes from knowing you've got them named.

4

♣♠♦♥

CONTEXT DENSITY

♣♠◇♡

Even as we're busy trying to break our enemies' codes, those devious scoundrels are hard at work cracking ours. In real-world poker play, defense against this would involve switching gears from time to time, throwing a little misdirection into the mix. Given the pace of play online, though, the fact that our foes are trying to profile us actually creates an opportunity to use against them the information they gather. To do this, we need to understand and exploit a little something called *context density*.

To weigh context density is to gauge the amount of information available within a given space of time. The more information that's available, the higher the context density is said to be. In television, for example, a show on public TV has higher context density than a commercial broadcast, where program content is interspersed with, and diluted by, commercials. Likewise, a medical periodical like the *New England Journal of Medicine* has higher context density than, say, *Men's Health* magazine, for the latter's hard data is watered down by ads for Lucozade and Trojan-ENZ. In the poker realm, if you were trying to gather information on how a certain foe defends his big blinds, and you went after this data in a ten handed game, you'd have 10 percent context density, because he takes his big blind one hand out of ten. In a six handed game, you'd be able to get meaningful stuff on this subject one-sixth, or 17 percent, of the time. Heads up, your context density on just this one subject rises to 50 percent, because your foe has to take the big blind every other hand. That's some thick context density. Thus we say . . .

PATTERNS ARE EASIER TO SEE WHEN CONTEXT IS DENSE.

But the number of players at the table is not the only factor in determining context density. Basically, anything that's not directly related to the strategic considerations of poker thins poker's context density. In realworld cardrooms and casinos, we find that context is broad but it's not dense. There's lots of information floating around out there—betting tendencies, body language, facial expressions, measurable attentiveness, and how people defend their blinds—but it's spread out over time and diluted by such information-poor irrelevancies as shuffling, dealing, pushing pots, rack fills, arguments, brawls, and CPR for heart attack victims. Online, hands don't just happen faster, they happen in an environment of very high context density, where the information stream is rich, deep, swift, and almost purely relevant. In this environment, we can reach conclusions about our opponents and make adjustments very quickly, while the relevant information is still fresh in our minds. We don't have to wait hours for certain exploitable situations to recur. Online, they may recur in mere moments.

It is this ability to make snap adjustments that gives us a powerful weapon to use against certain foes.

Imagine that you're playing in a full ring game against, among others, a frisky Joe who raises from middle position. You hold a bad ace and don't feel like getting involved in a reckless adventure, so you fold. But you notice that the guy winds up showing down 8♠-7♠, and you go to school on that, formulating the hypothesis that this foe likes to mix up his play by raising with middle suited connectors. In another lap or two, you see the same middle-position, middle-card raise, and you consider your hypothesis confirmed. Now you're on the lookout. Next time he makes that mid-lap raise, you can go to war with a wide range of hands, because you know that with a variety of overcard flops—whether you hit them or not—you can scare him off the pot with a bet.

Naturally, this trick works both ways. If you're the one making the mid-orbit, middle-card raises, your more focused opponents will quickly get hip to your tricks. This is not necessarily a bad thing, not so long as we understand that . . .

THIRD TIME'S THE ADJUSTMENT.

Third time's the adjustment. Give an attentive poker player one look at a move, and he'll wonder, *What was that about?* Show it to him again, and he'll form a postulate about the way you play. Make the move a third time, and he'll have a counter-strategy prepared. You yourself have often worked this trick in defending your blind against an inveterate blind stealer. The first time he steals, you let him get away with it because you don't know whether he has a real hand or not. The second time he steals, you label him a blind stealer. The third time he tries to steal, you're ready, and you play back at him.

Now here's the thing: In the realworld, such a sequence may take an hour or more to play out, depending on how long it takes your blind to come back around. In fact, only the very best, most attentive and retentive players will track the sequence and plan a response. Online, though, you can whip through three laps in ten minutes or less, and the speed at which certain situations repeat themselves allows even the most inattentive opponents to catch on.

Which is exactly what we want them to do.

In the realworld, we have to worry about our best foes not just cracking our code but also deploying effective counter-measures. After all, if they're focused enough and smart enough to detect our trends, they're also (possibly) focused enough and smart enough to anticipate our adjustments. Online, though, we can count on our worst foes having knee-jerk reactions to our play. They absorb our patterns without really understanding what they mean, and they react to those patterns without considering that we may be anticipating their reaction. On-line poker, then, with its sizzling pace of play and ultra-high context density, gives us the chance to victimize our foes by their predictable assumptions and flawed responses.

You attack a guy's blind. He folds. Two minutes later, you attack it again. Again he folds. Maybe he even does you the favor of chatboxing about it, protesting, u cant have a hand every time. Two minutes later, you attack again. This time he's ready to take a stand—but this time you actually have a hand. Yes, you're lucky to pick up a real hand at an opportune mo-ment, but you're also prepared to exploit the luck that comes your way. Should you happen *not* to pick up a real hand here, you merely refrain from attacking the blind. You know the guy is primed to play back at you, so you don't give him a chance to do so unless and until it suits your ends.

Can you think of other examples of "third time's the ad-justment" thinking?

>>

Here's one, from the end stage of a sitngo tournament.

Fortunately for you, you're down to heads up play. Unfor-tunately, your opponent currently outchips you by about 4 to 1. Given the size of the blinds relative to your stack, you know it's time to start making some all in moves and try to double through. Do you wait for a premium hand before pushing all in?

Hell, no.

You look for a semi-strong hand like A-middle or K-J, and push all in with that. Given the random distribution of hands, it's unlikely that your opponent has a better hand than yours at this moment. Even if he does, there's a range of better hands he'll fold here (e.g., little pairs and A-T) because this is the first time you've pushed, and his first impulse will be to believe that you have a quality hand. In the name of not letting you double up and get back into contention, he'll fold to your first all in stab.

Now, though, he's on guard. Now he's alert to the possibility that you've taken your small stack into *push and pray* mode. Good. This is exactly what you want him to think.

You swap the blinds back and forth a few times. Since you're playing online, this takes all of forty-five seconds. Then you pick up another semi-strong hand.

And you push all in again.

Of *course* he's suspicious. Of *course* he's wary. He thinks you're just trying to bully bet your way out of trouble. And, of course, you are. But he still can't call because, again, he probably doesn't have a hand, and, again, he can't discount the possibility that you do. So he folds once more. Even as he folds, though, he cements a picture of your strategy in his mind. He figures you for desperate. He concludes that you'll keep making desperation raises with semi-strong hands (or even no hand at all) and that all he has to do to beat you is to wait and call you down with a major holding. He might not even wait for all that major a holding, since the lower he thinks your raising standards have fallen, the lower his corresponding calling requirements will go.

Meanwhile, you're anticipating this adjustment, and you're right out in front of it. Having taken a couple of shots with indifferent hands, you picked up a couple of blinds before your foe was in the mood to call. Now that he's in that mood, you just wait to pick up a hand of real quality, something like Q-Q or J-J, go all in and hope to get a call from a worse hand like A-x or T-T. Will this happen? Sometimes. If it doesn't, you continue to joust and trade blinds, let some time pass, and create the impression that you've given up your desperation-raise strategy. Then you go ahead and *steal all over again!* Prime him to call, and manipulate him into calling with a worse hand.

Luck is a factor here, but not the way we conventionally think of luck. It's pure luck, for instance, to pick up pocket aces when your foe has pocket kings. Of course, the money will go in the middle. It's a no-brainer. What we're talking about here is something called *applied luck,* where you launch a sequence of actions leading to one conclusion if the cards break your way, but a totally different conclusion if they don't. With applied luck, it doesn't really matter if you get lucky or not, since you have a plan for every eventuality. Plus, no matter what happens, you've got your foe leaning the wrong way because you're anticipating, or actually dictating, his adjustments.

Consider the orphan flop trifecta.

An *orphan flop* is something like 8♣-3♦-3♥, a forlorn little waif featuring no straight draws or flush draws, and not likely to have hit anybody's hand. These orphans are just looking to be adopted by the first person who bets. If that person is you, your foes will naturally be incredulous. Incredulous or not, though, the first time you go the adoption route, they can't be sure where you're at, and in their uncertainty they'll often give you the benefit of the doubt and fold. If you bet at the next orphan that pops up, you turn incredulity to suspicion— and you do so by calculating design. *This guy is a lying sack of sushi,* your foes now will think, *who thinks he can adopt every damn orphan that comes along. I'll show him!* It's the "I'll show him" part of their thinking that's important. They postulate that you'll bet at all unwanted pots and now plan their little response. Next time you bet at that orphan, they decide, they're gonna raise you no matter what they have. That'll teach a lying sack of sushi like you a lesson!

But you know this. You know they've made an adjustment—it's just the adjustment you've guided them to. And you're already a step ahead. When the next orphan comes along, you'll either have a piece of it or you won't. If you miss it completely, you won't bet, and you'll be content to have adopted two orphans out of three with virtually no risk. But if you happen to have hit the flop, look where you're at: You can bet a strong hand into opponents who are primed to counter-attack—probably with less of a hand than they folded the last two times you tried!

Again, you're relying on applied luck: adapting your strategy to the actual cards that fall. If they fall your way, great. You're in the catbird seat. If they don't . . . that's great, too. Your fold in this situation just tells your foes, *See, guys? I don't attack every orphan that comes along.* Which, of course, just lends more credibility to the steals you later launch.

It's all about balance, adaptation, response to circumstance, and staying a step ahead. Thanks to context density, your balance and adaptation are quickly rewarded in ways they just usually aren't in b&m games. In the realworld, it can take so long for the orphan flop trifecta to play out that your inattentive foes can't be counted on to remember what you're doing and to make the adjustments you want them to make. As previously noted, the cardroom players most likely to suss you out are your best, most attentive enemies. They'll make adjustments, but not necessarily the ones you want. Online, weak minded opponents will acquire a sense of how you play your orphans without even realizing it. The notion will be forced into their heads that you're getting *way* out of line and you must be stopped. Because the pattern presents itself to them in so short a space of time, these weakies are both more likely to make the move you want them to make and less likely to see it for the trap it is. You can train them like Pavlov's dogs. They'll fold when they should raise, call when they should fold, and basically give you everything they've got.

Like all orphan attacks, the orphan flop trifecta works best against few foes because the fewer foes you face, the less the chance that one of your enemies has a real hand. So pick your spots. Can you think of other spots where applied luck, plus context density, can put you into a position to manipulate the few or the many weak minded foes you face?

>>

Here's one you see a lot online, especially in short handed play. Someone makes a raise and two players call. The flop comes A-x-x. The first player to bet at this flop is certainly representing an ace, which the other players may give him credit for—at first. If he goes too often to this same well, soon his foes will stop believing he has the ace and start putting him on the steal he's making. If you're the one betting into the naked ace, count on your opponents yielding to you the first or second time, but *not* the third. Again, they're more likely to follow this line of lockstep thinking online because they're much more likely to see an A-x-x flop several times within the space of their modest attention spans. In the realworld, the only opponents retaining information about your theft attempts are the very ones you'll have most difficulty manipulating.

I don't want to give the impression that your internet opponents, as a class, are less skillful and more easily beaten than your realworld foes. This may be true, simply because online poker is the port of entry for thousands of new players every day, and new players, as a class, are less skillful and more easily beaten than experienced ones. But that's not really the point. In both online games and b&m games, you will find a distribution of strong players and weak ones, and you will naturally make more money by avoiding the strong ones and engaging the weak ones. That's Poker 101, as I'm sure you already know:

DON'T CHALLENGE STRONG PLAYERS: CHALLENGE WEAK ONES— THAT'S WHAT THEY'RE THERE FOR.

Nor do I want you to adopt something like "third time's the adjustment" with the force of religious conviction. Some foes adjust more quickly. Others never adjust. In all cases, it's a matter of nuance, timing, and knowing your foes. But the thing about context density is that it creates a circumstance unique to online poker, one in which your weaker foes can be exploited in a particular way.

For this reason, online poker requires us to think strategically not just about each bet and each hand but about each hand within the flow of hands recently seen and those we can reasonably expect to see soon. If it's true that "third time's the adjustment" (and against some players it certainly is), you should plan to bet at many flops whether you hit them or not, just to put yourself in position to win big when you happen to hit your hand at the exact moment your foes have been manipulated into showing some spine. If it doesn't happen during this sequence, it'll happen during the next one or the one after that. If it doesn't happen at all, well, you still have the benefit of being the active, aggressive bettor at your table, and that's never a bad thing.

Of course, you can't go slinging your bets around all day without *ever* having a hand. Consistent naked aggression makes you just too easy to trap. Here's a rule of thumb I use to moderate my aggressiveness and give my opponents ample opportunity to lean the wrong way:

STEAL TWICE, REAL ONCE.

Steal twice. Real once. Be bold and aggressive with your theft attempts, and be aware that every time you steal successfully you hasten the moment when your foes will play back at you. To reiterate, if applied luck breaks your way, you'll surprise them by having the goods. If it doesn't, no problem! Just dial back on your aggression until you find the opportunity to resume your manipulative ways. Thanks to context density, you have a strategy that will give you the confidence to play aggressively and outfox the foes you face.

5

♣ ♠ ◆ ♥

MY CODES

♧ ♤ ◇ ♡

When I first started playing cardroom poker, I would carry around a ratty little spiral-bound notebook and record in it observations that I considered interesting or handy about my foes. Interesting they may have been—Joe Sideburns likes to eat kimchi at the table, and then he farts bad—but handy? Not so much. Aside from the obvious irrelevancy, so much time would pass before I'd see a certain foe again (if, indeed, I ever saw him again) that whatever data I gathered about him was not directly useful.

Years later, when I started playing internet poker, I became a deep devotee of note boxes, those little pop-up text entry windows that let you record your thoughts and discoveries about the people you play against. Being a writer, and verbose by nature, I could get on some real note writing jags and soon overwhelmed those little boxes' space limitations.

> This guy's a total tool. He called three bets preflop with 6-9 offsuit, caught runner-runner straight cards then typed "6-9—lick me!" in the chat box. Well, bite me, DustyRoadApple, keep playing that crap and you'll lose all your money you assho

In the early days of online poker, you tended to see the same screen names in the same games over and over again. We were a close community of strangers, huddled in front of our respective VGA monitors and reaching out through dial-up modems (28.8 baud—*fast!*) to clutch one another's money on such primordial poker sites as Highlands Club and the long gone and little lamented Pokerspot. Night after night I'd pound away against familiar foes, and the book I made on them, at first on scrap paper and later in the note boxes, paid handsome dividends. The game was mostly short handed $3-6 limit hold'em, and once you discovered that a certain player would fold to a bet on any flop he missed, you really had a cudgel with which to whack him.

But . . . *après moi le deluge,* right? Dial-up gave way to DSL, ending the infuriating parade of disconnects that plagued on-line poker's pioneers. The World Poker Tour brought televised poker to the masses. The providentially named Chris Money-maker won the 2003 World Series of Poker, and the trickle of online players became a torrent, a flood. In such heavy and ever-changing traffic, is it still useful to make book? In my experience, yes, but I've shifted the emphasis of the notes I take and altered the reason why I take them in the first place. The question is no longer, "How can I use this information against my foes when next we meet?" but, "How can I use this information against my foes right now?" Even if I'm only sharing a sitngo or loitering in a cash game—and certainly if I'm playing a large-field tournament where I'll be with the same players until they or I bust out, or until the table breaks—I make the effort to open note boxes on all my foes and record whatever morsels of information I can glean. It may be that I'll be able to use this information in the next five minutes. It may be that I never will. In either case, I do enjoy the secondary benefit of keeping my head in the game. While I'm feverishly taking notes, there's literally no time for my nomadic mind to wander.

But if these notes are going to be helpful, I need to be able to do two things: write them quickly and apply them right away. To these ends I have developed a series of codes—shorthands and abbreviations—that represent large chunks of acquired information. My codes tell me in an instant and remind me as play continues what sort of foes I'm facing.

There is another, high tech, approach to all this, of course, and that's to integrate such sniffer tools as Poker Tracker, Poker Office, or Poker Prophecy into our play. These tools are incredibly useful, though somewhat daunting, and you can read in appendix B how to get the most out of them. For now, though, let's stick to the low-tech method. With nothing more than your native intelligence and a few quick keystrokes, you can make surprisingly insightful book on your opponents.

In the following pages, you'll find some of my codes, along with explanations of what they mean and how they may be generally applied. As I describe these players and situations, think hard about how *you* would describe them, because the codes you devise for yourself, spoken to you in your own idiom, will ultimately be much more useful to you than the ones you get from me.

CB = CONTINUATION BET

A continuation bet is the bet that a preflop raiser makes on the flop. Many players feel morally bound to make this bet whether they've hit the flop or not, because they perceive (and rightly so) that if they don't follow up preflop raises with postflop bets, their vigilant opponents will start taking advantage of their postflop timidity. CB typed into a player's note box alerts me that I've seen continuation bets from this particular foe. If I've also seen him make such a bet and ultimately reveal a hand that missed the flop completely, I'll amend my code thus: CB/B (for continuation bet/bluff). Now I know for sure that he doesn't necessarily have to have a hand to bet the flop.

A continuation bet without a hand is a strong move. Not all players will make them, and those who do make them reveal themselves to be aggressive and canny. Thus, a simple CB or CB/B in my note box tells me more than just how this preflop raiser handles his postflop obligations; it informs my entire perception of him. From this one note I can assume a certain minimum level of awareness, expertise, and fearlessness. Not to put too fine a point on it, strong players make CBs and weak players don't.

The beauty of putting your foe on CB tendencies is the license to speculate it yields. If the price is right, you can call his preflop raises with almost anything, knowing that if you happen to hit the flop, you may very well find yourself ahead in the hand against an opponent who has nothing but the hidebound determination to bluff off some chips. Call him on the flop, raise him on the turn (or bet if he checks), and take down a pot that you otherwise would have missed.

Would you be better off just folding your marginal hands and waiting for better opportunities? Against an unknown foe, sure—but this is a known foe. Thanks to your codes, you have intelligence on him, an edge you can exploit. Now you can call behind his raise with 8-7 suited, knowing that if the flop comes something like 8-J-3, he'll feel obliged to bet into you whether he has a jack or not. Most of the time, of course, he won't have a jack (for the flop misses any given player two times out of three, and if he's holding a jack he'll hit that specific pair less than one time out of five). If he bets without a hand, he's just playing into your strength.

Now naturally there's no guarantee that you'll hit the flop and he'll miss it or that the flop won't come so scary—high suited and straighted, say—that you'll have to let your undercards go whether you think he's hit or not. But folding to a continuation bettor is not necessarily a bad thing, since it emboldens him to try the trick again. Thanks to context density, he'll retain a mental snapshot of you as someone who folds to continuation bets. Next time he makes one, if you're fortunate enough to have hit your hand (or bold enough to bluff) you can raise and take him off his hand.

I'm second guessing myself right now, because it seems as if I'm advising you to play crap hands, and that sort of advice leads to loose play and reckless adventures. Know what? That's a chance we'll both have to take. Internet poker, as we've already discussed, is about deciphering your opponents' patterns and then getting out ahead of them. Tabbing someone as a CB player and giving him a chance to hang himself (okay, there's no law that says you have to do it every time) is just a step you take toward taking over the game.

YO = YIELDS ORPHANS

We've already talked about orphan flops, that is, certain combinations of cards that are hard to have a piece of. Typical orphans contain a pair of small cards plus a third unconnected offsuit small card. 7-7-2 rainbow is the classic orphan flop, in that it offers no straight or flush possibilities, and it's unlikely to have hit the cards in most sensible players' hands. Usually, whoever bets first into this flop is going to take the pot because even if the other players know the first bettor is a baldfaced thief, what can they have to defend with? A good ace? A small pair? These hands play well against someone who attacks orphan flops, but—and here's the key—most players don't have the stomach for such a fight. Most players find it easier just to yield the orphan and move onto the next hand. You know they do because they're chatboxing nb—nice bet—even as they fold.

I want to know who and where these players are. I want to know which of my foes will surrender a flop without a fight. So I routinely bet into orphan flops, not just to win the pot but also to collect this important information. In the ideal circumstance, I will have raised preflop and seen the flop against just one opponent. If the flop comes orphan—and in the fast-

paced online environment it happens often enough to matter—I'll go ahead and fire away. If my foe folds, I'll add the ini-
tials YO to my note box profile of him.

Now I have information, and information is power I'll bet
at the next orphan that comes along—8-4-2 rainbow is another example of an adorably adoptable flop—and I'll keep
betting at them until my foes show some spine and demonstrate the willingness to play back at me. Some never do.
Others only do when they have a real hand. Meanwhile, I've
reinforced my aggressive image and not to beat the dead horse
of this, but that's never a bad thing.

Is there profit in this play? Let's do the math. Say the blinds
are $1 and $2. You make it $6 to go. You get one caller and the
blinds fold. Now there's $15 in the pot. An orphan comes, you
bet it and your foe folds. You're $9 ahead. Next orphan, you bet
again and win again. Another nine bucks. The third time you
attack an orphan, your foe raises, either because he has a real
hand or because "third time's the adjustment." You surrender
your $6 investment, leaving yourself twelve bucks to the
good. If your foes yield the majority of orphans, you'll definitely see a profit here. And if they *don't* yield the majority of
orphans, well, you'll find that out pretty fast and only attack
orphans against those players when you actually have a hand.

Remember also that you're not just money to the good,
you're also *data* to the good. Players who earn the YO designation are defining themselves for you as timid, cautious players
not looking for a fight. On those rare occasions when they
play back at you, you can more confidently credit them with a
real hand and get out of their way. No harm in surrendering to
a raise; there'll be another orphan along in a minute.

Don't be too loose in your definition of orphan flops.
Something like T♥-T♠-9♠ is *not* an orphan flop. Not only does
it have straight and flush possibilities, but it hits playable (by
internet standards) hands like J-T and A-9. Save your attacks
for true orphans, and collect your profit and information accordingly.

AO = ATTACKS ORPHANS

You obviously want to know which of your opponents are frisky enough to go after orphans like you do. Any time you see someone betting into a low ragged board, especially if he was the preflop raiser, you should provisionally assign him the AO value and append his note box accordingly. If he routinely attacks orphans, be on your guard and proceed against this foe with caution, for he's not a maniac or a reckless bluffer, just someone who knows enough to grab an uncontested pot. He's both aggressive and informed, and his AO designation in your text box warns you to anticipate not just orphan attacks but a whole array of tricky strong moves from this guy.

As keen as you are to attack orphans yourself, it's situationally useful (e.g., early in a tournament) to lay off an orphan or two, just to take the temperature of the table. As with the continuation bet, a player who goes after an orphan and subsequently shows down a less than stellar hand is telling you something very important about his general approach to the game. He wants to outplay his opponents. He's looking to be involved and he won't necessarily wait for quality hands. Looking at someone who attacks orphans is (or should be) looking at a mirror of yourself. As such, you'll need to plan a response to this player, one that uses the information stored in your codes, plus an awareness of how you would view the situation if you were the attacker. (Here's where your mind reading skills come in handy.) If he's truly betting with nothing, he's giving you a prime opportunity to steal from the stealer.

First, let others at the table be your straw men. Stay out of confrontations with the AO player and let him take down a couple of uncontested pots from other players. Then look for an opportunity to get involved in a pot against him. Since he hasn't yet seen the move you have in mind, he'll assume that you're just another cally Wally who will likely roll over for him. He has become accustomed to collecting orphans without a fight. If the flop comes orphan and he bets, he'll be surprised, and probably surrender his hand, when you reraise. Why wouldn't he? He's never seen you make a reraise bluff before, so the first time you play back at him he must necessarily credit you with a hand.

You may think it highly unlikely that the right sequence of orphan flops will present itself to you here. You might be right—but there's always *some* sequence of flops going down. Looking to steal from the stealer is just one of the many programs you should be running, and just one of the various opportunities your avid note taking is preparing you to exploit. In any case, everyone who plays poker is looking for cards that fit their hand. You're doing that, too, but not *just* that. You're looking for cards that fit your hand . . . but also cards that fit your plan. And if you know your foe is an AO player, you've got a plan in place if the right situation arises. It makes all the difference in the world.

TTT = TICKLE THE TROUT

This note tells me I'm up against an opponent I have previously teased or trapped—tickled, in my vernacular—into making big mistakes for big bets. Generally, a TTT designation indicates a weak, loose, and unsophisticated foe, one who can be led down predictable paths to certain ends. In a typical TTT scenario, you'll find a foe who will call a raise with inferior values, get stuck on the hand if he catches a piece of it, and—in the best of all possible worlds—bet into you when you have the best hand. Such players are relatively rare in this wonderful internet poker world of ours, for they and their dead money tend not to last long. But while they yet swim, these fish are worth noting and hooking.

Say you start out with something like A♣-T♣, raise preflop, and get one trouty caller. The flop comes 9♣-8♣-3♥. You have the nut flush draw, overcards, and a runner-runner straight draw, so of course you bet . . . let's say about two-thirds pot. Trouty calls, and you figure him for a good nine or a good eight (though being a trout he could easily be on a bad nine or a bad eight, or a draw without correct odds). The turn is your bingo card, the 4♣. Holding the nuts, you check. Here's where Trouty distinguishes himself from your more sensible foes. An astute player would at least consider the possibility that you bet on the flop with a flush draw, hit your hand, and are now trapping. But Trouty will not. He'll draw the opposite conclusion. He'll read your check on fourth street as a sign of fear— fear that *he* holds the flush—and will obligingly bet into you. Whether you raise him now or pop him on the river is entirely up to you, and entirely dependent on how big a trout you reckon him to be. But the point is that some players will fall for the simplest plain deception, and it's your job to identify and exploit these foes.

It's characteristic of trouty players to ignore the completion of straight and flush draws. When the flop comes J-T-x, the turn is a brick, the river is an ace, and a raising war breaks out, they seem only dimly aware of the possibility that someone might have entered the pot with K-Q. Likewise, they're susceptible to the *stealth ace*, a known phenomenon where a player holding pocket kings or pocket queens will encounter a flop like A-7-3 and be utterly unable, somehow, to see the ace that's out there.

TTT, then, is shorthand for: *weak, loose, clueless; attack!* And you'd better attack fast, because this is one player who will not last long in the game.

FNL = FAST 'N' LOOSE

Many internet players distinguish themselves by their wide open, aggressive style. Maybe they're viscerally disconnected from the fact that they're playing for real money. Perhaps they believe that fast 'n' loose is a winning style of play (it is, but only within limits). Or maybe it's just the fearlessness that comes from long exposure to and deep experience with internet poker. For whatever reason, you'll find FNLs, the reckless gunners of poker, to be much more plentiful and prevalent online than you will in realworld games. For the sake of defending your bankroll, you need to know who they are and how to neutralize or evade their turbulent play.

When I see someone getting involved in lots of pots, raising a lot, or otherwise trying to take over the table, I provisionally label him as FNL. From that point forward, I'm on the lookout for all the warning signs of FNL behavior: frequent preflop raises (with or without a real hand), attacking orphans, strong continuation bets, and pushing draws. If he confirms himself as genuinely fast and loose, and not just seemingly so due to a hot run of cards, I start looking to identify the limits of his aggression. To borrow from my terminology in *The Killer Poker Hold'em Handbook,* I need to know if I'm dealing with a genuine maniac—a real poker kamikaze—or only a *fakiac,* someone who appears to be wildly out of control but really is sensible and can therefore be made to behave sensibly.

To find out, I'll look to get involved with him, play back at him, and see what he does. In the way of all bullies (both the real ones and the *faux* ones), he expects other players to lay down for him, and a sudden, unanticipated reraise will be an authentic test of his mettle. Suppose he raises from middle position and I reraise behind him. If he lets go of his hand, I've confirmed that he's FNL enough to have raised in the first place with a hand that can't take real heat, but also sensible and flexible enough to get away from that hand when he thinks he's beat. If he does lay down, I'll add two notations to his record. First, I'll note RWC (*raises with cheese*) because I've confirmed that he doesn't need a real hand to bet, since if he'd had a real hand, he wouldn't have laid it down when I reraised. I'll also add CBRO (*can be raised off*), indicating that he's not so stubborn as to stick with his cheesy cards once he's been caught, or even *thinks* he's been caught. These three pieces of information—FNL and RWC but CBRO—define this guy as a dangerous player, but someone I can probably outplay, given what I've learned.

Now, it's possible that the notion of reraising someone when you yourself don't have a hand, and just for the sake of gaining information, makes you nervous. It might strike you as a needless waste of valuable chips. After all, what if he doesn't slow down? What if he takes your probing reraise and throws it back in your face with a reraise of his own? What information has your bet bought then?

Well, possibly the information that this is a player you can't stop. That you need to stay out of his way. That the only way you can realistically beat him is to lay back and trap. That maybe you should just change games. This seems to me to be quite a lot of information gleaned from a single reraise, even at the cost of some chips. If you're afraid to raise for information (never forgetting that you might actually win the pot when you do), then you probably won't prosper against FNL players, or even anyone. The raise is the basic weapon of poker. If you only use it when you have the best hand, or only use it as a club to beat other players off a pot, you're not appreciating its nuance. If information is power, then the raise is a power tool.

Look at it this way: If you always knew for certain how your opponents acted, you would certainly be a winning player. Since you can't always know for certain, the best you can hope for is to triangulate on your targets, give yourself a general sense of their tendencies, and then work to refine that general sense into a more specific one. We've already talked about this in terms of detecting and decoding your foes' patterns. With info-raises such as this, we're just taking our data processing to a higher level. In the manner of active sonar, we're "pinging" our targets to define them more clearly. A single well timed information raise can gain you the data you need to win many bets, or save many bets, against a given foe later in the session, or in the tournament, or tomorrow. That's why you want to know not just whether your opponent is fast and loose, but where, exactly, the limits of his recklessness lie.

RRR = RAISES 'R' REAL

For every FNL player out there, there's at least one timid (or by his lights solid) player content to play a game of "get the goods, bet the goods." Because they play a simple, straightforward game of poker, these players are, among other things, terribly consistent in their action. Whenever I'm up against a player I suspect of being this kosher, I take note of his raises, and correlate them with the hands he shows down. Just one or two "real raises" are enough to earn the designation RRR in his note box. These three letters warn me that when this player raises, I'd better have a damn good reason to get involved, because he's probably betting with the best hand, or at least the one he thinks is best.

Does such a player never bluff? Well, not never. Raise into him enough times, for example, and he'll eventually just get cranky and raise back out of frustration or spite. But here's the philosophy I adopt in dealing with players like this:

KOSHER UNTIL PROVEN FRISKY.

Once a player shows me that he has the hand he's representing, I give credence to his raises, and I'll continue to credit them until he shows me something different. If he starts raising with suspicious frequency, or gets caught stealing (by me or by somebody else), I'll modify my RRR designation. But not before. Most players don't warrant it. Players of a certain mindset are simply, consistently, incapable of betting or raising unless they have a hand.

This doesn't just mean that they don't bluff. It also means

they won't seize the opportunities that present themselves over and over again in internet play. They don't attack blinds—unless they have a hand. They don't adopt orphans—unless they hit the flop. They don't reraise FNLs—unless they've got a monster. It's mostly this unwillingness to exploit exploitable situations that reveals the RRRs for what they are: true value players who bet their hand, their whole hand and nothing but their hand, so help them God.

The beauty of these players (from our point of view) is that they give so much and ask so little in return. They'll fold every time we put pressure on them, except for those rare times when they actually have a hand. And then they'll obligingly signal their strength by pushing back. We can comfortably get out of their way, knowing that we may have given away a few chips, but to a player who will likely soon give them back. And if we're wrong, if the RRR player is essaying an infrequent and uncharacteristic bluff? More power to him! He's still folding too frequently to our naked steals, and he's still staying true to his nature by not stealing when it's his turn.

RRR, then, says much more to me than just "raises 'r' real." It delineates a whole class of play. It tells me that a given foe is trying to play correctly according to the well-known selective-aggressive formula. He's probably doing alright in the game—not going big, not going home—although he's missing out on some of the opportunities that his friskier playmates routinely exploit. And he's no threat whatsoever to attentive opponents, who see his raises coming a mile away.

CD = CAN DRAG

Dragging is the word I use to describe slow playing, sandbagging, hoover bets, and other forms of entrapment, including, I suppose, dressing in drag. To drag is to retard your betting—drag it—in hopes of dragging other people's money into the pot. It turns out that even players who can't bluff very well for reasons of nervousness or fear can drag fairly effectively, and it's worth exploring why.

To bluff is to represent strength when you're weak, and to drag is to represent weakness when you're strong. These different types of deception carry with them very different emotional values. In the dragger we find confidence. He knows he has a big hand and he's just trying to get the most value out of it. If he gets caught, oh well, he didn't maximize profit, that's all. The bluffer, however, may be feigning confidence, but knows he's engaged in chancy activity, and if he gets caught he'll be punished by having some chips taken away. It stands to reason, then, that bluffers, as a class, tolerate (or maybe even enjoy) dicey situations more than draggers. Both the bluffer and the dragger is practicing deception, but the dragger is practicing safe deception. Some players simply can't manage the other kind at all.

Playing online, I'm constantly on the lookout for trappy players. When I see someone sandbagging or slow playing, I bang a CD designation into his box. Now I know that he's at least capable of that. If he's also an RRR type, I've got a pretty clear picture of his play. His raises already don't scare me; I know how to get out of the way of those. Now I'm onto his calls and check-calls as well. If I feel he's dragging, I can simply slow down and decline to bet his hand for him.

He may, of course, be just garden variety weak-loose, calling with an inferior hand and begging to give his money away. This would not surprise me, for players who can only drag and not bluff are likely to have holes in other areas of their play, such as, well, calling too much with inferior hands and giving their money away. Still, that's why I take notes, so that I can make a more informed judgment as to whether a call is just a call or the slow playing of a big hand. If my note box tells me that I've seen this player drag before, I can appropriately weight the possibility that this little CD player is practicing the only deception he can muster.

I confess to a certain disdain for the draggy player. It's not that he's doing anything wrong; to the contrary, he's not do-ing *enough* wrong. If he can only drag and not bluff, he's sim-ply not a complete player. He either hasn't yet acquired the nerve or the knack for the bluff, or it's just not in his nature to practice such scary chicanery. As Annie Duke says, "If you don't get caught with your hand in the cookie jar sometimes, you're not playing the game right." Players who drag only and never bluff are just too afraid of getting caught.

WCWC = WILL CALL WITH CHEESE

We talked just now about garden variety weak-loose players and the sorts of errors they routinely make. Like everything else that passes before our eyes online, this is behavior we can identify, codify, and store for later use—in this case, to press and bet for value against players who have made it clear that they'll make calls they simply should not make.

You see these players online all the time. Some of them, just new to the game, are merely inexperienced and haven't yet learned how to gauge their chances. Others are action junkies, and would rather waste their money than waste their time watching a hand they're not in. Still others have been se-duced by odds. Knowing, for example, that Q-8 is only around a 2 to 3 underdog to A-9, they jump willy-nilly into almost any pot.

Now look, there are plenty of times where it's correct to play cheese. If the pot odds genuinely justify a call, call. If you're up against a player with strong CB tendencies, it's fine to get involved with, shall we say, "creative" holdings, because you know if you hit your hand you'll get paid off. But these are strategic considerations apart from just the basic mistake of calling with inferior values.

The WCWC designation alerts you that you're facing an opponent who will victimize himself in a variety of related ways. Seeing him make bad loose calls in one circumstance, you can anticipate provoking similar errors in other areas. Say, for example, you watch *BizzyBee* bumble into a pot that's been raised and reraised in front of him. This time he gets lucky, flops two pair, and eventually shows down a surprising winner, 8-5 offsuit. In such circumstances, some players berate this dondo in their chatbox. (Always a mistake. Haven't they heard? *Don't tap on the glass!*) But while others are loudly lamenting their misfortune, you're calmly writing WCWC in the appropriate place. Next time this Wally's in the big blind, you know you're pretty free to go after him with anything half good because you know that someone who can get into a multiply-raised pot with 8-5 offsuit is unlikely to have strong compunctions about defending his blind with ragged hands.

It's a funny thing about loose preflop callers: They frequently turn tight on the flop. Down there on the level of their root psychology, I think they see calling preflop as a bit of an adventure—*who knows what wonders the flop may bring?* When the flop brings disappointment, as it so often does, the adventure is over and they surrender their cards. You see this pattern frequently in a WCWC player—loose call preflop, tight play postflop—and if you have him thus designated in your note box, you know what to look for every time you two square off.

OTHER CODES

Here are some other codes I use to describe players or situations I run into routinely online:

- HC = *he controls*. This is a player whose betting is creative, strong, and unpredictable. Much as I hate it, he has the power to rule our confrontations.
- IC = *I control*. This player is passive, predictable, and susceptible to my strong moves. Obviously, I'd rather play against an IC player than an HC one.
- CRR = *calls 'r' real*. Some players won't get involved un-

less they have a real hand or a real draw. I like to note, and know, who these players are.

- BBP = *bets bottom pair*. Conversely, some players consider any piece of the flop a license to bet. They present natural trapping opportunities.
- DD = *drives draws*. A DD player bets his straight and flush draws, either for the fold equity that's in it or just because he's frisky.
- RWJ = *raises with junk*. Very aggressive preflop. This can be a dangerous player since it's hard to put him on a hand.
- NB = *naked bluff*. This player has demonstrated the ability to put in a big bet with no hand whatsoever.
- CTC = *content to check*. This player will happily check it down and can often be moved off the pot with a bet on the turn or river.

Note that some codes complement others. RWJ tendencies are likely to be found in FNL players, for example, and RRR and CRR designations often go hand in hand. And as I've said, some players who can drag will never bluff—but then again, some will. So if your note box shows CD, DD, and NB, say, you'll know that you're facing a player who brings the full package.

Codes like these, of course, can only take you so far. Good players will switch gears, and bad players will play inconsistently. Sometimes someone will surprise you by making a completely uncharacteristic move. What you think is a trend will turn out to be an aberration. And you will certainly *Heisenberg* your foes; that is, change the way they play against you by the way you play against them. Still, it's better to have your foes encoded than to attack them (or let them attack you) blind. If you're not making book, you're wasting one of online poker's most golden opportunities. It's even kind of fun.

Pause for a moment now and reflect on the types of players you routinely face. What fanciful names or shorthands can you apply to them and their style of play? Give it a whack. It costs nothing to try, and the information you give yourself now may earn you, or save you, some big bets down the line.

>>

If you're having trouble calling to mind specific players or specific playing types, just save this exercise for the next time you play online. A single table sitngo is a good place to work on your encoding chops, because the players are there for the duration, until they bust out or until the sitngo ends. Make it a point to open every text box and to enter at least something in all of them. Notice how this activity keeps your head in the game. Over time, you'll make do with fewer and fewer actual recorded notes, and your minimal keystrokes will become stoked with meaning, but for now there's no substitute for a little creative spy work.

Codes such as these are essentially keys that unlock large files in one's brain. They represent, and trigger memories of, the collected observations we've made and conclusions we have drawn. While you may find it helpful to use my codes in your note-boxing efforts, your own codes will do more for you because, as I said, they speak to you in your own idiom. Furthermore, the effort to create names for the tendencies or behaviors you observe can only strengthen your awareness and improve your ability to make reliable assessments on the fly. Plus, "to name a thing is to own a thing." Once you've got some poor cally Wally dialed in as a CD RRR YO with WCWC tendencies, there's really not much he can do, apart from getting very lucky, to keep you from taking his dough.

PART II

♣♠♦♥

SITNGOS

♧♤◇♡

6

♣ ♠ ♦ ♥

PLANET SITNGO

♧ ♤ ♢ ♡

Is it possible to devise a single comprehensive strategy for beating sitngo tournaments? On the face of it, no. How could one strategy apply to the many varieties of sitngos—multi-table, ten handed, six handed, and heads up—and to the different degrees of knowledge and ability found at the different buy in thresholds? Nor could an approach to the languid pace of a regular sitngo fit neatly into the breakneck framework of turbo play. Furthermore, some people argue that no single strategy can be applied across the breadth of poker sites because the style of play varies so greatly from site to site. Some sites, they'll tell you, are loose; others incredibly tight. Some sites, it is anecdotally claimed, feature wacky madness like five players going all in on the first hand, with one player quintupling through—and *still* playing badly enough to finish out of the money. To me, this seems like a particular brand of fish story: *Man, you should have been here yesterday; they were biting and they were* big!

Even after adjusting for confirmation bias, no single strategy is perfect for all sitngos simply because no two sitngos—even those on the same site with the same structure—play exactly alike. The mix of players changes; nor can even the same players be expected to play the same way from one match to the next. Some will consciously make adjustments. Others will just get tired, tilty, or distracted and act in unexpected ways. Nor do *you* stay the same. The focus and concentration you bring to your first sitngo of the day is quite different from what you show in your tenth in a row.

So the overall strategy for sitngo success is this:

STAY FLEXIBLE.

Stay flexible. Be ready to adapt. It's great going into a game with a game plan, but your game plan shouldn't lockjaw your thinking. Rather, it should be the platform on which you stand to make strategic adjustments as circumstances require. You might, for example, have the very sensible idea of staying squeaky tight through the first rounds of play, only to discover that several players will reliably surrender their *limpets* (limp bets) to raises. In the name of sticking to your system, you would forego the free money that these weakies are offering you here, and that would be wrong. Per Ralph Waldo Emerson, "A foolish consistency is the hobgoblin of little minds." Stay flexible. Adapt.

In all events, your global approach to sitngos should be guided by your deep understanding of the mindset of your sitngo foes. You will discover, if you do not already know, that sitngo aficionados are a far cry from their cash game counterparts. To stretch an analogy to the snapping point, sitngo players are to cash game players as light beer is to absinthe. Yes, the sitngo fan likes his action, but he likes it in safe, measured doses. So measured, in fact, that we can make the following assertions about most sitngo players:

- They aren't in it for the money.
- They're risk averse.
- They make mistakes.
- They feel fear.

These assertions guide our strategy as we prepare to seize and subdue Planet Sitngo. But are they valid? Let's test.

MOST SITNGO PLAYERS AREN'T IN IT FOR THE MONEY

Does this surprise you? Do you disagree? If so, I would ask you to think about what motivates you to play in sitngos. Name, if you can, the things you like about them.

>>

Here's what I get when I go sitngo:

- Tournament experience
  - I can look at a lot of situations and try out a lot of different approaches
- Limited time commitment
  - Within the hour it'll be over and I can move on to other things
- A viable "exit strategy"
  - Unlike cash play with its temptation to play "just one more orbit," when the tournament's over I can organically end my online session
- Enjoyment
  - Winning a sitngo is a fun and interesting intellectual exercise
- And, oh yeah, the money
  - Limited reward, granted, but reward just the same

But there's a problem with the money. From a profitability point of view, it just doesn't add up.

A $30 ten-way sitngo pays 50 percent for first place, 30 percent for second, and 20 percent for third—$150, $90, and $60, respectively. If all ten contenders were exactly equally skilled, each would finish in the money an average of three times out of ten. In ten matches, then, theoretical player *SitnGoGoBoots* puts in $300, finishes first, second, and third one time each, and out of the money seven times, wining an average of $100 per money finish for a total take of, well, $300. For the average player (which most players are, by definition) sitngos are a break-even proposition.

Except they're not.

Because we're not just putting up $30 per match. We're also putting up an entry fee. The fee may vary from site to site, but $3 is typical for a $30 sitngo, so that's the number we'll use here. It costs us $330, then, to win our average $300. Is that a good deal? Hell, slot machines pay better.

I'm not telling you anything you don't know, I know. You did the math of this a long time ago. So did I. So did *SitnGoGoBoots*—but he rejects absolutely the notion that he's a merely average player. He's *much* better than average, he figures, and his win rate must be much better than three times out of ten. If *SitnGoGoBoots* had hard data to back up this claim, I might buy it, but it turns out that his evidence is not evidence at all but really just vague memory. Still, let's give him the benefit of the doubt. Let's say he wins four times out of ten. Now he's pulling in $100 x 4, or $400. His net profit after ten sitngos is $70, a whopping $7 per match. And how long did each match take? On the order of an hour, right?

Hmm. What's minimum wage these days?

"You're still underestimating me," says (a now somewhat defensive) *SitnGoGoBoots*. "I don't win just four out of ten matches I play. I win half! At *least!*" At *least*, huh? Okay, let's say he does. Let's say he wins $500 for every $330 he puts in play. Now he's pushed his win rate up to $17 per match. That's an okay number, I suppose—*if* he's telling the truth and *if* he can keep it up, which I doubt, not because I'm a natural cynic but just because most players overstate their win rate and underreport their downside. Even if every word from this guy were gospel, can't someone smart enough to win half his sit-ngo matches—"at *least!*"—generate more than $170 per ten-hour day doing something, almost anything, else?

The question is entirely rhetorical. Every sensible player, even the entirely rhetorical *SitnGoGoBoots*, knows that he's not going to get rich a sitngo at a time. Still, some do try—by playing many sitngos at once. They reason that if they can beat one sitngo for $17 an hour, they can beat four simultane-ously for $68 an hour. Now, $68 an hour is an ample wage, but this win rate is predicated on the assumption that one can consistently money in 50 percent of the sitngos one enters *while playing four at a time!* I'm not saying it can't be done, but I'd want to see a player's books before I accepted his claim.

Yet, we all play anyway. We thousands of average (and we few above average and we few below average) players flock to sitngos many, many times a day, each of us with at least some awareness that we're betting with at least some the worst of it. Why do we do it? What do we get from the sitngo experience if not profit?

Can the answer be as simple as this? It's fun.

Sitngos are fun. And that's why most people play.

It's fun to match wits and strategy against nine other play-ers (or five or even just one). Better yet, it's fun on a fixed in-come. No matter how many sitngos a day we play, especially if we play the small ones, we can't lose a lot of money fast. We may not get rich, but we probably won't go broke. We can have fun all day, and maybe even make it pay (a little).

That's why most sitngo players aren't in it for the money. It's not that they don't want to win a lot. It is rather that they don't want to *lose* a lot. Even if we know we're consistently giv-ing away some equity, it's a price we willingly play for the low-variance, low-volatility, high-enjoyment realm of the sitngo.

MOST SITNGO PLAYERS ARE RISK AVERSE

Many sitngo players become fans of the sitngo's slow gamble after memorable unpleasant experiences in cash games. Somewhere along the line they went through the horror (and haven't we all?) of seeing the bottom drop out of their bankroll in the frenzy of online cash play. For whatever reason—bad luck, bad play, superior foes, narcotic cough medicine—they found themselves in *QFM*, quick flush mode, where money flowed through their hands like water, and their fingers sprouted calluses from so frequently and repeatedly punching the *buy more chips* button. In the manner of watching a train wreck, they saw the tragedy unfolding but were powerless to stop it. Next thing they knew, they were riding the virtual rail, or else dwelling in the cellar of micro-limit cash games, trying to rebuild.

They solemnly vowed not to let that happen again.

And sitngos came to their rescue. Because no matter how badly they played a sitngo they couldn't do worse than bust out and lose their buy in. If they wanted to lose more, they had to find a whole other sitngo and wait for it to start. While on some sites, notably Party Poker, the wait can be less than the time you've spent reading this sentence, still there's a qualitative psychological difference between the dark thought of a cash game player on a losing jag—*"Just one more rebuy will turn this nightmare around"*—and a sitngo player trying to pull himself out of a similar slide—*"God, I played that match badly; screw it, I'm going to bed."* In simplest terms, it's easier not to start than it is to stop. It's easier to decide not to enter another sitngo than it is to exit a cash game that's kicking our ass.

Sitngos, then, apply the brakes to a losing player's play. True, you can bet yourself broke on the first hand of a sitngo and find yourself in a second one seconds later, but that's not the way most players go about it. They want to get their money's worth. They want to put themselves in a position to win, and while there are a venturesome few who adopt the strategy of *double or done*, most sitngo fans are fiscally cautious. How do we know this? Because if they weren't, they'd be mixing it up in the higher volatility cash games, where the roller coaster ride is steeper and faster, and the thrill is that much greater, or more dreadful as the case may be.

Knowing this about the sitngo habitué—that he prizes limited risk and correct play—how would you characterize his approach to the match?

>>

How does that compare to your own as you understand it now?

Here's how I see the typical sitngo player in action: Tight by nature, he's doing his best to play correctly according to his notion of correct play. Particularly in the early stages of a tournament, I take his raises to represent real hands because I know he wants to bet with the best of it. If he suffers a setback, though, it's hard for him to right himself. His streak of fatalism will lead him to believe that he's in the midst of yet another doomed sitngo; he'll give up. Then look for him to squander the rest of his chips on a reckless adventure, a hopeless bluff, or a dim hope. Impatience or despair, it seems, often trump caution.

But caution is the controlling idea for many sitngo competitors. Having made their investment, they don't want to squander it. This means that they'll rarely go all in without the best of it, and also that, when faced with an all in bet, they'll lay down many hands they should play. Their entire approach is informed by *fear,* the fear of losing everything on the turn of one or two cards. If you merely embrace risk while those around you eschew it, you'll have a sizeable strategic edge in sitngo play.

MOST SITNGO PLAYERS MAKE MISTAKES

It's hard to play perfect poker. If you lack training, discipline, and experience, it's damn near impossible. Since the vast majority of internet poker players are relatively recent arrivals, and therefore may lack experience, we can expect most of them to miss playing perfect poker by a fairly wide mark. This does not mean that we should underestimate them, for we may be fairly well wide of perfect poker ourselves. It does, however, mean that we can look for them to make mistakes and we can seek ways to exploit those mistakes.

This is particularly true in the sitngo realm because many players rightly recognize such tournaments as opportunities to deepen their understanding of poker in a situation where the cost per mistake is relatively low. If you run into kicker trouble with a bad ace in a cash game, for example, and it costs you half your stack, that's real money out of your real pocket. Make the same enthusiastic error in a sitngo and you may have lost some chip equity, but you haven't lost any money—at least not yet. If you're still alive in the tournament, you still have time to right the ship.

For someone raw in poker, then, sitngos are a thorough-going godsend. When your $10 or $20 entry fee can buy you an hour's worth of real poker experience against real poker foes, it's an offer you almost can't refuse. Better than books! Better than the free-play tournaments where, since no real money's at stake, no real play seems to take place. Better, certainly, than the high-volatility cash games where, even in the realm of modest buy ins, experienced players go through newbies like a sneeze through cheap Kleenex, and the cost of learning quickly leaps high.

So now we have a whole class of sitngo players who are bound to make mistakes, some of which include: overbetting small pairs; chasing draws without adequate odds; entering a pot with something like A-J after a raise and a call; making loose calls into unraised pots with third-rate holdings like K-6 suited; bluffing off their chips, and getting blinded out. What other errors would you expect these newbies or near-newbies to make during their first halting circuits around poker's grand track?

>>

Again, I mean no disrespect to these anxious tyros. They're doing something really right by taking measured steps into the game. They've found a way to avoid going too far, too fast, and risking their bankroll at a time when their bankroll is most at risk. But if I'm playing in a modest buy in sitngo, I will anticipate that a certain number of my opponents don't yet quite know what correct play is. Thus, if I make a preflop raise without an ace and the flop comes A-x-x, I won't necessarily bet at that flop because I won't necessarily count on my foes to know enough to put me on a good ace and lay down a bad one. By contrast, when I have, say K-Q and the board shows K-x-x, I'll go ahead and bet, and bet again, knowing that inexperienced holders of K-J or K-T will call me down and pay me off.

Newbies in sitngos, then, offer us many marvelous targets of opportunity, so long as we gauge their skill level accurately and don't engage in wishful thinking. We must also be mentally prepared for the times when others' mistakes cost us pots or even our tournament lives. Many is the experienced sitngo player who has walked away disgruntled, muttering, "I would have won if my opponents hadn't played so badly." This guy should know better. In the long run, he will make money (and win sitngos) at the direct expense of other players' mistakes.

And in the sitngo realm you'll see lots.

MOST SITNGO PLAYERS FEEL FEAR

Once you start a sitngo, the money you paid to enter is no longer yours. You'll get it back, and then some, if you win the sitngo, but if you finish out of the money, it doesn't matter whether you finish tenth, sixth, or fourth; that money is as gone as cheap gas. And yet, many sitngo players have an almost sentimental attachment to their buy in. Against all logic and reason, they fear to lose money they've already spent.

You see this phenomenon during two distinct periods of the sitngo tournament. It appears first early in the tournament, when people are playing tight, trying to play correctly, and trying to get "their money's worth" from their buy in. This makes no sense on its face, of course; if you finish out of the money, your net return is the same whether you last one hand or 100. I suppose it could be argued that the newbies who are buying tournament experience do actually get a better return on their investment by lasting longer in the sitngo, but what sort of experience are they gaining? How to play too tight in a sitngo and last just long enough to finish out of the money?

The second, and highly exploitable, time you see the fear factor in sitngos is when the table gets close to the money. Again, most players' thinking is often spurious here. Having come so far in the tournament, they now think that they have more to lose, not just in terms of money but also time and effort, none of which they want to go to waste. This will have predictable results. Can you name them?

>>

Players will play too tight. They'll look off gambling opportunities when they clearly have the best of it, or when the odds justify getting involved. They'll do everything in their power to avoid busting out on the bubble—one place off the money. You might have someone with a middle pocket pair, for instance, who won't get involved against someone he suspects has overcards because he hopes to find a better place to get his money in or, more likely, hopes that others will bust out and he can back into the money without actively putting his tournament life on the line. I'm not saying that it's always correct to take that coin flip, but it *is* always correct to make your decisions for sound strategic reasons and not for fear of losing money that's gone.

But most sitngo players are risk averse and most are prone to mistakes. These two characteristics come together in the end stages of a sitngo and cause many players to clench and clutch and dream of pocket aces. If you're willing to gamble at that stage, if you simply recognize that your entry fee is no longer yours to lose, then you put yourself in position not just to make it into the money but to make it into the money with a controlling interest in chips. Then, when you get down to the final three . . .

Ah, but we're getting ahead of ourselves. Before we get to the final three, we've got the whole sitngo to play through. Let's play through one together now, here on these pages. We'll examine some key moments and crucial decisions of a sitngo, en route to the discovery that winning sitngos is not so much a matter of playing every hand correctly (for the vast majority of them play themselves) but of playing a few critical hands just right.

7

♣ ♠ ♦ ♥

SITNGO À GO-GO

♧ ♤ ♢ ♡

Like snowflakes, no two sitngos are exactly alike. Yet, some situations do recur, and the lessons we learn from events in one sitngo we can apply to other sitngos and other situations. In any case, the particulars of a given hand aren't nearly as important as the underlying thought processes that guide our decisions and inform our conclusions. In the name of exploring those situations and growing those thought processes, let's browse a sitngo together, hit its highlights, and discuss reactions we might have, strategies we might use, and moves we might make.

Okay, here we (sit and) go. We're playing a ten handed $50+5 NLHE sitngo on pokerbeatsworking.com. The time is 11:00 P.M., at least where we live, though of course for our opponents anywhere it could be anywhere. In any event, this is for us a late night recreation, a little dose of vitamin p before bedtime. As such, we know why we're here: to have fun by testing ourselves against the challenge that poker and our foes present. Still, we're determined not to be the typical sitngo junkie. We intend to play alert, aware, fearless, and mistake-free poker, to take appropriate risks, and to win the money if we can.

As the tournament gets underway, we find ourselves facing

a mixed bag of players, about half of whom we already have some notes on.

NAME	SEAT	NOTES (if any)
Dealerzchoiz	1	Kosher Timmy, RRR
Skip Loader	2	
GreeeeeDeeeee	3	FNL, RWC
54321claudia	4	
Killer Poker (us)	5	
Wooly Bully	6	Frisky, HC, AO, DD, CB
cantcount05	7	
IownU666	8	YO, CBRO
Charley-Davidson	9	Cally, tilty, IC, TTT
Mylittlepony	10	YO, WCWC

We don't get involved in the first hand, but two sure do. With blinds at 10 and 20, *Charley-Davidson* opens in early position for 60. *Wooly Bully* raises to 120. Everyone else folds and Charley reraises all in. Wooly calls. 9♥-T♥ for Charley, K♥-K♦ for Wooly. With two hearts on the flop and another on the river, Charley doubles through to 3,000 in chips and Wooly is out.

Off the top of your head, how big a dog was Charley on this hand?

>>

Not that you have to rely on the top of your head. Sites like CardPlayer.com, Pokulator.com, and many others offer on-the-fly odds calculators, and there's no reason why you can't keep one of these handy gizmos open on your desktop while you play. While it's better to have these numbers memorized (the pocket kings are about a 4-1 favorite here, if my memory serves), one of the real beauties of online poker is how a twenty-inch monitor, a fast microprocessor, and a big butt-load of bandwidth can compensate for flawed or inadequate memory. Are you making the most of the fact that you're playing *online?* If not, why not? Keep an odds calculator handy.

So Wooly took a bad beat and he's eliminated. We don't much mind this outcome, because our notes tell us that *Wooly Bully* is a formidable player whom we'd just as soon see gone. As for *Charley-Davidson*, the fact that he'd go all in on the first hand with 9-T suited suggests that he might not be the type (to say the least) who can cling to an early big chip lead. We'll look for opportunities to get involved with him and get him stuck on a hand. We'll also note in passing that he may be playing double or done, an approach favored by those who'd rather take a shot at a dominating chip position than compete from the middle of the pack. If they bomb out, they figure, there's always another sitngo waiting in the wings. I have seen no evidence to suggest that this strategy is successful in the long run, but many players swear by it, and those who use it should be identified and tagged, for their opening huge moves are often made with far less than premium values.

Nothing much happens for the next few hands. This is typical of the first lap or two of a sitngo. Apart from the explosive fireworks of kamikaze pilots like *Charley-Davidson,* most sitngo players like to start slow and spend some time sussing one another out, not a bad plan, especially against unknown foes. To watch others' confrontations is to go to school on their tendencies and tactics and gain valuable information for free. Furthermore, as you no doubt know, all online poker sites offer *hand histories*: records of every action on every hand. Are you aware that this includes the *starting hands of everyone who calls the final bet?* Even if those cards aren't shown on your game screen, they are revealed in the hand history, and from such data you can glean critical insight into your foes' starting, calling, and raising requirements. Therefore, it makes sense to be patient and observant early on. With information, as with action, try to get more than you give.

With the blinds still at 10 and 20, for example, *Skip Loader,*

GreeeeeDeeeee, and *cantcount05* hook up in a hand. *Skip Loader* opens for a raise and the other two call. The flop comes A-A-K and everybody checks. They also check a jack on the turn and a three on the river. *Skip Loader* turns over T-T and takes the pot. Here's what the hand history shows.

Showdown:

Skip Loader shows T♠ T♥.
Skip Loader has A♥ A♣ K♣ T♠ T♥: two pair, aces and tens.
GreeeeeDeeeee mucks cards.
(GreeeeeDeeeee has Q♦ 4♠.)
cantcount05 mucks cards.
(cantcount05 has 8♣ 7♣.)

Based on shown cards alone, we learned that *Skip Loader* will bet a medium pair in early position, but won't make a continuation bet into a flock of scare cards. Through the hand history, though, we also learn that the other two will call raises with inferior values; that *GreeeeeDeeeee* may be the last float on the clueless parade; and that *cantcount05* seems disinclined to drive his draws, at least into a dominating flop. We add the appropriate notes on these players—WCWC for both, at minimum—and adjust our play accordingly.

It's wise not to over-interpret such scant data. *GreeeeeDeeeee,* for example, might be trying to mislead us with a single bad loose call, or he might have clicked the wrong button by mistake. And *cantcount05* may make that call with middle suited connectors early in the tournament but not later on. Still, the first phase of a sitngo tournament offers the opportunity to gather all sorts of information, and if we're careful not to invest too heavily in its meaning, it can give us snapshots of the players we face, snapshots we absolutely must have and develop if we're going to make informed choices against them later on.

In any case, the early portion of a sitngo is a good time to avoid reckless adventures, because the scant advantage of collecting low-denomination chips of swiftly diminishing value doesn't measure up against the downside of getting trapped and beaten. To put it another way, for sitngos (and really for all tournaments) . . .

PATIENCE IS PRECIOUS
WHEN CHIPS ARE CHEAP.

This may seem counterintuitive at first. After all, shouldn't you feel more comfortable taking a flier on a low quality holding when its inexpensive to do so? Maybe . . . but the problem with cheap flops is how costly they can get. Suppose you decide to make a *what the hell* call with J♠-9♠ in early position. Suppose even that nobody raises. Now the flop comes J-x-x. Do you love your hand? If you push in a lot of chips and win, great. But if you push in a lot of chips and lose, your stack will be eviscerated; maybe halved; maybe altogether gone.

During the early stages of any tournament, the risk of losing far outweighs the reward for winning. No matter how big a pot you win when chips are cheap, the value of those chips will be quickly degraded by the rising blinds. In that sense, it almost doesn't matter whether you win early pots or not. But it *does* matter if you lose them, for you could leave yourself crippled or riding the rail. So, early in a sitngo (or, again, any tournament) you want to avoid trouble hands like A-J, K-J, K-Q, Q-J, and suited connectors. Even J-J is not a premium hand early. Practice patience: No one wins a tournament in round one anyhow.

Here's another hand from the first level that illustrates this point. *Dealerzchoiz* makes it 60 to go from early position. It's folded to us and we hold 4♣-4♠. What do you think we should do?

>>

I'm gonna like folding here. The best hand for us to compete against would be something like A-2 offsuit (or, *mirable visu*, pocket twos or threes) and we have no reason to believe that *Dealerzchoiz* would raise with such cheese. Our notes on him tell us that—RRR—his raises are real, at least so far as we've been able to see in the past, so his likely raiseworthy holdings are good aces, big overcards, or an overpair. It's interesting to note that a player who *does* raise with cheese is more of a threat to our 4-4 than we might imagine. While such a frisky critter might give us the gift of a bet with A-2 offsuit—in which case we're better than a 2-1 favorite—he could also be out of line with something like Q-8 suited, almost exactly a fifty-fifty shot against our puny pocket pair. But as I said, we know (or think we know) *Dealerzchoiz* to be a kosher player. If we choose to get involved, therefore, we're probably a small favorite against big overcards or a big underdog to an overpair. So why get involved? We really need to hit a set here, and if we do there's no guarantee that we'll get paid off. Similarly, we might be looking to bluff, and there's nothing wrong with that, but if we're out to bluff, who cares whether we have 4-4, 2-7, or a partridge in a pear tree?

I'm not advocating timidity; when you get the goods, bet the goods, right? But a sensible approach is called for here. It won't kill us to fold, and the information we might amass by watching others go to war will be worth more to us in the long run than the few fresh chips we could accumulate here. There's nothing wrong with playing snug early. Leave it to others to batter one another and reveal themselves to you.

Many players find their patience tested here. After all, they didn't join a sitngo just to *sit*. They want to *go!* And folding hand after hand after hand is not their idea of a good time. Usually, they respond either by joining multiple sitngos or they loosen up their starting requirements. I propose a third path: Redefine fun. Take your pleasure not in action but inaction. Consider every correct fold a win. Consider every piece of captured data a win. Practice patience to a sublime degree, and then take pride-unto-glee in the patience you have.

So we let the laps pass, and the only hand we've played so far was 9-9 on the button. We raised, everyone folded, next case. We still have about 1,500 in chips, and no one has much more except *Charley-Davidson,* who still leads but has come back to the pack at about 2,500. We imagine that our foes (if they're paying attention to us at all) read us as basic Timmy. The blinds have gone up to 20-40 when we find ourselves in middle position holding K♥-Q♥. We might not have called with it, but when no one opens before us, we're sure gonna raise. We make it 120 to go, our standard 3x big blind opening raise. Only the little blind, *Mylittlepony* calls. From our notes on him, we know he's capable of making loose calls, but since he called out of the small blind it seems more likely that he has at least a little something-something here. Since we've been so sparingly involved, he'll credit us with a strongish hand, and therefore probably has a strongish one himself. Of course, people have different ideas of what "strongish" means, but we'll make the tentative assessment that he's got approximately T-K or a middle pocket pair. Anything below that, he'd probably dump; anything above that, he'd probably raise.

The flop comes A-7-4, two-suited, and Pony quickly checks. The speed of his check doesn't tell us much about his hand's value, for he could be checking weakness or slow-playing strength. But the fast check does tell us one thing: He knows where he's at in the hand. If there were some doubt in his mind—should he or shouldn't he drive a draw, for instance—he might have taken a couple extra beats to settle on his check. Thus, we can put him on a hand that's either clearly strong or clearly weak.

While we're on the subject, let's take a moment to remind ourselves not to give off this tell ourselves. Our online foes don't have much to go on in picking off tells, and the pace of play is one of the strong indicators they turn to first. So we're well served to wait a few seconds, and the same number of seconds, every time before we act. This will allow us to disguise necessary delays when our path is not clear and we have to think things through. In other words . . .

BE CONSISTENT IN THE
TIME YOU TAKE TO ACT.

Okay, the flop either hit him very well or missed him completely. At least that's what we think right now. We'll update our assessment as the hand goes forward. Every time he acts or doesn't act, he's giving us information, and it's our job to integrate this information into a global view of his hand and intentions. This, by the way, is why we really should have no trouble practicing patience. With so much to think about—assuming we choose to think about it—there's no end to our mental agenda. Okay, now there's 280 in the pot, and we each have stacks of around 1,500. Should we check or bet, and if bet, how much?

>>

First, let's update our thinking. Our foe's quick check suggests a clean miss or (less likely) a slow-play disguised as a miss. He's probably not on a straight draw because he probably didn't call preflop with 5-6 or 2-3. He might have called with a suited king or queen, though, so he might be on a flush draw. We certainly don't want to give him proper odds to call, so let's fire in 200 here. It's a good, solid bet, about two-thirds the size of the pot. If our foe calls with a draw, he's calling 200 into a 480 pot, and so getting a 2.4-1 return on investment (ROI) on a draw that's worse than 4-1 to hit on the next card. If he's sensible and on a draw, he'll fold. If he's on a draw and he calls, he's making a mistake.

Guess what? In most cases, your single foe will fold to this bet. He'll rarely be on a draw; he'll rarely be on anything at all.

Remember that in Texas hold'em, it's really hard to make a hand. Two unpaired cards improve to a pair or better just a squidge more than one time out of three. Most of the time, then, the flop is either a complete whiff for your foe, or else a draw, which your two-thirds pot bet will price him out of taking. The only hands you truly fear here are the unlikely flopped set or the somewhat-less-unlikely A-x. But if he doesn't have an ace, you're in terrific shape, for a crucial reason: You raised preflop, and raises look like aces to most players.

I'll say it again, because it's a Big Idea:

RAISES LOOK LIKE ACES
TO MOST PLAYERS.

Are you aware of this? Do you know the importance of this? Every time you raise—no, seriously, *every time you raise*—your opponent figures you have an ace. In fact, probably you do have an ace, because the so-called premium hands in hold'em are ace-big and big pocket pairs, and there are many more ways to hold ace-big than a big pocket pair. So raises look like aces to most players because, hey presto, most raises *are* aces. Since you raised preflop, your opponent can easily put you on an ace and get away from his hand.

I want to underscore this point because it draws the distinction between sensible tightness and heedless timidity. You don't want to make random bets or get involved in reckless adventures, but neither do you want to hold back out of fear. If you check on the flop, you're just asking your opponent to take the pot away on the turn, no matter what he has. That's no way to win at poker: not tournaments; not cash games; not strip poker with the nice neighbors.

Of course, while people raise with aces, people *call* with aces as well, and there's no reason why *Mylittlepony* can't be holding an ace right here. That's why the two-thirds pot bet is so handy. It's big enough to get the job done—drive out the draws and the pure whiffs—yet small enough that we can get away from our hand with most of our stack intact if our opponent plays back at us, which he probably will if he's on a good ace or better.

But that doesn't happen here. We make the routine continuation bet and *Mylittlepony* makes the expected fold. Hand over. Next case.

Before we move on, though, let's note what we learned just here. Quoting Virgil, the great Roman poet that neither you, I, nor anyone we know has ever read, *audentes fortuna juvat,* fortune favors the bold. Therefore be bold and . . .

WIN THE HANDS YOU'RE SUPPOSED TO WIN.

Moving on . . .

While the tournament is still nine handed or ten handed, we'll typically see approximately a lap or a lap and a half at each level. Forty or fifty hands in, then, we're gonna be looking at blinds of 30 and 60, and if there haven't been a bunch of eliminations up till this point, we're bound to see some now, as the escalating blinds start to exert pressure and foment raising wars.

54321claudia gets enthusiastic about pocket jacks, runs into *GreeeeeDeeeee*'s pocket aces, and exits the field. You see that a lot.

IownU666 slowplays a flopped straight and erases *cantcount05*, who had the misfortune to hit two pair. You see that a lot, too.

Charley-Davidson crashes and burns when he pits his big stack against *Skip Loader*'s slightly bigger stack, and his Q♣-Q♥against Skip's badly dominated A♥-Q♦. Charley's a 7-3 favorite, but—wouldn't you know it—a diamond flush gets there. This happens rather rarely, but to hear Charley whine about it in the chatbox (as he noisily decamps) you'd think he saw it all the time. Nor does he seem to remember that he owes his own sitngo life to a similar suckout against *Wooly Bully* on the very first hand. Online players characteristically have selective memory, heavily slanted in favor of "the other guy gets all the luck." It's our old friend confirmation bias again. People remember the brutal beats because they sting, whereas the times their favored hands hold up, or when they're on the receiving end of Dame Fortune's largesse, they consider it to be uneventful; the natural order of things. People are funny like that.

We, meanwhile, are planning a radical shift in strategy. Having stayed squeaky tight through the 10-20, 15-30, and 20-40 levels, we're looking to loosen up considerably at 30-60 and above. We're not going to get all cally—we never like doing that—but we are going to be much more aggressive in attacking the blinds. With the escalating price of poker, this becomes an absolute necessity, but also with the decreasing number of players, it becomes a viable strategy. At this point, we're looking to open any unopened pot whenever we have two half-decent cards or even just good position and reason to believe that the blinds won't defend. Here's where context density comes to our aid. Just fifteen or twenty minutes ago— very recently in our opponents' minds—we were playing so tight as to be practically absent. The tournament had a much different character then, and paid a much higher premium on patience, but many of our foes will not take this into account. They've got us pegged as solid and snug (or timid and weak) because we've played so few hands and, for a little while at least, they'll give respect to our raises that, frankly, our raises won't deserve.

As we slip into blind-stealing mode, we also adjust the size of our bets. Early on, if we came into a pot we came in for about three times the big blind because we generally wanted to thin the herd. Now we don't have to worry about that so much, for the herd will thin itself. It's smaller to begin with, since three or four players are gone, plus we're starting to get within sniffing distance of the money, so our foes will naturally start to tighten up. Also, as the blinds continue to rise, even a minimum bet starts to represent a fair whack from a stack, especially a short one. With this in mind, we'll stop opening for three times the big blind and instead open for just double.

This flies in the face of conventional wisdom, which says that anything less than 3x the big blind is a wimpy bet, just looking to get run over. In this case, though, conventional wisdom is if not all wet then at least a little damp. With betting, as with screwdrivers, it's always a case of the right tool for the right job. The bet we're looking for is one big enough to send the desired message, but not so big that we over-commit ourselves to the pot. With so much fold equity built into the situation, thanks to the rising blind-to-stack ratio and to our foes' default unwillingness to get involved, a bet of twice the big blind is generally big enough to get us what we want.

Mostly, we don't want anyone to call, and most of the time that's exactly what will happen. Eventually, though, our foes' picture of us will shift from snug to frisky. They'll become convinced that we can't have a hand every time we raise, so they'll lower their own starting requirements in the name of finding an opportunity to mix it up. What they don't realize is that we've fine tuned the size of the pot to serve our postflop plans no matter what happens. If they fold we win, but if they don't fold we don't lose much.

Case in point: The blinds have just jumped to 50 and 100. We're in late position with Q-9 suited. We've had good success with our blind steals, but we know that our foes are getting peeved at our commando ways. Sure enough, we make our standard (at this stage) opening raise of twice the big blind, and *Dealerzchoiz* decides to come in. Our stack sits at about three grand; his at about two. With our minimum raise, plus his call, plus the blinds, there's 550 in the pot. No matter how the flop comes, we're going to make a bet in the 350-400 range. Again, this is a bet with a certain amount of clout, especially since *Dealerzchoiz* can't be certain that we won't also bet the turn. Yet, if he wakes up with a real hand here and raises back, we can get away from our hand with relatively little damage done.

It's a one-two punch of a certain devastating power: We raise with any half-decent hand. If we get one caller, we bet two-thirds of the pot no matter what. Most of the time we'll win either before the flop or on the flop. If we get raised and we don't have a hand, we'll usually fold. If we're just called, we pause to reconsider the situation. We'll bet the turn if we still think we're ahead. Otherwise, we'll shut it down, check it down, and fold if we have to. Since we raised the minimum preflop, and shaped the size of the pot postflop, we're able to get away from the hand with most of our stack still intact. We get maximum bang for our betting buck.

Just for the sake of argument, see if you can construct an argument for betting much bigger preflop. In particular, tell me why this doesn't expose your stack to unnecessary risk.

>>

You may be wondering why it's correct to bet the minimum before the flop but not after. It has to do with pot odds. If we make a flop bet of 100 into a pot containing 550, we're pricing all draws and speculators right into the pot. Moreover, we really *are* telegraphing weakness with a weenie bet and asking to get raised out. An advantage of making the minimum raise preflop is that it reduces the size of a two-thirds bet on the flop. Say we'd raised three times the big blind preflop and gotten called. In that case, there would be 750 in the pot, and our two-thirds bet would then be 500. If we get played with here and have to break off our drive and/or surrender the pot, we will have lost 800 in chips. Starting with a minimum raise, or *min raise*, we hazard a pre- and postflop total of just 550 or 600 to do essentially the same job. Our goal is to get the most reward for the least risk, and this betting sequence is designed to achieve that goal.

Okay, our slash-and-burn style of play serves us well through the elimination of *Skip Loader* and *IownU666*, and now we're down to the bubble. A snapshot of the final four:

NAME	CHIP COUNT
Dealerzchoiz	3,800
GreeeeeDeeeee	5,300
Killer Poker	3,200
Mylittlepony	2,700

Poker, as we know, rewards the fearless, and right here on the bubble is when our fearlessness will reward us most. Suppose you're holding pocket jacks in the big blind. *Dealerzchoiz* and *Mylittlepony* have folded, and *GreeeeeDeeeee* pushes all in from the small blind. Would you call here or fold? What would your reasoning be?

>>

A lot of players give up their hands in this situation, but I can't really validate that choice. Granted, pocket jacks are problematic. As the saying goes, "There are three ways to play pocket jacks—all wrong." But let's consider the situation a little more fully. We're short handed, which means that relative hand strength has dropped. An all in push from the small blind carries some clout when you're at a ten handed table, especially if there are many limpers in the field. Four handed, though, with folds in front of him, the small blind needs almost no hand at all to make this move. He knows that most of the time the big blind will hold a weak hand (because most hold'em holdings are weak). More to the point, a call from the big blind here would put that player's tournament life on the line, and this is the crux of the small blind's thinking. He's counting on the big blind to cower out rather than risk bubbling off. This further decreases the chance that the small blind is pushing a monster here. And of course there are only three hands that beat J-J in this situation. If you fear to run into an overpair here, or even just fear to get unlucky, you're being way too timid for the circumstance. Get your money in the middle. In almost all cases you'll have the best hand. Where appropriate, then . . .

DON'T FEAR THE BUBBLE.

People do, though. They fear the bubble. They hate, loathe, and fear the bubble, and resent it for being the place where their dreams are dashed. We've already discussed the fallacy of this thinking: how a bubble finish pays exactly the same—nothing—as first out. Still, people get caught up in the mindset. They fret the time and effort they've invested in the sitngo, and fret the risk of having nothing to show when they've gotten *oh so close*. First, don't fall prey to this thinking. Second, recognize when your foes might be counting on you to cower out, and evaluate their likely hand strength accordingly. If it turns out that they do have a huge hand here, well, that's bad luck and that's just poker, but most of the time, this single sensibly derived big call is all it takes—also exactly *what* it takes—to make the money.

One thing you should certainly have at this point is a good, strong read on all your remaining foes. At minimum, you should know who's tricky and who's straightforward. This knowledge will inform your next critical decisions, which decisions you want to make with thoughtfulness and care. After all, while we're not afraid of bubbling off, all things considered we'd much rather money through.

GreeeeeDeeeee, having run into our pocket jacks and our fearlessness, is now short stacked and imperiled with less than 2,000 in chips. We're in the chip lead at 6,000 or so, and *Dealerzchoiz* is next with about 4,000. The blinds are 150 and 300. Now that we're four handed, and the chips have been consolidated in the hands of the few, we're back to raising three times the size of the big blind. Always asking ourselves how big a bet we need to make to achieve our goals, we find that a raise to 600 doesn't have quite enough muscle to keep a stack of 4,000 or 5,000 from making a loose call. So we make it 900 or even 1,000 to go. This, we find, is sufficient to pressure the blinds and move them off their indifferent holdings. Such is our intention when *GreeeeeDeeeee* folds and we, holding A-7 suited, make it 900 to go on the button.

But oops, *Dealerzchoiz* comes over the top for all his chips. Now we've got a decision to make.

We know we've been raising a lot of pots, and it's not out of the question that *Dealerzchoiz* could be raising us back here just to put us in our place. He'd love to get us off our raising jag, if only to leave the door open for his own promiscuous blind stealing. But we have to ask ourselves one question: *Why did he reraise all in* here? A reraise is a strong move, and a reraise bluff is a play that few players can make, especially on the money bubble. He may have been thinking for the past several hands that he'd like to reraise us, and he may have been looking for an opportunity to do so. We can reasonably conclude that he's found his opportunity now.

So what does he have? What would you need to have to reraise all in at this juncture?

>>

I would expect to find him with at least two unpaired big cards. Any middle pocket pair is a candidate, as are, of course, big pocket pairs and good aces. One thing I don't put him on is a pure bluff or even a *variation raise*, something like middle suited connectors. If this is a move he's been waiting to make, he's been waiting for good cards to make it with.

A lot of players see red in our situation. They take the reraise as a personal affront and fill their heads with much unnecessary and unproductive emotional noise. "How *dare* he!" they think, all huffy and insulted. Their egos thus engaged, they'll jump through all sorts of mental hoops to convince themselves that the raiser is lying, naked bluffing, and just begging to be called and destroyed. We're much better served with a quick, dispassionate analysis here. We need to decide, based on our experience of this player and our notes on him, how strong a move he's capable of here. What we need *not* to do is to consider his attack personal. In other words . . .

KEEP YOUR EGO OUT OF IT.

The other guy doesn't hate you, and he's not trying to prove his moral or tactical superiority. He just wants your money. Look, there's no place anywhere in poker for dick measuring contests, but there's *really* no place for it here, when you have a reasonable chance of winning this sitngo. If you think your hand's worth a call, call. But "I'll show you!" is no reason to go to war. Worse than silly, it's self-defeating.

In fact, of all the hands *Dealerzchoiz* might reraise with here, a naked bluff is the only one we can comfortably compete against. Any ace he feels like raising with is likely to be a better ace than ours. Any small pair has a small edge. Two unpaired *tweeners* (cards in between our ace and seven, for example Q-J) are only a slight underdog. And big pairs are just a mess, dominating us either a little, a lot, or *quite* a lot. Hey, it wasn't a mistake to raise with A-7. Seizing the initiative is rarely terribly wrong in poker. But when our foe comes back over the top for all his chips, we *have* to credit him with one of two things: either he has a strong hand or he's made a strong move. If he has a strong hand, there's no reason to get involved. If he's made a strong move, why not just acknowledge the excellence of his play, adjust, and wait for a better opportunity? This latter path is easy to follow *if* our big, fat, hairy egos don't get in the way. Let ire leak in, though, and we'll find a way to persuade ourselves to call him down. Next thing we know, we're on the rail, and how does the ol' ego feel now?

So we duck *Dealerzchoiz*'s counterpunch here and the tournament goes on. Perhaps emboldened by his successful reraise, he goes on a little raising spree of his own here and actually succeeds in putting *Mylittlepony* out of play. Hallelujah! We've made the money!

Good times.

Now what?

Now we're in a situation where, probably, all the chips are going to go in the middle before the flop. The blinds are usually so high at this point that most bets represent a thick percentage of a player's stack, and either the first bet or the first raise will pot commit *somebody*. The guiding principle here is this: If we're going to get all our money in anyhow, we might as well get it in early, either with the best hand or with the benefit of a full board to draw to. If we have the best hand, we want the money in the middle while it's *still* the best hand, and if we need to hit to win, we'd like our full five shots to do so.

Such a circumstance arises just after the blinds hit 200 and 400. We have 4,400 in chips, and we're on the button holding A-K offsuit. We should probably push all in right here, hoping to pick up the blinds without a fight and move on. Due to a momentary lapse of reason, though (perhaps we're *un peu fatigue?*), after a whole sitngo of strong, solid poker we suddenly decide to get cute and just flat-call. Greedy us . . . rather than raise big and be satisfied with the blinds, we prepare a snare. I can think of two ways this is wrong. Can you?

>>

If we just call here, we give the small blind a cheap flop and the big blind a free one. A-K offsuit is a favorite against any one random unpaired hand, but *not any two*. Flat-calling, then, is an open invitation to get ganged up on. It's also an open invitation to get raised. While this may be the exact trap we were trying to set, it loses the advantage that opening for a raise has—the chance that the others might fold. Fold equity is huge three handed. Every time you swipe the blinds, that's another three hands you can survive without shrinking your stack. To put it another way . . .

IF THEY FOLD,
YOU DON'T HAVE TO GET LUCKY TO WIN.

But they don't fold. *Dealerzchoiz* completes in the small blind, and *GreeeeeDeeeee* (the chip leader at this point) raises to 2,000. We're kind of surprised that he didn't go all in, since he's committed a third of his stack anyhow. Did he make a mistake, or is he trying to get cute, too?

Of course, with *Dealerzchoiz* still live behind us, we need to think about what he might do after we act. Will he join the party? Probably not. Unless he slowplayed a huge hand in the small blind (of diminished likelihood since we hold an ace and a king) he'll probably be content to sit back and watch his foes go to war, reckoning that no matter who wins, he'll be ticketed for second place money at least. So we figure *Dealerzchoiz* for a fold, especially if we decide to reraise all in.

Which is what we should do. First of all, folding is out of the question. Against any pair except aces or kings, we're no worse than a 5-4 underdog, and the pot is giving us roughly correct odds for that draw. Against any hand that's not a pair, we're ahead so we definitely want to be involved. But having flat-called once already, we don't want to do that again. If we did, we'd be committing half our stack to the hope of hitting an ace or a king on the flop. Should that not happen, we might have to put in our last 2,000 on a draw. If we do hit the flop, we might not get paid. So we go all in. In the worst case, if we're chasing a pocket pair, our full chip commitment gives us five cards to catch up. And if our foe was frisky and out of line, we put him to the difficult choice of calling with the worst of it or folding and surrendering the chip lead. We sorta made a mistake by flat-calling on the button, but *GreeeeeDeeeee* sorta made a mistake by not raising all in, so in this little "mistake perfecta," we can reraise all in, close out *Dealerzchoiz,* and put *GreeeeeDeeeee*'s feet to the fire as well.

But before we push in our chips, let's double check our decision. Could we reasonably fold this hand and wait for better times? Well, sure, but down to 4,000 in chips, we face the unpleasant prospect of having the blinds whittle us down until we're forced to make a move with something smelly like K-9 suited or worse. To find a better place than this for our money, we'd need to catch some big luck, and soon. Why not take the luck we have right now? We'd have been better off going all in at the first opportunity, but as this is the situation we now find ourselves in, we need to make the best of it.

So we push. *Dealerzchoiz* folds. *GreeeeeDeeeee* calls. He has pocket jacks. Those problematic pocket jacks. Lucky for him, he hits a jack on the flop. Lucky for us, the flop also contains a queen, and when the turn is a ten and the river a brick, we've doubled through.

Now that we have over half the chips, we can afford to be patient. It would be a perfectly viable strategy to kick back for a few hands and let our foes sort themselves out. Either they'll balance out their chip stacks into two relatively weak chip positions, or else one will be eliminated. We hate neither outcome. However, it's equally viable to keep up the pressure. Remember that it takes more of a hand to call than it takes to bet. We might raise with K-J, for example, whereas, wary of an ace, we'd let that hand go to a raise. Likewise, our imperiled opponents will now want to avoid confrontations with us. Each is hoping the other will bust out first, and their mutual timidity could play right into our hands.

As it happens, though, this tournament doesn't end like that. Rather, after sparring for a few desultory hands, we all end up going all in. A-J for *GreeeeeDeeeee*, 8-8 for *Dealerzchoiz*, and A-Q for us. The flop and turn come rags, and a queen on the river seals the deal. We cash $250, for a $195 profit—not bad for one hour's work.

If you think I'm stacking the deck of this sample sitngo to deal us a win, well, maybe I am. But look, no one wins tournaments, not even little sitngos, without getting a little lucky. This is especially true at the end, when weak players have been eliminated and those who remain can't be expected to make foolish blunders (except us with that A-K, but oh well). Skill and strategy put us in a position to win. After that, we try to get our money in with the best of it and hope our hands hold up. So, yeah, I dealt us a win.

Would you prefer a bad beat?

To recap:

1. *Take measured steps early.* Take time to figure out your enemies' proclivities. Play only premium hands or premium position early on, but when you do play, play strongly. Try to be the one betting, rather than the one calling. Remember that if they all fold, you don't have to get lucky to win.

2. *Go strong to the middle.* The middle rounds of the sitngo—the fourth, fifth, and six levels—are when you want to turn up the heat. Radically change gears and go into aggressive blind stealing mode. If someone plays back at you, give them the benefit of the doubt, for you don't want to call off all your chips against a made hand. Keep showing muscle till someone shows some muscle in return.

3. *End time is big time.* Look for opportunities to put your whole stack in the middle with the best of it. If you can't raise all in, you probably shouldn't get involved at all. While there are exceptions—the occasional foe who will let himself get nibbled to death, for instance—the last round of a sitngo is truly the time to "go big or go home."

4. *Shape your bets.* As blinds rise and players get eliminated, continually rethink the size of your raise. Preflop, look for a raise that's big enough to drive out the riffraff, but not so big that you get stuck out on a limb. Adjust your bets so that if you have to fold, you still have a stack that can do battle.

5. *Be in it to win it.* Recognize that the spurious fear of losing an invested effort will cause others to play tighter than they should on the bubble. Not only don't fall prey to this flawed thinking but also use it to your advantage and play bully when the money gets close.

Oh, and by the way, if you're disappointed that we didn't have a nice, leisurely examination of heads up play back there, don't fret, for we're going to do that next.

8
♣ ♠ ♦ ♥

SINGLE COMBAT

♧ ♤ ◇ ♡

There's a popular perception that bad beats happen more often online than they do in realworld play. This is true, but only because *all outcomes* happen more often online. Though we seem to be routinely victimized by suckouts ranging from improbable to jaw-dropping, the fact is that we're no less lucky online than we are anywhere else. Still, given the frequency of astonishing bad beats online, it's no wonder that many of us wish we could suck the luck from poker. This can never be, of course, for it's luck that gives the punters a prayer. But wouldn't it be nice to find a form of poker that tilted the balance in favor of skill and away from the jaw-dropping suckout?

That form exists. It's called match play. You find it online and almost nowhere else in the poker realm, and while it doesn't eliminate luck completely, it does reduce the impact. Consider that in a ten handed poker game you have to worry about nine other players sucking out at your expense. Even six handed, there are five potentially lucky slackjaws arrayed against you. In match play—a heads up, winner take all, no limit hold'em tournament—you only have to worry about one player slaying you with Dame Fortune's magic bullet. Does it make a difference?

All the difference in the world.

TWO SHOCKING OBSERVATIONS

Let me offer, if I may, two observations about you and your current relationship to match play.

1. You're afraid to play heads up
2. You shouldn't be

If you're already not afraid to play mano a mano, then I apologize for tarring you with that brush, but for many of us the fear exists and it's real. It dates back to our earliest days in poker when most of the people we played against were, in fact and in fairness, a whole lot better than us. Being less skilled than our foes, we found safety in numbers. We played hit-to-win poker, looking to call along into volume pots and win lots of chips when the cards made us an offer we couldn't refuse and our cleverer foes couldn't refute.

Maybe we dabbled in short handed games, but many of us bailed, or watched others bail, as soon as the game got short. We encountered, and soon acquired, an almost fetishistic aversion to short handed play. As for heads up, we played it rarely, if ever. Realworld casinos don't generally spread short games or heads up games as there's not enough money in the rake to justify the commitment of a dealer and a table. If we did play short, we always seemed to find ourselves up against that one rapscallion who had a knack for getting under our skin and getting us leaning the wrong way. We'd be calling when we should raise, raising when we should fold, and generally hating the world. With hands, hands, hands coming fast, fast, fast, we found that we lost at explosive rates, and quickly got tired of that. So we retreated to the safety of our full gang game and our volume pots, and what we hoped would be our fair share of the luck. And there we stayed, stuck.

Stuck in luck.

Yuck.

But look, our rookie days are long gone. We've played (at a rough estimate) six gazillion hands of poker since then. We've long since stopped fretting over bets and raises, wins and losses. We've acquired a sublime appreciation for the long run. We know that quality decisions matter most, and the more of these we make the better we will do. We've learned how to get our money in with the best of it—which makes it that much more frustrating when those who get their money in with the worst of it seem inevitably to drag the pot. We're aware that it's only confirmation bias making us think we have the *worst luck in the world,* but still: How many times have we picked up pocket aces in a full ring game, gone to war against a big field of cally Wallies, and gotten called down and trampled by someone's ridiculous cheese? It's enough to make one contemplate seppuku. But that's not necessary, not when heads up play offers you the simplified task of beating just one other player's luck and skill.

You may be thinking, *Yeah, but what if he's better than me?* Trust me: he's not. First, he's likely to be an action junkie, drawn to the promise of involvement on every single hand and plagued by the problems of patience that action junkies have. Second, since most online players are of indifferent ability—just as most realworld players are—if you're an above average player up against an average (or worse) player, you have a competitive edge. Third, you *are* an above average player, and not just because you're reading this book, but just because you're reading, studying, and thinking about your game, which is more than most poker players ever do.

Can you think of some innate advantages you'd have against an average opponent in heads up play?

>>

I can think of several. You're more thoughtful, more disciplined, and more self-aware. (You know how to read minds.) You're fearless and bold and . . . well, that's enough sunshine up your butt for now. The point is, the attitude you should carry into single combat is one of *supreme arrogance.* For real edge in one-on-one clashes, there's no substitute for the rock-ribbed certainty that you will dominate and crush all comers.

THE MATCH PLAY MINDSET

You may think that this arrogance is unwarranted or inappropriate, but I see it simply as a tool, a means of psyching oneself up for battle. Remember, arrogance is what confidence wishes it were, and confidence, we know, is a poker player's supreme ally. If I still haven't made your blood boil for heads up action, let me put it another way: You have been challenged. The gauntlet is down. I put it to you that if you're really as good as you (and I) think you are, then you should be able to prove it in match play poker, the purest form of poker there is. If you think you're smarter, more disciplined, better informed than your online opponents, then you have, it seems to me, almost a moral obligation to isolate them, engage them in single combat, and pick them clean.

As I said, match play is something you rarely find in real-world cardrooms and casinos. There have been some televised heads up tournaments, and these have been enthusiastically greeted, but the format really only finds a home online, where so many players are the aforementioned action junkies and where the pace of play at a full table, even at internet poker's hasty pace, is yet too languid for their ADD-addled brains. They want a hand and they want it *now!* With heads up action, they're either in the hand or about to be in the hand, a situation they find deeply satisfying.

So know this about your heads up foe: He wants action. Patience is a problem for him. Why, you may be wondering, can the same not be said for you? Know what? Maybe it can. That's okay. There's nothing wrong with being an action junkie so long as you know it, admit it, and own it. But recognize that there are various kinds of impatience in poker.

Some kinds will hurt your cause severely in match play. Other types . . . not so much.

It's a form of impatience, for example, to want to play a wide range of hands. For reasons we'll discuss, that's fine in match play, where most holdings present you with some kind of opportunity to win (or steal or adopt) the pot regardless of the cards you hold. It's a different sort of impatience, however, to be in a hurry to win. Your impatience to defeat your foe may cause you to put yourself in coin flip (or worse!) situations for all the chips. As you'll see, in match play there's only infrequently a sound strategic reason for pushing in your whole stack. It's usually just raw impatience that makes us make that move.

A third type of impatience is the *impatience to hit a hand*. You might, for instance, persuade yourself to take a slim draw against your single opponent just to scratch the itch to win, or just to see the (virtual) look on his (virtual) face when you smack him with a surprise holding. This type of impatience is particularly toxic in match play. If draws are death in no limit hold'em, they're doubly deadly heads up.

Impatience, then, need not be a problem for you when you play heads up, so long as you know what sort of impatience you're dealing with and how to deal with it effectively:

- Impatience to be *involved* can be served. The whole point of match play, in a sense, is that you get to (have to) play most hands.
- Impatience to *win* should be tempered. You just need to win. You don't need to win right now.
- Impatience to *hit your hand* must be quelled. The biggest satisfaction is not hitting your hand, it's leaving the table with the other guy's cash.

And what combats inappropriate impatience? Goals. A clear sense of your purpose in playing. You're not there to have fun. You're not there to kill time. You're not there to show off. You're there to *win the match,* and you'll do whatever it takes, no matter how long it takes, to achieve that goal, without a single shred of self-indulgence. That's the mindset I'm talking about, and if that's a mindset you're prepared to embrace, then you're ready to make match play your own private, profitable playground.

THE RISK–REWARD RATIO

When you turn your attention to match play, you have to abandon much of what you know about conventional nine- or ten-handed ring games. The strategies that serve you well among the multitudes—notably your canny hand selection and your standard attacker-aggressor approach—require not a major revision but a general chucking-out-the-window. Likewise, you have to rethink what you think you mean by discipline.

In ring games and full table tournaments, discipline is mostly about deciding not to chase when pot odds don't warrant or deciding not to enter a hand in the first place. In match play, discipline is almost always about deciding not to make or call a big bet that can effectively put the outcome of the match on the line. Discipline, in other words, is more about thinking ahead and considering the consequences of being right or wrong in key situations. This kind of decision making is all about risk versus reward, and not all that much about who has the best hand.

Let's say it's the first hand of the match, you hold pocket fives and you know for sure that your foe has A-K offsuit. Though this is commonly called a coin flip, it's really not, not unless the coin's weighted in your favor to the tune of 55 percent. Nevertheless, your opponent goes all in. Should you call? What do you think?

>>

Pure math says call, for if you could take this wager a million times you'd happily do so, knowing that the inexorable law of averages would grind you out a profit. But this isn't a million matches, it's just this one, and though you have slightly the best of it now, you may have *much* the best of it later. Your risk and reward, then, are just about even. But you don't want just about even. You want things *way* in your favor. If you're smarter than the other guy (and we're operating under the assumption that you are), you should have no problem folding your hand in this marginally positive situation. You're not desperate. You're content to prolong the match until your superior analytical skills and decision making ability wear him down and defeat him.

If you call this bet, you're gonna need luck to win the match.

You don't *ever* want to need luck to win the match. You want the *other guy* to need luck to win.

When you encounter coin flip situations in match play, keep the risk-reward ratio in mind. *The risk* is that you could lose the match. This is not a catastrophe, but it's sure not the outcome you're going for. *The reward* is that you could win the match, but—and here's the key consideration—you'll probably have a better chance, or even a *much* better chance, to do that later on.

Coin flip situations are the bread and butter of no limit hold'em. Over and over again on TV and in our own play, we see the best hand and the best draw go to war, with a slim tilt to one side or another. In match play, as I hope you'll soon see, it only occasionally makes sense to put yourself in a coin flip situation. That's why it's fundamental to match play strategy that you should . . .

AVOID BETTING LOTS OF CHIPS ON COIN FLIPS.

Save your chips for when you're an ample favorite. You'll find ample opportunity for this.

THREE GAME STATES

Poker, we know, is a zero sum game. Every dollar someone wins, someone else must lose. (Actually, it's less than a zero sum game, in that the house is extracting its cut, but let's let that go for now.) In match play, zero sum becomes an exact mirror image: What you win I lose, to the penny. Given this see-saw situation, there are three possible game states in match play: about even, way ahead, or way behind. As you're about to see, the state you're in greatly informs how you go about your business.

All matches start, and most matches continue for some time, in the game state I call the BFM, or *Big Fat Middle*. It's the convention on several online poker sites for heads up play to begin with chip stacks of 1,500, and that's the convention we'll use here as well. In such matches, the BFM ranges from about 1,000 to 2,000 in chips. It's possible to close out an opponent from the BFM. For instance, a flopped straight against a flopped set is likely to get all the money in the middle. But that's a rarity and an exception. In the BFM you should not be thinking about winning the match via lightning stroke, but about building your chip stack up over two grand . . . seizing the high ground, as it were.

Once you have that high ground, you're in the SAP, or *Swoop And Pummel*, zone. The SAP zone stretches from 2,000 in chips to, well, all of them. Once you're in the SAP, you have two goals. The first is to stay there, and the second is to conclude the match. In other words, get 'em down, keep 'em down, and polish 'em off.

In the other direction, if you've been knocked down below 1,000 in chips, you're said to be in the HRN, or *High Risk Neighborhood*. In this game state, you strive to survive, to build up your stack, and to crawl back to the BFM. If it's early in the match and you're high in the HRN zone, you're not in terrible shape, but if the tournament has been running for a while and the blinds are high, or if you're down below 600 in chips, then you really are on life support and looking to make bold (read: desperate) moves. The HRN is a bad part of town and you don't want to spend any time there at all if you can avoid it. This may sound self-evident, but it's not. No one wants to lose any hand, but you can lose many small hands without jeopardizing yourself in the way that one ill-considered bad call will do.

Match play, then, is less about big moves than about a slow, steady grinding away at your opponent's position as you attempt to move him into peril and then knock him out. With this in mind, the importance of individual bets, especially small bets, is greatly reduced. In general, any bet that doesn't eventuate a change of state is almost irrelevant, apart from the information you might derive from it. In fact, the information is often more valuable than the chips themselves. Let's take a closer look and see why.

During the first round of play, in an unraised pot containing forty chips, you find yourself facing a typical orphan flop of 2-T-T rainbow. You go ahead and fire a pot size bet at it. This bet is of little consequence because it's not big enough to shift the game state. But if your foe lays down to it, he identifies himself as a YO player, someone who yields orphans, and you now have a piece of key data. Later in the match, when the blinds are high and the money in even an unraised pot becomes significant, you can attack similar orphans confident in the knowledge that your foe has demonstrated a willingness to yield. Except as a function of what you learn, then,

SMALL BETS DON'T MATTER
MUCH IN MATCH PLAY.

If the bet is large, that's a whole other thing. Suppose in that same scenario someone made an improbably big overbet of 600 and got called. That bet shifts the balance of power, moving one player into SAP and the other into HRN. You don't want to risk shifting states, ever, if there's a reasonable chance that you'll be going the wrong way. Small bets are for information and can be used liberally. Big bets are for termination and should be used sparingly: only when you feel you're in boss command in the hand. Never casually put yourself in peril. If you do this one thing right, you'll have a massive advantage over most match play foes you face.

A BIT ABOUT THE BLINDS

It's well known that the ratio of blinds to buy in affects the way tournaments play out. If you get a lot of chips relative to the starting blinds, then the tournament is said to be "slow" and have a lot of play in it. This structure favors intelligent, thoughtful, attentive players, giving them plenty of time to unravel their opponents and beat them by dint of superior skill. If the blinds start relatively high, or rise relatively quickly, or both, then the tournament is said to be "fast," in which case players are forced to make big moves sooner and luck holds greater sway. As it happens, the blind structures of most heads up sitngos favor the skilled player to an almost ridiculous degree. An exception to this would be the turbo or ultra turbo versions you find on various sites, where the blinds escalate every five minutes or even less, but in the main in match play you have plenty of time to lay back and pick your spots.

In a typical (non-turbo) heads up match, the blinds start at

10 and 20, presenting a very generous 75-1 ratio between the big blind and the starting stack of 1,500. Blinds rise relatively slowly, usually every ten minutes, again depending on the site and its particulars. This might seem like a blistering pace compared to realworld tournaments, but remember to measure time in internet terms where hands take seconds, not minutes, to complete. Heads up, it's possible to see something on the order of seventy-five hands before the blinds bump up.

That's plenty of play, then, and plenty of time for your foe's weaknesses to reveal themselves. Recall the immortal words of Mike Caro, "Everyone takes turns making mistakes in poker. The trick is to skip your turn." This wisdom is doubly wise in match play. Simply make fewer mistakes than your foe and the generous structure of the match will give you generous edge to exploit.

In such circumstances, where you have a big starting stack and gently rising blinds, you can afford to be *very patient*. There's no hurry! You can wait and wait and wait for favorable situations to emerge, and while you're waiting you can study your foe intently, decipher his codes, and solve the puzzle he presents. Further to this, remember that both players are taking blinds on every hand. In full table tournaments, one aggressive pirate can snag more than his share of the blinds and threaten those who don't fight back. In match play, however, if two heads up players surrender their blinds with similar frequency, a rough equilibrium is established, an equilibrium that may last until the blinds rise so high that such genial blind swapping is no longer possible. In heads up play, no one wins on blinds alone. Don't be afraid to let your foe steal some blinds, and don't feel too much urgency about stealing back. Remember that blind bets are small bets, and small bets are inconsequential here.

LIFE IN THE BFM

When the match begins, and periodically throughout its ebb and flow, you'll find yourself relatively even in chips with your foe. During such times you are like a sumo wrestler, trying to push your opponent toward the edge of the ring. As we've discussed, there's not much equity in small bets, but that doesn't mean you won't be involved. Move your foe toward the HRN by creating pots big enough to win and then winning them. In other words, for the sake of controlling the match in match play . . .

BUILD THE POT,
THEN TAKE IT AWAY.

To achieve this end, you should be prepared to fold all your trash hands, but to raise with almost everything else. Yes, even hands like Q-8 offsuit. Even J-T. Remember that there's only two of you, so those hands are better than even money against your single opponent's random hand. And even if you're an undercard underdog, say J-T against A-Q, you're not in *that* bad of shape—only about 3 to 2 the wrong way. Sure, every now and then you'll run into a big pocket pair and find yourself a 4 to 1 or 5 to 1 underdog. But big pocket pairs only come up about one hand in fifty. So relax and be bold. In other words, raise.

Raise with any ace.

Raise with any two big cards.

Raise with middle suited connectors.

Raise with middle pocket pairs.

Raise with big pocket pairs.

For heaven's sake, raise with pocket aces.

Raise, raise, raise, raise, raise, raise, raise.

Am I making myself clear?

And when you're done raising preflop, plan on betting out on the flop. Your preflop raise signaled the strength of your hand, and you can therefore "own" most flops and capture most pots—pots made big enough to be worth winning thanks to your preflop raise.

I know what you're thinking. I often think it, too. *If I raise, raise, raise, raise, raise, won't my foe figure out that I don't always have a hand?* Of course he will, if he's not entirely brain dead. He just won't know *when* you don't have a hand. And he'll never know exactly *what* kind of hand you don't have.

Are you raising with pocket aces or 7-8 suited? He doesn't know.

Do you have K♥-J♥ or 9-9? It could be either.

If you only raised with great hands, he'd put you on great hands every time you raised. If you raise with great hands and fair hands alike, he'll never know where you're at. So raise. Raise consistently and raise aggressively. Raise with any two decent cards in the small blind and raise with any big hand in the big blind if your foe has just called from the small. Raise to disguise the strength of your strong hands when you get them. Raise because your foe will either fold or loosen up and call too much. Raise because the truth is revealed under pressure, and the pressure you put on your foe will reveal the truth of his playing style, calling requirements, ability to defend, willingness to reraise, and much more. Raise to take control because control, above all else, is what successful match play requires.

If you get reraised, as you eventually will, then you can slow down and reassess the situation. But that will happen less frequently than you might think, because most players try to play a heads up match according to the selective-aggressive principles of full ring games, and *that's just wrong.* Most of the time they'll just fold or call. If they do reraise, it stamps their hands as quality cards—RRR—and you can proceed with appropriate caution from there. Either that, or it stamps them as frisky, tricky players, capable of reraising with nothing, and you can proceed with appropriate *extreme* caution from there.

It's liberating, I think you'll find, to find yourself in a poker game where your raising requirements are so loose. What a change from full ring games, where folding is the default action, and twiddling your thumbs is standard operating procedure. In match play, not only can you play *lots* of hands, you can (and should) play most of them for raises. You get to be *involved* and you get to be *in charge!* Good times!

Of course, you're not raising with *everything*. Some hands are genuine trash hands and should not be played except for free in the big blind. These include:

Up-downs. An *up-down* holding is something like K-3, Q-5, J-4. These half-hands are just trouble. If you hit your high card, you've got kicker problems and can't feel comfortable driving on the flop. If you hit your low card, you've got overcards to worry about and are likewise stymied in your betting. The only way you love these hands on the flop is if they hit you twice, but if you're holding K-3 and the flop comes K-7-3, say, how likely are you to get paid off? The only hands that can call you and lose are good kings or pocket pairs, and those hands probably raised preflop so what are you doing in the pot in the first place?

Little Poison. Little cards—5-3, 8-2, 7-4, for example— are little poison in any hold'em game, but they're double trouble in match play because while they may have the lead on the flop, they're vulnerable to almost any card that comes off on the turn. Suppose you complete the small blind with 6-2, and the flop comes 6-5-4. You've flopped top pair with an inside straight draw. Congratulations! At this point you're only vulnerable to overcards, sixes with better kickers (and they're *all* better kickers), and bigger straights, not to mention sets and overpairs laying in the weeds. Fold. You don't need the grief.

Bad Aces. Bad aces are a special case. You want to raise with them often, but call only rarely. If you raise, you invite your foe to call with the worst of it (which he'll have most of the time). But given that most players raise with good aces, as they should, if you call with a bad ace, you run the real risk of being badly dominated. The only flop you can really love is one that gives you two pair, and then you'll only get paid off if your foe has a better ace *and* he gives you action *and* he doesn't outdraw you. Again, there are so many favorable hands you can get involved with that trouble hands like little aces are best laid down to a raise.

There are other hands you can fold: middle suited connectors, paint with mediocre kickers, even small pairs if you feel your foe is either tight enough to bet only with a better pair or strong enough to squeeze you after the flop.

One benefit of folding trash hands is that it lends a little more credence to your raises. If you dump your true junk and raise with most of the rest, you'll have a high enough fold frequency that you won't look like a total maniac, but yet be raising often enough to seize control of the match. Also, you'll be in almost every pot you enter with at least a little something-something for the many, many times you do get called.

Here's the sort of betting sequence I'm going for—the rhythm, if you will—in the opening moments of a heads up sitngo, when the blinds are 10 and 20 and control has yet to be seized. I'm holding A-9 in the big blind. My foe, a typical Timmy, completes the small blind. Now there's 40 in the pot—and I raise another 40. Already Timmy is peeved, because, action junkie that he is, he's looking to see a lot of cheap flops. That won't happen on my watch, guaranteed. And he'll know it right away. If he folds, I capture the blinds and move on. If he calls, though, there's now 120 in the pot, and that's a pot worth winning.

Almost no matter what the flop is, I'm going to come out betting. High, low, or middle I'm going to represent that the flop hit my hand with a bet of about 80 into a 120 chip pot. It's our old friend the two-thirds pot bet again, big enough to

get Timmy to fold, but small enough to limit exposure, should
he happen to wake up with a hand. Most of the time he'll fold
right here. Why? Because most of the time he'll whiff.
Remember . . .

IT'S HARD TO HIT A FLOP!

Two-thirds of the time, unpaired cards don't connect with
the flop. Two-thirds. Every two hands out of every three.
Inevitably, inexorably, inescapably. This, it seems to me, is the
great unspoken truth of poker, and it's a truth critical to victory in match play. If your foe is used to playing at full tables,
he's used to *somebody* hitting *something* on the flop. Heads up,
though, mostly nobody hits nothing. So bet most flops as if
you own them. Your foe will know you're lying sometime,
maybe even most of the time, yet still not be able to call, because what does he have that can beat you? Bottom pair? It's
hard to go to war with bottom pair, especially when you're
calling and not leading. Will he get involved with a draw?
Fine. Draws are death in no limit. No, in most cases he'll find
it more prudent to withdraw, hoping to get lucky on a subsequent hand and pick up something he can trap you with.
Perfect. Now you've got him playing hit-to-win. Now you're
in control, and you've also picked up sixty chips. That's an insignificant sum in and of itself, but it's a step in the right direction . . . a step toward pushing his big sumo butt out of the
BFM and into the HRN.

Before we move on, I'd like to ask you a question: What (if
anything) scares you about playing as I've just described?

>>

If you're like most people, you'll have at least a little trouble coming off your selective-aggressive full ring game mindset (or appropriately snug full table tournament mindset) and

getting into the ultra-raisy mentality appropriate to match play. It's okay to have those feelings, and even to honor them. Now ignore them, and get ready to come out swinging!

DEATH FROM ABOVE

Any time you have more than twice as many chips as your foe, you're ready to swoop and pummel and deliver the knockout blow. You may think that the way to do this is to continue making the same promiscuous raises you made in the BFM. Surprisingly, this is not the case, because the deeper in the hole your foe gets, the more likely he is to reraise for all his chips. It's a sensible move on his part. He certainly doesn't want to let himself get blinded off, nor does he want to limit the effectiveness of his dwindling stack by sticking in separate bets, or by flat-calling raises preflop only to have to surrender on the flop or turn. (Some players will do this; it's a terrible mistake and they should be punished—with raises—for their sins.) While this will definitely result in his taking an all in flier on second rate hands like K-9 suited and little pairs, you should be very reluctant to call with second rate hands of your own. You have him on the mat. Don't let him up.

Your foe knows that he can't afford to get halfway involved with weak hands and that every loose call further cripples his stack. At the same time, he's hoping to get the rest of his money in with the best of it (or not so much the worst of it) while his diminishing stack still carries some clout. He needs a coin flip for all his chips, and he needs to get lucky. You don't need the coin flip, and you don't need the luck. All you need is wait him out. You won't have any trouble doing this because (if he's playing correctly) he'll either be folding or raising all in, and thus will be established another rough equilibrium. In this equilibrium you have very much the best of it, for you can bust him but he can't bust you. So if he starts getting crazy-raisy with his all in moves, go ahead and let him. He's offering bait you don't need to take. You want to keep him in peril, and he simply can't get out of peril a blind at a time, not if he's folding his trash hands or folding to your quality hand raises. The *only* way he can escape his predicament is if you let him double through.

Obviously, you'll be happy to call him with your big pocket pairs, where you might be as much as a 4-1 or 5-1 favorite. But for the rest of your holdings, think before you act. Your short stacked foe is likely to move all in with any pocket pair, for instance, and if you don't have a pair yourself, you're never a favorite to win. Sure, you'll win your share of coin flips but, again, why give him a chance to get lucky? Simply refuse to call his all in bets and you neutralize his only offensive weapon.

You, on the contrary, have a variety of arms in your arsenal. In the SAP position, you can:

- Make pot size raises preflop from the small blind button.
- Raise from the big blind if he makes the mistake of just completing the small blind.
- Complete the small blind with ragged hands, looking to flop a monster on the cheap.
- Bet into many flops, recognizing that your short stacked foe can't make speculative calls for the last of his chips.

In all events, remember that you have the luxury of time, a luxury your foe doesn't have. He needs to get his money in sooner rather than later. He's looking for any pair, any good ace, any *fair* ace, or any two unpaired wheelhouse cards. Let him make his all in moves. Willingly sacrifice your blind every time you don't have a premium hand. The more you refuse to play back, the more emboldened he'll become, coming over the top with progressively weaker hands. Eventually, your cards will make you an offer you can't refuse and you can get your money in with a big pair or a dominating ace.

Again, see things from his point of view. He knows that the

only way out of trouble is to bet himself back into the match. He's counting on you to become impatient or annoyed, to lose your discipline, or to get greedy. Don't give him the satisfaction. Attack when he seems weak, retreat when he seems strong, and don't bother calling his all in bets—even if you think he's fully bluffing—unless you have a superior hand. *That's* how you'll finish him off.

But what if the shoe is on the other foot . . . and that foot is on your neck? Let's take a look at that unhappy happenstance now.

THIS BAD NEIGHBORHOOD

Any time you have less than a third of the available chips, you're at risk for busting out. The risk is less if the blinds are yet low, or you're on the high side of the HRN (900 to 1,000 in chips) because you can still afford to wait and pick your spots. If the blinds are high or your stack is low, though, your match life is on the line. Be prepared to make a move.

And what is that move?

A big push to the center.

Go all in.

I've already suggested that it's a mistake to fritter away a small stack on flat calls and half measures, but let's see how bad a mistake it is. Suppose it's the third round (blinds 20 and 40), you have 450 in chips left, and you hold something like A-8 suited. If you make it 100 to go and get called, you really need to see an ace on the flop to feel secure about either betting or calling. If an ace doesn't come, and of course most of the time it won't, you'll either have to bet and hope or check and fold. Say you choose the latter course. Now you're down to 350 in chips and in *really* bad shape. Your stack is gutted, verging on useless. Within a very few hands you may have to take a stand with something worse than A-8 suited. And even if you double through, you're still stuck in the HRN. That's why it's vital that you not adulterate the limited strength of your short stack by parsing it into separate bets. You need to be swinging that club while it's yet a bit heavy. This is the way the world ends: not with a whimper but a *bang!*

It's okay to fold your medium hands preflop and wait for something stronger, but keep in mind that how long you can wait is determined by the size of the blinds and your opponent's aggressiveness in attacking them. What's *not* okay are a lot of loose calls and small raises. Being short stacked, you won't be able to play creatively after the flop. You have to hit to win. Since you have to hit to win anyhow, it might as well be on *your* terms, with a hand of *your* choosing—and for a meaningful sum.

How big a hand do you need to go all in? This depends on your stack size, the tournament stage, your read on your foe, and your sense of his willingness to call without a premium hand. Favor pairs and aces with at least medium kickers, but be prepared to go with any two court cards as well. Adjust your push-in requirements to the size of your stack. The fewer chips you have, the less you can afford to be picky. Desperate times, as they say, call for desperate measures.

When you push all in, there are just three possible outcomes.

- Your foe folds.
  - You win the blinds but you're still imperiled.
- Your foe calls and you lose.
  - Game over.
- Your foe calls and you win.
  - You're back in the hunt.

(Okay, *four* outcomes; you could split a pot.) Clearly, you're going to have to get lucky, or at least not get unlucky, to get back in the match. That's what happens when you're short stacked and imperiled, and that's why you should be very chary about calling bets big enough to put you in this jam in the first place. And again, while it's not desirable to have to rely on luck, at least see to it that *it's worth getting lucky* if you do. Suppose you play pocket tens for a small raise, the board comes rags, you bet, and he folds. Your hand held up. You were lucky . . . but your luck *only earned you the blinds plus your small raise*. And it didn't get you out of peril.

As urgent as the need may be to put your whole stack in play, yet there's no cause for panic. This is something many players will do in this situation, though, especially if their only experience of heads up play is at the end of a full table tournament. When a big tournament gets down to heads up, both stacks are often imperiled because the blinds are always quite high. In match play, you can be heads up and short stacked and still not in terrible shape because the blinds are yet relatively low. Remember this: When you're in the HRN, you *do* have to move your whole stack all in, but you may have time to pick your spot.

It will frequently happen that you're up against a cagey foe who knows better than to pay you off when you go all in. In that case, you might have to resort to smaller preflop raises and hope to get lucky a different way, by catching a bettable piece of the flop. But don't be surprised if he punishes you by making a big reraise. The best thing to do with the HRN is just not go there in the first place, and no I'm not being flip when I say that. It's a bad neighborhood—the worst. You *can't* control the action and you *can* be eliminated from play. So while you're yet in the BFM, do everything in your power to stay there. Avoid reckless adventures. Don't make promiscuous loose calls, and especially don't call big reraises with inferior values. Sure, your foe might be bluffing. If he is, give him credit for a good play and get out of his way. You'll have other opportunities to whittle away at his stack, but *not* if you put yourself in a situation where you have to hit to win. That's a recipe for match play disaster.

TRUE FACTS OF MATCH PLAY

No matter which playing zone you find yourself in, there are some fundamental truths of match play worth noting, and while we've covered some of this ground already, these points are so important that they bear repeating.

Loose Calls Are a Must to Avoid

Look at it this way: Either the other guy has a hand or he doesn't. When you make loose calls, you're investing your hope for the match on guessing right or drawing out. If you guess wrong, miss your draw, or cower out and fold to subsequent pressure, your loose calls will cripple your stack. So long as your stack is healthy, you've got a good chance of winning the match. Why put yourself at a disadvantage, just for the sake of catching the other guy in a lie or giving him a bad beat? To win in match play, you absolutely don't need to do either.

Say you've got T-9, looking at a flop of K-Q-9, when your foe makes a pot size bet. What are you hoping for when you call? Either that your nine is good or that you'll improve. Maybe you're right on one count or the other. You still don't need to call. Why? Because match play offers many, many opportunities to win chips where *maybe* doesn't enter in; where you *know* you're ahead in the hand. In any case, when you're calling you're not in control, and you should always strive for control.

You can play cozy without playing too tight. Recalling that small bets don't matter in match play, you can get involved in hands all over the place. But only get involved for big bets when you have the best of it. Let the other guy make the bad loose call. The structure of the tournament is such that you can win most matches without ever making a call on a guess. Be patient. Never make a loose call and you need never imperil your stack.

You Almost Never Need to Bluff

Yes, you'll raise preflop with a wide variety of hands, and yes you'll make continuation bets on many, many of those flops. But that's just the matter-of-fact act of building a pot and then taking it away from a foe who usually can't call. I don't consider that stuff a bluff.

Here's what I consider a bluff (and why I consider it grief): With blinds of 10 and 20, I call my opponent's min raise with pocket eights. The flop comes A-K-Q and he bets eighty chips into an eighty chip pot. I raise another 200. Now *that's* a bluff. Unless I know my foe to be an inveterate bet-at-anything type who has already shown great willingness to fold to a reraise, I'm really counting on him being able to get away from his hand just because I tell him to. Not too many players are exactly that smart or exactly that dumb. Most will call, either to see what the turn brings, or to dare me to fire again, which I'll have a great deal of trouble doing, especially if the turn is coordinated to the flop. Some will even raise me back, and then of course I'll have to fold.

That's a pretty pass I've brought myself to. To win 160 chips I risked 200, when I could just as easily have folded and gotten away from the hand for the negligible price of 40 chips. Not only that, I've revealed myself to be a naked bluffer, which will serve me ill later on when I try to claim the orphan pots and ragged flops that I consider to be mine by right.

Stay out of trouble! Don't fret that they won't pay off your made hands and don't feel like you have to "advertise." Most of your foes are too loose and cally by nature, being action junkies and all. Heads up poker offers so many opportunities for straightforward *get the goods and bet the goods* play that a bluff is not only an unnecessary cleverness, its a ruinous self-indulgence offering precious little upside and a big, ugly downside drop.

You Don't Have Odds for Any Draw

How could you? You're heads up all the time. One on one, you almost never have sufficient volume in the pot to adequately compensate your draw. You might argue implied odds: that if you hit your draw on the turn you'll get paid off.

Maybe . . . but most players are wary of scary boards and unlikely to pay off your made hands. However, they'll happily bet at you again if it looks like you're on a draw that missed.

Suppose you flop a straight draw and your opponent bets forty chips into a forty chip pot. The odds don't come close to justifying a call here, for you're worse than 4-1 to make your straight on the turn, and the pot is offering just 2-1. It's early in the tournament, though, so you figure, what the hell, you'll take a flier, try to catch lucky. But the turn is a brick, and your opponent now bets 120. You've put yourself in a lose-lose situation. If you call, you're throwing good money after bad, and if you fold, you've peed away chips you didn't need to lose. *Just don't chase!* What could be simpler than that?

Now, occasionally you'll find a foe who does you the favor of underbetting the pot and pricing you in. If that's the case, by all means call. Someone who bets the minimum, say 20 chips into a 120 chip pot, is offering you correct odds for your call and just begging to get drawn out on. He's making a mistake. And what do we do with mistakes? Punish them.

Also: Don't make them. To avoid making them, acknowledge the atavistic urge that leads to chasing in the first place. We *know* that the odds are against us, but we can't help fantasizing about delivering a crushing blow with a huge hidden hand. I hope you understand by now that the knockout blow is not necessary in match play. Just keep grinding away. Keep betting with the best of it and stay out of dicey situations. By degrees, the game will go your way.

But There's Nothing Wrong with Driving Draws (Thanks to Fold Equity)

Let's imagine that you and your foe are both on flush draws. If you made a bet, he'd be out of line to call, for he wouldn't have proper odds. But you wouldn't be out of line to bet, because your outs include not only the chance of completing your hand but also the chance that your foe won't call.

Fold equity has tremendous application in heads up play, where you need to see just one other player giving up without a fight. To take a gross example, you can't count on much fold equity in a ten-way pot, since several contenders will probably have playable hands. Against one foe, though, fold equity lets you semi-bluff with pretty much wild abandon. You love to put your foe into a position where he's wrong to draw (because he doesn't have odds) and wrong to fold (because neither do you). That's why in match play, as in most of poker, it's much better the bettor to be. If you're driving a draw, what you're really driving is your willingness to bet. The draw, in a sense, is gravy.

So be on the lookout for opponents who will chase when they shouldn't. Unless they're craftily setting you up for a reraise bluff—such players are rare, but they do exist and should be duly noted—you can make driving at draws a part of the package you use to muscle your foe into submission.

Never Show Cards

Some players insist on showing the cards they've folded, or showing their winners after you fold. I suppose they do this either to demonstrate how smart they are or how pretty their big pocket pairs are. Other players like to show bluffs, either to make themselves feel majestic, to induce incorrect play, or just to cheese you off. To me, showing me your cards only shows one thing: that you're a doofus who shows cards.

Never show cards. *Never.* If you have to show what a good laydown you made, then your ego is running the game and you have no business playing at all. Goodness! If you show me a good laydown, don't you think I'm going to give you the opportunity to make another one, whether I have a hand or not? Talk about handing me a club to beat you with!

As for showing bluffs, yes it's boastful and yes it's vexing, but it's counter-productive to your ultimate goal. After all, who do you want to show bluffs to? Foes who are too tight and who need loosening up. If your foe is playing too tight heads up, he's making a big mistake you certainly don't want him to stop making. Maybe showing your bluff will put him on tilt—*maybe*—but it seems just as likely that you'll put him on guard. *This guy thinks he's got my number,* your opponent will think. *I'd better work harder to play correctly.*

Mostly when people show hands they're not doing it for strategic reasons. They're just doing it to feel better about themselves. If they're boastful, I let 'em boast. If they're irksome, I let 'em irk. All they're really showing me is hard evidence about the way they play, the way they think *I* play, and their underlying state of mind. More clubs. More clubs to beat them with.

Rarely Just Complete the Small Blind

Either you have a hand or you don't. If you have a hand, build a pot you can take away. If you don't have a hand, don't get involved. The problem with just completing the small blind is that you give the big blind a free look at the flop. He doesn't have to decide whether to play his crap hand or not, and if he has a quality hand, you give him free rein to raise. Yes, you're seeing the flop in position for the minimum (unless he raises), but if you like your positional advantage so much, why not leverage it by bumping up the bet? To repeat: If you just call in the small blind, you're getting a discounted flop, *but the other guy gets it free!*

Sometimes I'll just complete with a medium pair if I'm looking to bait my opponent into raising so that I can reraise all in. This is *not* a bet that wants a call. It makes most of its profit from getting a surprised and seemingly trapped foe to fold. If he does call, it's likely to be with big overcards, so I'll be a slight favorite. Note that this play works whether my opponent calls my all in bet or not, but it works *best* when he folds, because then, as desired, I get to win without luck.

I'll also flat call with small pairs, hoping to hit a set. Here's a situation where implied odds are both real and relevant. If I sneak into an unraised pot with pocket threes and hit a three,

I may be able to get my foe to go off for most or all of his chips. But if the flop misses me I'll never initiate action. I'm happy to check down that little pair. All I have in mind is to flop a set. If that doesn't happen, I'm done with the hand. I won't spend another dime, even if I think my little pair is the best hand. There's too much risk and not enough reward.

One thing I *don't* do is flat call with pocket aces, kings, or queens. Many players like to trap with these hands, but I see two flies in that seductive ointment. First, you might let a trash hand hit a lucky flop. Second, the pot you win is likely to be small. Are you concerned that if you raise, the other guy will fold and you won't get paid off? That shouldn't be a problem, not if you've been raising with appropriate frequency, because your raise with big tickets will look no different than the workaday raises you make all the time. Besides, a flat call from a player who *never* flat calls is highly suspicious. I wouldn't pay it off, would you? So go ahead and put in a raise with your big pairs. Give your good hands a good chance to win some chips.

Don't Bluff Rivers

Early in our poker careers we learned not to bet on the river when the only hands that could call us could beat us. This wisdom is especially apt in match play, where loose calls are rare (because incorrect) but where trap plays are common. So don't open the betting on the river unless you think you have the best hand *and* you think a worse hand will pay you off. If you bluff here, you're just walking into match play's most common trap: the check-raise on the river with a made hand.

There are several possible outcomes if you bluff on the river, and most of them are bad. Your foe could:

- Lay down a better hand. (That one you like.)
- Lay down a worse hand. (No profit in betting.)
- Call with the best hand. (Ouch.)

- Raise with the best hand. (Double ouch.)
- Raise on a bluff. (Ouch squared, because you're bluffing and now can't even call.)

I can't even see bluffing in desperation if it's the only way to win the pot. If you can make a bet sufficient to be credible and scary, you still have a big enough stack that you can afford to be patient and fold. If you don't have enough chips to bet big, or if you choose not to bet big, you're just inviting a call, and what kind of bluff is that?

Traps Are More Common Than Bluffs

Bluffing with bad hands and trapping with good ones are two sides of the same deceptive coin. But, as previously noted, there's a big emotional difference. When you trap, you trap with confidence, knowing that your deception is backed by a solid hand. When you bluff, you know that you're running the risk of getting caught and that getting caught may imperil your stack or your future in the match. With this in mind, expect your deceptive foes to be more likely to be deceptive by trapping than by bluffing. It's simple human nature. Trapping offers great reward for little risk, whereas bluffing offers great risk for maybe no reward.

Suppose you're on the button with A-K, looking at a flop of 7-7-8. Your foe checks, so you try to adopt this orphan by making a pot size bet. Now he comes back over the top for all his chips. Is he trapping or is he on a naked resteal bluff? All other things being equal, put him on a trap—the safer sort of deception—than on a bluff. It's better to surrender a pot than to squander your chips on a wrong guess. Remember, you never want to guess for all your chips, and in match play you almost never have to.

Hold His Feet to the Fire

Poker is a game of incomplete information. Heads up against your unseen foe, you're both sort of stumbling through the dark. If there are tough decisions to be made, *let your foe be the one to make them.* Don't chase. Don't make loose calls. Don't call big bets. The structure of match play is such that you'll have plenty of opportunities to make bets with the best hand, *but only if you're patient.*

The guy who bets has two edges: He can win without a fight, and he can force his foe to make a wrong choice. This may be stating it too strongly (but then again it may not so I'll go ahead and state it anyway): *If you're not the one making the bet, you shouldn't be in the pot.* This wisdom, by the way, bicycles to every corner of the online poker world, and indeed the realworld poker world as well. Superior players force inferior players to make tough decisions; that's what makes them superior. If match play did nothing but get you into the habit of betting more and calling less, it would be doing you a service indeed.

Make Book on Everyone

Since you're only facing one foe at a time, it's vital that you know what he's capable of and where his strengths and weaknesses lie. Take extensive notes. At minimum, keep track of your wins and losses against him. Have you beaten him more than he's beaten you, or the other way around? Also note his tendencies: Does he drive draws? Does he yield orphans? Does he attack them? Can he make a big call with less than the best hand? Can he make a big laydown?

The universe of online players is quite large. You might go a long time between bouts with a known foe. But when you *do* face a known foe, you need to know your history against him; if he's smart and conscientious, he certainly knows his against you.

The foes I like to face best are ones I've never faced before. I don't know for sure that they're inexperienced at match play, but I *do* know that they have no experience against me. The first time I play against anyone, I hit him with my standard package of promiscuous raises and frequent postflop bets. I note how he responds and make adjustments accordingly. If I'm up against a Timmy, I'll turn the heat up even further. If I'm facing a Wally, I'll slow down and only bet with a real hand. If I encounter someone as frisky as I am (or friskier— they're out there), I'll play defense until I figure out where his weaknesses lie.

Everyone has weaknesses. Match play gives you plenty of opportunity to study your single foe at close quarters and find his flaws. Eventually, you'll see something you can use: *He drives his draws twice,* or *he won't bet bottom pair,* or *he drags big pairs.* Whatever he gives you, you take. Information is power, and the information you gather and store will give you the power to win the match.

Don't Give More Action Than You Get

I first learned this lesson back in the old days of $1-3 seven-card stud in Las Vegas, where I experienced the grief of squandering chips on calls against ultra-tight players who wouldn't return the favor. I'm not saying that your match play foes are ultra-tight, but the match is a delicate balance. If you consistently pay off on second best hands, or pay off real hands that you believe to be bluffs, you'll quickly find yourself in the HRN, struggling to survive. If a foe is pushing you around . . . *let him!* Get out of his way, but get out early in the hand, when the cost of folding is cheap. Credit him with real hands, even if you think he's bluffing. Remember that everyone does too much of something. If he pushes too hard, eventually you'll get the chance to trap him with a real hand and push back in a big way.

In a similar vein, if you're drive bluffing into a foe who's too willing to call, break off your drive. Bet the flop, sure, but if you get called, think long and hard before betting the turn. In other words, don't double drive into foes who stubbornly cling to their hands. Fruitless bluffs are as bad as overly optimistic calls in the sense of giving more action than you get.

>>

As you can tell from this lengthy discourse on match play, I'm quite a fan of the form. The way it takes normal poker strategy and turns it on its ear is something I find endlessly fascinating. And matching wits in single combat against a single foe is a challenge I don't seem to tire of. Plus, it's the perfect break in my workday routine. Twenty minutes later, I've been there and back.

Then there's the luck. I do believe that match play is the least luck driven version of poker there is. For this reason, interestingly, some players might not like it. In a full ring game, they're free to blame bad outcomes on bad fortune, rather than their own bad play. To play heads up, however, is to lose the luxury of this lie. If you play great poker, match play will prove that you do. If you suck, match play will prove that, too. This turns out to be a level of unblinking honesty that some players would rather not face.

For those of you who haven't tried match play, I encourage you to give it a go. It will show you a lot about yourself: the limit of your patience and discipline, your endurance, and your ability to stay tough in the face of adversity. Plus it's fun. Hand after hand after hand after hand, it's just flat out fun.

PART III

TOURNAMENTS

♧♤◇♡

9

♣♠♦♥

FULL FIELD TOURNAMENTS— EARLY

♣♤♢♡

When internet poker first sprang to life, it was greeted with deep suspicion by many b&m casino operators, who feared that online poker would be the death of live play. Why, they fretted, would anyone still travel to play poker in cardrooms when they could play all the poker they wanted at home? So deep was their distrust of the online game that they refused to support it or have anything to do with it. Many clubs threatened to pull their advertising from magazines that promoted or even mentioned online sites. This clumsy attempt at restraint of trade failed miserably for a number of reasons, not the least of which was this: Online poker is *great* for realworld poker.

Online poker doesn't pull players from the realworld poker pool; it throws them in. It creates players, trains them, whips them into a frenzy of enthusiasm, and sends them out to do battle. Granted, quite a few of these players caught the bug from watching poker on TV. It's internet poker, though, that has given them what they need most: a safe place to take their baby steps, far from the glare of Doc, Ace, Lefty, and other crusty figments of their imagination under whose intimidating gaze they dreaded to have to learn the game. Were it not for internet poker, there would not be new and thriving poker rooms in casinos such as Caesar's Palace or the Golden Nugget in Las Vegas; nor 300 tables of action nightly at the Commerce Casino in Los Angeles; and certainly no 5,000+ person tournament fields like those at the 2005 World Series of Poker.

Which brings us to the subject of full field internet tournaments, those played either for cash payouts or as satellites into bigger tournaments. It is these tournaments, with their modest entry fees, massive number of entrants, and huge prize pools, that have provided the spawning ground for the new generation of poker enthusiasts, or obsessionists if you will. If a single table sitngo provides righteous bang for a beginner's poker-learning buck, the full field tournament is newbie nirvana. For just the proverbial fistful of dollars, one can pick up hours and hours of real poker playing experience, see hundreds of hands, weigh a whole vast array of tricky decisions, learn at an accelerated pace, and maybe even win some dough or a trip to a distant locale.

Apart from the learning and the cash, what draws many online poker players to big field tournaments is exactly the promise of that trip to a distant locale. On UltimateBet .com, for example, an investment of as little as $22 can earn an all expense paid trip to UB's signature tournament in Aruba, including airfare, lodging, and entry into the championship event. The vacation of a lifetime, and it's just a lucky tournament win away. Nor is UB the only one with the tropics in mind. Every year the Party Poker Million cruise puts hundreds of online players together aboard a cruise ship in the Caribbean or along the Mexican Riviera for a weeklong orgy of poker at sea. Other sites have other strengths. PokerStars specializes in sending qualifiers to the World Series of Poker. Two of its most luminous luminaries, Chris Moneymaker and Greg Raymer, won the Big One back to back in 2003 and 2004, and while that streak broke in 2005, 'Stars did send over 1,100 online qualifiers to the Show, a whopping 20 percent of the field.

For many players, then, their choice of which tournament or tournaments to enter online boils down to a question of where in the realworld they'd like to go play poker. These are practical considerations. Not to be (too) cynical about it, a player who wants to spend a considerable amount of time and money playing online may have less trouble convincing the spouse that that's a good idea if the end result is a white sand vacation, a ports-of-call laden cruise, or even just a trip to good ol' sin city.

And once they reach these destinations . . . it's party time! In a way that no one building the online poker paradigm could have anticipated, the community of online poker players has turned into a moveable feast of avid *reuniónistas*. Each year, players who have met one another at other tournaments in other places, or even those who only know each other's online identities, get together in Aruba, Las Vegas, Paris, Monte Carlo, or at sea, and greet each other as old friends. It's like a high school reunion, a biker rally, the Rainbow Gathering, or a podiatrists' convention, but with poker. For many online players, it's the high point of their year.

For those not interested in so-called destination satellites, there's no shortage of tournaments that offer straight cash prizes as opposed to buy ins to bigger events. With so many people playing online, these fields can become astronomically large, meaning that the chances of winning are quite small, but the return on investment is quite huge. Special events with million dollar guarantees are common, and winning one of these will certainly garner what James Clavell called "fuck you money." Even turning $40 into $2,500 in one of the endless parade of regularly scheduled daily online tournaments can sustain a player's bankroll and fund a new couch or color TV to boot.

Needless to say, it is the failure of the multitude that finances the triumph of the few. Some people go months between tournament wins; some never do win, and meanwhile their buy ins melt and morph into the prize pool that sends the winners on to realworld tournaments or to a nice, restful snooze on that couch. The realworld tournaments benefit hugely from this. If PokerStars contributed 20 percent of the field to the main event of the 2005 WSOP, then PokerStars players contributed 20 percent of the prize pool: more than

$11 million. That's a lot of losses for a lot of players, $100, $200, or $300 at a time.

All of which, then, begs the only question that matters: How do you win these things?

A TYPICAL TOURNAMENT

For the purposes of this discussion, we're going to assume a typical tournament scenario of, say, 500 participants in a tournament with a $200 buy in and a guaranteed prize pool of $100,000. A crude application of math skill shows that this tournament just exactly makes its guarantee; any fewer participants and the house would have to fund the difference out of its own e-pocket. Rest assured, though, that setting the guarantee in a full field cash tournament is an art well mastered by every online poker site. If they're offering a guarantee of $100,000 on a $200 buy in tournament, you can bet there'll be more than 500 players putting up their dough.

Don't forget the juice. As with sitngos, the house takes a cut from everyone. The higher the buy in, the bigger the entry fee will be; however, the cost of your entry fee may be proportionally lower in big events, since entry fees for cheap tournaments can be as high as 10 percent, but drop to as little as 6 percent or 7 percent for big ticket affairs. In our $200 buy in example, we'll be looking at juice of $15—$15 we'll never see again, win, lose, or disconnect. Many online players neglect to calculate the juice in deciding which, or more crucially how many, tournaments to play. This is a mistake, just as it's a mistake to ignore the tax on anything you purchase. Like buying a baker's dozen in reverse, you can end up effectively paying for thirteen tournaments but only playing in twelve.

Many people complain about the juice online, be it entry fees or the rake in cash games. They just don't see how the fees are justified. In realworld cardrooms, it's easy to spot where the overhead goes: to personnel, physical plant, rent, cards, chips, and seat cushions. Online, though, where's the expense?

All they need over at pokerbeatsworking.com is a server and some software, right? Sure . . . plus programmers and customer service reps, marketing staff, and administrators. And don't forget money for advertising and promotion. Those fish you love so much have to come from somewhere, don't they? And not for nothing, but an equivalent buy in tournament in the realworld could cost you up to 20 percent juice. Don't like it? Hey, neither do I, but what can I tell you? There's no such thing as a free lunch. On the plus side, you don't have to tip the dealers when you win.

Good news! The prize pool for this tournament is a healthy sixty players deep, meaning that more than 10 percent of the field will cash. As is typical, though, the big money is crowded at the top. First place pays 25 percent—$25,000 in this example—second pays 15 percent and third pays 10 percent. The numbers drop off the shelf after that, with tenth place earning a grand, thirtieth getting $500, and sixtieth just barely clearing a profit at $300. These are representative numbers; the specifics vary from site to site and from event to event. In any case, know this: Playing just to make the money in a full field tournament is a losing proposition. You could do much better playing in cash games or, probably, mowing the neighbors' lawns. Be in it to win it. Play for the top three spots—at least the final table—or save yourself some time and grief and just don't play at all.

You'll tweak this "be in it to win it" philosophy if you're playing in a destination satellite awarding a number of identical prizes. An online satellite for a big realworld tournament will usually hand out as many tournament seats, or tournament prize packages, as the prize pool allows. Suppose that instead of paying out a hundred grand in cash, our little sample tournament here awarded twenty seats to a $5,000 buy in event at the World Poker Open in Tunica, Mississippi. Why anyone would actually want to *go* to Tunica is beyond me, but that's neither here nor there (just like Tunica). In this instance, whether you finished first or twentieth in the tournament, you'd get the same payout. This consideration will engender some strategic adjustments that we'll discuss later. For now, just know that whether you're playing for cash or "valuable prizes," you're in for a nice long haul.

How long? A 500-person tournament will last four or five hours, on average. As the field increases, so does the time commitment, such that the largest online tournaments can go ten or twelve hours or more. You'll get a five minute break every hour or so, but mostly what you'll be doing is sitting at your computer for hour after hour, enduring tedium and retina burn, hemorrhoids, and attention deficit disorder, while waiting for hands you can play. No limit Texas hold'em has been described as "hours of boredom punctuated by moments of pure terror." I don't know about the terror part—the thought of losing mere money never scared me all that much—but if you're not mentally prepared for a lengthy wasteland of not very much going on, you won't do well in the full field biggies.

At this point, a certain seductive rationalization can creep in. If it's going to be that long and understimulating a stretch, we reason, we'll simply beguile the time with music on the radio, ballgames on TV, phone calls to friends or, hey, why not online play in cash games or even whole other tournaments? The flaw in this logic is not hard to spot. Your goal for a full field tournament is not just to play it but to win it, and anything that distracts you from what's happening on the screen in front of you will surely detract from your effort.

Concentration is called for, and concentration requires commitment. This commitment may extend to people other than yourself. It does you no good to give your all to a full fielder for many hours, and get deep into the event, only to hear at a critical juncture that the dog just threw up on the Berber, the toilet overflowed, or your mother's on the phone and she wants to talk to you *now!* A moment's loss of focus, resulting in one loose call or ill considered bluff, can undo the good and careful work of hours. When you play in a full fielder, then, you need to send the strong word, both to yourself and to those around you, that having made the decision to enter a big tournament and having paid the price to do so, you'll be doing *this* and *only this* until you're done or until you've won.

It's easy to send this message and to make this commitment when you're going elsewhere to play cards. If you leave the house, bound for a tournament at your local casino, your spouse, friends, and parents know, and you know, that the only thing you'll be doing during all that time is trying to win the tournament. If you're smart enough to turn off your cell phone (something admittedly I'm not always smart enough to do), you can have a pure, distraction-free tournament experience. This purity is much harder to achieve in your home poker environment, where the people you love may make careless demands on your time or Jehovah's Witnesses may come to your door. You must take pains to cloister yourself. You need a *do not disturb* sign. Here, use mine.

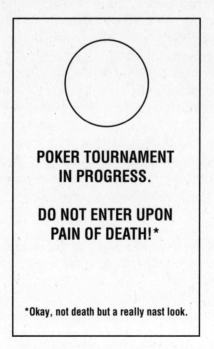

**POKER TOURNAMENT
IN PROGRESS.**

**DO NOT ENTER UPON
PAIN OF DEATH!***

*Okay, not death but a really nast look.

Thanks to the accelerated pace of play online, in an internet full fielder you'll see upwards of seventy hands an hour; more when the tables get short. Looking at all those hold'em hands can certainly take its toll. Just think about it. If you're really paying attention on every hand, you're: looking at your cards and evaluating their strength; responding to bets and raises from other players; integrating their actions into your evolving picture of how they play; reconsidering your situation in light of new information such as reraises, cards on board, pot size, and so on; experiencing the emotional tempest of both positive and negative outcomes; or just folding and waiting patiently for your next two cards. That's a lot of mental wear and tear, a much broader cranial assault in a much denser context than you experience in realworld tournaments.

To prepare adequately for such an assault takes thoughtful planning. It's not enough just to stock up on Starbucks and cashews. Are you rested? Have you eaten well? Have you cleared your desk, literally and figuratively? Did you spread the *do not disturb* word? Have you loaded your support software such as a sniffer and an odds calculator? In other words, do you have sufficient energy, clarity, dedication, freedom, and time to undertake the task at hand? Despite your best efforts, *fatigue will set in.* Absent your best efforts, simply save your money and do not play. You'll only be contributing to the prize pool for others, and what kind of fun is that?

Take a moment now and sketch the things you could do to improve your preparation for full field tournaments.

>>

I could play in the morning or afternoon, rather than the evening when I'm tired. Alternatively, I could turn my sleep schedule around so that I'm fresh in the evening, when many of the biggest and juiciest tournaments start. I could exercise and then take a shower before I sit down to play. I could eat

*healthful foods long on protein and short on carbs, to keep me
energized and alert, with my blood sugar in balance. I could
remind my wife that I'll be unavailable for the next several
hours. I COULD TURN OFF THE DAMN PHONE! I could
close my email program and web browser. I could get a pillow
for my chair. I could review my poker texts to put me in a
poker frame of mind. I could put on a sweater if I'm cold.*

Notice how much effort we're making just to be *ready to
play.* Quite apart from any actual strategy and tactics we might
apply in the tournament itself, this preparation provides us
with the baseline reserves of energy and awareness we'll need
to run the marathon to come. You might think of this effort as
"warming up" for the tournament, for, not to mix sports
metaphors too heinously, if you're a base stealing ballplayer, it
does you no good to read a pitcher's moves and get a great
jump off first base if you haven't adequately stretched, and so
pop your hamstring on your first stride toward second. In
every poker tournament ever played, most everyone walks
away busted, with nothing to show for their effort but a lot of
spent time and a new tale of woe. To be not among them,
make sure that your tournament starts well, before your tournament starts.

Our sample tournament begins with 1,500 in chips and
blinds of 10 and 20. With blinds increasing every fifteen minutes, here's what we can look forward to for the next four or
five hours of our lives:

ROUND	SMALL BLIND	BIG BLIND	ANTE
1	10	20	0
2	15	30	0
3	25	50	0
4	50	100	0
5	75	150	0
6	100	200	0

ROUND	SMALL BLIND	BIG BLIND	ANTE
7	100	200	25
8	200	400	25
9	300	600	50
10	400	800	50
11	600	1200	75
12	1000	2000	100
13	1500	3000	150
14	2000	4000	200
15	3000	6000	300
16	4000	8000	400
17	6000	12000	600
18	10000	20000	1000
19	15000	30000	1500
20	20000	40000	2000

Caution: There's no guarantee that the tournament will end in four or five hours. Some tournaments with extraordinarily large fields can drag on well past the time you had budgeted for your play. If you're planning on winning the tournament (and why would you enter if you weren't planning to win?) err on the side of needing *lots* of time. There's nothing worse than investing hours of your best mental effort in an online tournament, *making the money,* and then having the pressure of an impending deadline such as a family obligation or, you know, a job putting you off your game or making you play recklessly and bust out. In simplest terms, don't start what you can't finish.

I've described this sort of tournament as a marathon, and it is in the sense that you have to pace yourself and make sure that you're still as capable of making quality decisions at the end of the match as you were at the start. At the same time, a full fielder has the ongoing intensity level of a sprint, in that you have to be on your game from the first hand forward, for the choices you make early will very much impact how long you last and how high you finish. Apart from the obvious peril of an early rash action leaving you short stacked or pushed out, there's a specific quality of play you encounter early in full field internet tournaments, one that requires you to make sharp reads and strong moves from the get-go. This quality of play has a name, and the name is: dead money.

EARLY ROUNDS: THE DEAD MONEY DOESN'T LAST LONG

The many different kinds of dead money in the first stages of a full field online tournament all share a common lack of commitment, or ability, to play perfect poker. Absent a remarkable skein of luck, these players stand to give all their chips away, and it's incumbent upon you to gather your share before those chips find their way into tougher, more competent hands. Let's label some of the dead money types, and plan our attacks against them.

Kamikaze

As in sitngos, some full field tournament players are of the opinion that an average stack is no stack at all. These double-or-done desperados are willing to risk their tournament life, and tournament buy in, for a favorable chip position. They figure that if they get lucky and double or triple through early on, they can then wield their big stack like a big stick and take command of the table. This strategy is fraught with obvious holes, not the least of which is that most people play tight to start, so a big all in move is likely only to get called by a premium hand. While it can be argued that there's theft equity in going all in with ruthless abandon, the risk-reward ratio is all out of whack. It only takes one opponent waking up with pocket aces or pocket kings to send this kamikaze pilot spinning into the sea.

But that's his problem, not ours. Ours is just to figure out who these crash-and-burners are, and to make sure they don't take us down with them. Remember, third time's the adjustment. The first time he goes all in, credit him with a real, albeit overplayed, hand. The second time he goes all in, suspect him of seppuku tendencies. The third time he pushes, be ready to push back if you have a hand. Of course, there's no harm in just staying out of his way, because to call is to put your own risk-reward ratio in jeopardy. However, "fortune favors the bold," and if you know a player to be wildly out of line and you have a big pocket pair, you do have the option of taking a stab at his stack.

The Ill Prepared

It's hard to know why these players are so ill prepared—maybe they didn't realize how long the tournament would take, or maybe they're tired or just befuddled—but they're out there, and you should be willing to go after them. You'll recognize them by their promiscuous calls with hands of indifferent value. If you see someone getting involved in a raised pot with K-8 offsuit, you can be pretty confident that he either doesn't know better (see below: "Training Wheels") or just doesn't care about his tournament results. Should you be fortunate enough to have one of these players on your right, you can reraise, kick sensible players out of the hand, and then bet for value when you hit. About the only way these ill prepared players can really hurt you is if they get lucky, hitting a flop like K-8-x, for example, when you're holding A-K and they're on K-8.

The other danger is playing down to their level. If you know that your foes have soft starting requirements, you'll be tempted to soften your own. This is a good time to remember that patience is precious when chips are cheap. Just because the ill prepared are offering you their chips doesn't mean that you *have* to go after them. If their loose calls engender loose calls of your own, you run the risk of being played with by other strong players, whether they have a hand or not. In general, you don't want to get involved in reckless adventures early in a full fielder, but if the ill prepared cast their chips in your path, you should be ready to scoop them up.

Training Wheels

As you know, some players use tournaments as a means of learning poker and honing their skills. This isn't a bad notion, for, as previously noted, they do get to see a lot of hands and make a lot of decisions for a fixed price, and no matter how badly they play, they can't lose more than their buy in. They will, however, likely lose their buy in precisely because they lack the experience to play well, or even remotely correctly. They'll make predictable blunders like calling raises with hands like A-3 and Q-J, pushing little pairs, neglecting to make continuation bets, or, conversely, getting out ahead of their hands with bets too big for the situation. Use these flaws as a marker map. Note, for example, a player who takes draws when the odds don't warrant. If he'll make this rookie mistake, he'll make a whole host of related gaffes as well. Can you predict what some of these gaffes might be?

>>

Tyro money is easy money, and it's crucial that you identify it and grab it while you can. Judge these Timmies to be kosher until they give you cause to believe otherwise and figure them to be unwilling to call big bets. Bluff them, trap them, attack their blinds, and just generally try to destabilize their play. If they're too tight, encourage them to play tighter still. If they're too loose, do what you can to loosen them up even more. Don't be shy about throwing some chat their way. It's amazing how willing new players are to reveal their lack of tournament experience. Be friendly . . . then strip mine their stacks.

The Meek

Since it's considered appropriate full field tournament strategy to lay out for the first few levels and get involved with only premium hands, you'll see plenty of players at your table who seem not to be doing much of anything at all. It could be that they're distracted by some rerun of *Friends,* but it's more likely that they've made the conscious decision to sit on their hands unless something really stellar comes along. It's hard to get chips from such players because they so rarely willingly put them in a pot. Then again, it's easy to avoid paying them off, for they telegraph their strength through their tightness, and you can freely throw away most hands you hold when they raise.

Of, if they come in for a raise, you might decide to mix it up with them, for their snugness creates an opportunity for you to do battle. Yes, you'll be waging war against a hand that's stronger than yours, but you'll likely know what *type* of hand it is. Avoid calling with hands like A-Q or A-J because the preternaturally tight player will most likely be raising with big pairs or big paint, hands that dominate and crush your second-rate aces. But if you call with a junk hand like 8-7 suited, a flop like 8-7-3 puts you in position to take someone with pocket aces off his whole stack. This ruse does require luck, but again we're talking about applied luck not random luck; a plan, in other words, looking for a place to execute. It also assumes that you're savvy enough to get away from your hand if you miss. If you lack this knack, then just play tight, patient poker like everyone else.

Speculators

A certain brand of tournament player considers the road to heaven to be paved with speculative hands. He loves to limp into volume pots and try to flop a monster, especially early in the tournament when he feels that such speculation is within his budget. This approach has some merit, but only if the rest of the table cooperates. If the speculator limps too frequently, savvy opponents such as yourself will come to recognize this and punish him with big raises he has neither the hand nor the stomach to call. Sometimes—it's not all that uncommon, really—you'll find yourself at a table filled with such flop seekers. Let them have their multi-way pots a couple of times, just to make sure that you're reading them correctly, and then plan on making a big raise, either from late position or from the blinds, and sweep all those loose limpets into your stack.

Should you happen to get called, beware of flops that come highly coordinated to straight draws or flush draws, because these are just the sort of flops that the speculators are fishing for. If you encounter such a flop, you'll have to decide whether to drive at it and make the speculator pay or back off, hoping to check it down but prepared to surrender if need be. However, if the board comes scary high, such as A-K-J or K-K-Q, go ahead and bet it like you own it. Speculators will have a hard time calling unless they're speculating with a hand that exactly fits the promise of the flop. In any case, speculative callers are just another brand of weak-loose player, and you should consider it your duty to take their chips away.

We've looked at some characteristic types of dead money that you'll find in big online tournaments. Can you think of any others and can you think of ways to exploit their definable defects?

>>

Dead money, like water, finds its level. While it's not uncommon for a given flawed or unschooled player to run well for a while and accumulate some kind of stack, the fact is that full field tournament structures almost inevitably weed out the weak, especially online where so many players are new to poker or simply not up to the challenge they face. Figure that by the fourth or fifth level, the easiest prey will have been picked off. Since it would be a shame to let other players get all these chips, you should play the first few rounds with the stated goal of identifying and exploiting the obvious flaws of your foes, while such obviously flawed foes yet dot the terrain.

Sadly, not everyone you face in the first rounds of tournament play will be so obligingly generous with their chips. There are plenty of skilled players out there, too, and they are to be evaded, avoided, or trapped as the situation demands. Fortunately, they have characteristic and identifiable patterns of strength, so we can pretty easily figure out who's got the real poker *nous*, or ability, and how to avoid giving them our chips. We'll take a look at these strong players next.

In the grim Darwinian jungle that is online poker, there are bound to be some players out there more skilled than us. I understand that some people prefer to battle such players either for reasons of ego or because they believe that knowledgeable players are actually easier to defeat than cally Wallies who don't know enough to lay down when they're beat. Well, that's just gogglebox nonsense! Sure, you can put good players off a hand, but they can do the same to you, and if they're fearless, creative, and cunning, then you're going to have to be all those things as well, just to hold your own. So let's now note some tournament types to be respected and figure out what to do with them when they grace us with their malign presence.

Ready Teddy

A ready Teddy is someone who came to play. He has carved out appropriate time for the tournament he's in, and he's prepared himself mentally for the task at hand. You won't know immediately who these players are, except that they'll be folding more than raising, and raising more than calling. They'll also hit you with unexpected check-raises in unlikely situations and maybe even throw stop-and-gos at you from the blind. (A stop-and-go, if you don't know, is where you call a raise in the big blind and then bet out no matter what the flop.) In all events, if you feel like you're up against players playing the players instead of the cards, you're among the ready Teddies.

With or without appropriate sniffer software, you should be able to make ample book on such players, for they probably play lots of tournaments and therefore leave abundant data trails to follow. And naturally if the site you're on maintains a leader board, and such players occupy top spots, you'll further know they're players you mess with at your peril. I'm not saying you're not as good as them. I'm just saying that in the early stages of the tournament when the field is yet full of weakies, it doesn't make sense to tangle with foes of known expertise. There will be plenty of time for that as the tournament matures. Try to mislead them, either with your own play or your chat. If you can lay a trap they'll fall into, fine; otherwise, concentrate on the task at hand, which is avoiding hard players while exploiting soft ones.

Pseudokaze

Just as there's a difference between a manic and a fakiac, so also is there a difference between a real tournament kamikaze and someone merely playing that role. It's often hard to tell one from the other because they both delight in the grandstand overbet. But whereas the kamikaze is generally going all in with his overbet, the pseudokaze prefers to make a *squeeze raise*, something large enough to intimidate foes into folding, but not so large as to cripple himself if he happens to run into a real hand. The pseudokaze also likes to make a huge raise into a lot of limpers, figuring that their limps show weakness and his big raise shows inarguable strength. He's likely to have a hand, but not *that* much of a hand. His equity comes from the times everyone folds and he scoops the limpets.

If you have a pseudokaze on your hands, you'll need to tighten up your raising requirements a squidge, because you don't want him reraising you (to the tune of 400, say, when the blinds are 10 and 20 and you've raised to 60) and making you an offer you can't accept. However, if you know that he likes the big reraise, and if you sense that he's over-applying the tool, go ahead and bait him with your big hands. You can either raise in front of him, inviting the reraise, or, if there are a lot of limpers, join the limpfest in anticipation that he'll use his grandstand overbet tool. If he does, you can whack him back with a huge reraise and hope that he has no stomach for the fight or that your hand holds up. Recognizing that this will probably put your tournament life on the line, though, there's nothing wrong with just not getting involved. Yes, you're letting another straw stir the drink, but in the early stages of a tournament, that's really not so bad. Also be aware that a player capable of a big reraise probably has other arms in his arsenal. Like the ready Teddy, he's playing the players and exploiting whatever tendencies or weaknesses he finds . . . including yours.

Lurking Scholars

There are players out there, you know, who are absolutely obsessed with their sniffer software. I'm not saying they go so far as to sleep with a copy of Poker Tracker under their pillow, but who knows? In any case, they don't just log stats for games and tournaments they're in, they also launch set-and-forget data miners for hour after hour on site after site, making extensive and telling book on foes they may never even have faced. Then they dissect those stats for information about folding frequency, defense of blinds, and the all-important

VPIP, voluntarily putting money into the pot. Based on this information, they may know that several of their foes at any given tournament table are too tight, too cally, too aggressive, too weak, too whatever, and they adjust their play accordingly, on the fly, in real time, with their sniffers open on their desktop, guiding them as they go.

If you find that you're routinely being attacked by a player who seems to be leaving everyone else alone, it may very well be that you've been sniffed. In that case, you have two problems on your hands. First, you won't be sure he's a lurking scholar unless he's kind enough to blurt it out. Second, if you play according to past patterns, even seemingly correct ones, your consistency will absolutely slay you; yet, if you compensate by veering too far from correct play, you'll be making intentional mistakes, and that can't be good, either. Given that you must vary your play, try taking different paths through those situations in which multiple options are correct. Sometimes defend your blinds; sometimes let them go. Sometimes raise with your pocket jacks; sometimes just call. Lurking scholars are formidable foes, and the sad fact is that if someone has a solid line on your play, you're going to have to be a little (or a lot) unpredictable to throw him off the scent.

Consistent Inconsistent

Strong, solid players identify themselves in the early tournament stages by making a lot of standard-size raises with a variety of hands. Not content just to sit and wait for big tickets, they're attacking the pot from all positions, and since they raise the same amount with strong hands and speculative hands alike, they're very tough to put a confident read on. Watch their postflop betting. If they make continuation bets only into the sort of flops that preflop raisers are supposed to hit, like A-K-x or Q-Q-J, they're probably just betting with the best of it. But what if they're likewise willing to CB into orphan flops or middle scare flops like 8-7-6 two-suited? Are they banging on with overcards, or did they raise with one of their *package hands* like 8-7 suited and happen to hit the flop hard? You've got a conundrum on your hands.

Let's dwell on package hands for a second, for it's a concept of some importance to the consistently inconsistent, and to we who must defend against them. Most players raise with strong hands; that's a given. For the sake of deception, some creative (and therefore dangerous) players add a few modest hands into the mix, notably middle suited connectors. They're not ignorantly out of line with their raises, they're just spicing up their standard raising package—hence the expression "package hands." This deception definitely works, and sometimes you can walk right into a nightmare, if you happen to flop top pair, say, and your consistently inconsistent enemy is in there with an unexpected and utterly hidden two pair. Against such tricky foes it's often best just to steer clear. If you don't feel like you've got this problem solved, let it be someone else's problem instead.

Braveheart

A most difficult foe to face, and face down, is one who plays to win, but yet is not afraid to lose. Far too many tournament players are more interested in extending their tournament run than in taking appropriate risks for the sake of building their stack and/or putting their opponents to the test. A fearless player, then, is a rare and formidable enemy, especially if he's not just courageous, but also creative, attentive, flexible, and deft. His willingness to put his tournament life on the line gives him the potential to get you leaning the wrong way, and if you lean far enough, you might tip over and fall, for the braveheart player adheres to one of poker's simplest, best strategies:

BE THE ONE WHO KNOWS,
NOT THE ONE WHO GUESSES.

By playing aggressively, by attacking relentlessly, and by trapping, bluffing, betting, and check-raising with equal abandon, he puts other players back on their heels and puts his opponents to one hard decision after another. If such a player enters the pot before you, you may have to fold hands you would otherwise play. Occasionally, you can use his fearlessness against him by feigning weakness and trapping when he gets out ahead of his hand. In general, though, unless you're similarly unafraid—yourself a braveheart, that is—you'll find it very tough to go toe to toe with this foe.

In the early stages of a full field tournament, there are certain players who just give me fits. Bravehearts are particularly troublesome to me—but they might not be that much of a challenge for you. I would ask you, then, to think about the sort of foe you hate facing most. What is it about him that drives you nuts or leaves you feeling impotent or lost? That he reraises your raises a lot? Calls too much? Doesn't respect your bets? Won't take your bait? Steals pots on the river? Contemplate this question in depth. The answers you arrive at will reveal much to you about where some holes in your own game lie.

>>

You may get the impression after reading this chapter that I advocate a cautious-unto-timid approach to the early phase of a full field tournament. That's not it, though, not exactly. What you want to do is profile your foes, categorize them as strong or weak, dangerous or safe, and then parse them further into some of the subcategories you see outlined here (or develop on your own). It's usually only hubris, ego, or greed that makes us want to tangle with the most fearsome foes we face. If you can get into the habit of being selectively aggressive, not just selective in terms of cards but also in terms of targets, you'll put yourself well ahead of the game and well prepared to move into the middle phase of the long, challenging (but hopefully rewarding) tournament journey you're on.

10
♣♠♦♥
FULL FIELD TOURNAMENTS— MIDDLE

♧♤♢♡

In the middle stage of a tournament (commencing around the fourth or fifth level in the example we're using here, though as late as the seventh or eighth level in other common online structures), the blinds will climb high enough to start putting the squeeze on players who have not succeeded in building their stacks. Thanks to rising blinds, medium stacks turn into small ones, and the pressure mounts on small stacks to take some sort of stand. Just like in realworld tournaments, a full field internet tournament has a natural ebb and flow, one keyed to the way stacks rise and fall in relation to the blinds. With the accelerated pace of play online, this shift from comfort to peril can happen quite quickly. The first time you'll see it (again, in this example) is between the third and fourth levels . . .

ROUND	SMALL BLIND	BIG BLIND
3	25	50
4	50	100
5	75	150

. . . which finds the blinds increasing by a full 100 percent. Where a typically tight player with a dormant stack of 1,500 could still afford to be patient with the big blind at 50, when the blind doubles to 100, he instantly has only fifteen big blinds left, and that's not enough to feel very much at ease. Furthermore, if your table has a couple of empty seats—some kamikazes punched holes in the ocean, say—you may be playing only seven or eight handed for a while, bringing the blinds around that much more quickly. Now you have a lot of suddenly jumpy players, looking to double up to survive the tidal onslaught of the blinds.

The field as a whole is still quite large, which means that the average chip stack is relatively low. This is why stacks become imperiled: There just aren't enough chips to go around. Those with endangered stacks must necessarily make big moves, not all of which will work out. The early part of the middle stage, then, will see the first big flurry of bustouts, and with the bustouts comes an interesting phenomenon, that of chips reconsolidating in the hands of fewer players. The average stack size rises, and those players who haven't busted out find themselves once again with a little breathing room. The tidal pressure of the blinds is momentarily eased.

This, then, is the pulse of tournament poker. When the average chip stack is small, relative to the rising blinds, you'll see a quickening of the pace of play and a large number of bustouts. When the average chip stack is large, relative to the blinds, the pace of play slackens as the remaining players recognize that they can practice patience once again. Since this is the internet, the tournament pulse beats faster than it would in the realworld. In a fifteen-minute round you might see the pace change literally within minutes, with typically the first half of the new blind level forcing players to the wall and the second half giving respite. For this reason, you'll want to keep an eye on the tournament clock, as well as the blinds and antes. Expect that every time the blinds go up, some players will panic. Forced by rising blinds into making moves they really don't want to make, a lot of players will be shifting into push and pray mode. Others will start limping more, hoping to get some looks at some cheap flops, catch lucky, and get back into a decent stack situation. Be ready to exploit both acts. Your A-K will play terribly well against someone making a desperate all in bid with A-Q or A-J, and your late position raises will sweep the limpets more effectively if the limpers are on relatively short stacks and making semi-desperate plays for cheap flops. Just beware that you're not reraising *too* short a stack; if a given foe is pot committed, you only want to invite him in for the rest of his chips if you hold a hand that plays well against his desperation call, say pocket nines on up.

MIDDLE ROUNDS: MISTAKES NOT TO MAKE

No matter what plays you make, profit will not come all that easily now. By the middle rounds of a tournament, most of the egregiously dead money has been cleared from the field, and those ill-protected chips have been shipped to players more able to defend them. For this reason, assume from the middle of the tournament forward that your foes basically know what they're doing and that you won't be able to beat them on their gross errors alone. Naturally, you want to keep your eyes peeled for others' mistakes, but expect those mistakes to be subtler, more situational, harder to spot, and harder to exploit.

What follows are some slip-ups you can count on seeing in the middle tournament rounds. As we examine these errors, consider them from both sides. Think about how best to take advantage of them, but also police your own play and make sure you're not falling victim to them. The middle stage is a minefield. Make a crucial mistake at a critical time—or even just allow yourself to lose track of where you are in relation to the antes and blinds or other stacks—and you will find that it's a stage you can't get past.

Overplaying a Big Stack

There's never a good time for reckless adventures in tournament play, but some of your foes will be tempted into predictable ones, particularly if they're running well through the middle stages. Enjoying the good fortune of a big stack, they will make a concerted effort to take over the table by dint of promiscuous bets, resteal raises, and other muscle moves. This tactic may work for a while, but it's easy for a big stack to get overconfident and, well, carried away.

Consider this scenario: Someone with a big stack has been successful in making frequent preflop raises and stealing more than his fair share of the blinds. Now he picks up A-Q offsuit and continues his rapacious ways with his standard preflop raise. This is not a bad move with a not-too-bad hand, especially when the table is laying down for him. This time, though, he encounters an all in reraise from a small stack in the big blind. Mistakenly considering this a vain attempt to slow him down, our big stack adventurer falls into a logic hole of a certain kind. He reasons that *(a) my foe is just being frisky, (b) he probably doesn't have much of a hand, and (c) I can afford to spend some chips to find out.* And he finds himself up against A-K or a big pocket pair. Blammo! His stack takes a hit, and his pride, judgment, and patience all take a hit as well. On the next hand, he tries to resume his thieving ways with something like J-T suited, runs into pocket queens, and, well, you know the rest.

To avoid this error, just don't get carried away by your own PR. You may be running well, and you may be running the table, but that doesn't mean you're invincible, especially with trouble hands like A-Q, which usually get reraised by, and play poorly against, A-K and big pocket pairs. Most of a big stack's muscle comes from the reluctance of other players to contend. As soon as someone shows willingness, you should consider that a warning bell and be prepared to slow down.

In attacking someone making this mistake, just two words:

Be bold. If you're fortunate enough to pick up a big hand when a bully's on a rampage, don't play cute by just calling and planning to trap him later. Raise him back! He has already trapped himself and will be highly unlikely to let go of his hand. Don't worry that this one time he has pocket aces. Maybe he does, but that's poker. However, given the recent frequency of his raises, it's more likely that he has a semi-strong hand like A-Q, or maybe much worse, and you'll be getting your money in with the best of it.

Neglecting the Ante

I'm not talking about forgetting to post your ante, for of course the software takes care of that. No, I'm talking about failing to take into account the impact that the introduction of antes will have on your stack. In our example, the antes kick in at level seven—and note that at that level the blinds do not rise. An inattentive player here will consider only the blinds and think he's getting a respite, for how significant is a lowly quarter chip coming off your stack?

ROUND	SMALL BLIND	BIG BLIND	ANTE
6	100	200	0
7	100	200	25

Pretty damn significant when it comes off your stack every hand. Even a quarter at a time, you're going to be paying 250 per round in antes, nearly as much as the combined blinds. That's a sum that cannot be ignored. From this point forward, then, smart players will be counting the cost of a lap and constantly updating that sum in their minds as the number of players at the table changes and/or as the blinds and antes increase. Those paying less attention will continue to consider stack sizes only in relation to the blinds.

At level six, for example, a ten handed lap costs 300. If you're sitting on a proud stack of 10,000 chips and thinking only of 300 in blinds, you might enjoy the smug satisfaction of holding fifty big blinds. As soon as level seven kicks in, though, the price of poker goes up to 550 a lap, and the size of your stack is relatively halved. Fail to take this into account, and you'll still be playing as if you had a dominating large stack, when, in fact, you don't. Compound this misjudgment with, say, a careless overbet or two, and you can find yourself on the virtual rail before you know what hit you.

When the antes kick in, then, make it a habit to calculate the total cost of each orbit and measure that number against the size of your stack. Think about how many orbits you could survive at this level if you folded every hand. This figure is a little misleading because you probably won't see more than a couple or three orbits before the next increase (unless you're very short handed, and then you're taking more blinds). The number will nevertheless tell you roughly whether you're in good shape, fair shape, or poor shape and how to adjust your play, according to the following chart:

NUMBER OF ORBITS YOU CAN SURVIVE	STATE OF YOUR STACK	STRATEGIC STANCE
<5	Imperiled	• Highly selective • Look for a favorable spot to move all in
5–10	Adequate	• Standard selective/ aggressive • Look for hands you can drive
11+	Strong	• Loose/aggressive • Try to take control of the table

Warning: This is a rule of thumb, or table of thumb if you like, and like all things thumb it runs the risk of smashing itself with a hammer. You need to consider your relative stack size not just in terms of the cost of an orbit but also the aggressiveness of the players at your table, the frequency of ground skinners (uncontested folds to the blind), even how long people take to act. Also try to keep in mind whether you're playing early or late in a given round, for the closer you get to a blind increase, the more potentially perilous your situation becomes.

The other number you need to know is how much goes into the pot on each deal. Know this number exactly and adjust the size of your raise accordingly. Players who fail to take the antes into account will frequently underbet preflop. In the case of 100 and 200 blinds with ten antes of 25, for example, it would be a mistake to bet just twice the size of the big blind, for you'd be creating a pot of 950 chips and offering attractive pot odds to a wide range of hands that figure to have card odds in the neighborhood of a coin flip.

A more appropriate bet is one exactly the size of the blinds and antes combined, the reason for which has a very interesting underlying logic. Suppose that for two hands in a row you raise preflop to 550, the size of the pot in this example. The first hand, everyone folds and you win. The second hand, someone reraises all in and you fold. How much have you won. Nothing. How much have you lost. Nothing. But—and here's the key consideration—*how is your image?* That's right: You look like a dangerously aggressive bettor. Though you're betting on a break-even proposition, you give the impression of taking control of the table. You earn, in other words, a tremendous amount of *image equity* on a virtual freeroll. Further to this, in the middle stages of a tournament, when all but the endangered short stacks are inclined to avoid big confrontations, you may very well win more than one out of two of these preflop forays and show a long-term profit on the play. So adjust the size of your bet to the size of the blinds plus antes, and look to steal (more than) your fair share.

Not Monitoring Stacks

Someone chasing the aforementioned image equity may be making preflop raises with anything or nothing at all. I have no problem with junk raises here; if you think you can fold the field, then 2-7 is as good as A-A. But when you're raising on a blind steal, or for image equity, you must always keep in mind the stack sizes of the players yet to act, both those in later position and those back in the blinds. Attractive stacks, from your point of view, are ones neither too large nor too small. Betting into big stacks, you risk getting reraised by someone who can potentially bust you. Betting into small stacks, you invite calls or all in reraises from desperate players making stands with half-hands. If you've made a junk raise in this situation, you're just giving your money away.

All it takes is looking, you know. It's not like the numbers are hidden. They're right there on the screen. You don't even have to guess your way through stacks of chips, as you would in a realworld tournament. And yet, day after day, tournament after tournament, we see players stepping in this hole. They raise with their Q-9 or J-T, blithely unaware that the big blind is down to less than one lap's worth of chips and, basically, already pot committed. Sure, the big blind could have undercards in that situation, but undercards are usually around a 2-1 underdog to unpaired overcards, and the combination of blinds and antes could very well give a short stack adequate odds to call. Note the stacks! If you see someone who looks like he has to go all in, either have a hand that matches up well against a desperation caller (such as a good ace, a fair pair, or court cards) or save your steal raise for another time.

Very large stacks are likewise problematic. For one thing, large stacks are usually found in the hands of strong, active players. Granted, the occasional Timmy will build a big pile on luck alone, but generally those who accumulate lots of chips know what to do with them, including coming over the top of your raises. This is more likely to be the case if the big stack is behind you, rather than in the blinds, for he'll figure his position into the equation. Only a very tricky, very brazen player will make pure bluff reraises out of the blinds. Again, if they know the value of a big stack, they know to wait for more favorable cards and situations. When they're behind you, though, and if they've got you covered by a ton, you're sticking your head in a certain noose every time you make a sizeable opening raise. Make sure you have a hand that contends and not just some egregious cheese; alternatively, reduce the size of your raise so that if you get reraised you can get away from your hand.

This may sound contradictory to what I said earlier about always opening for a pot sized bet when antes are involved. Since I've already cited Emerson and the foolish consistency bit, let me just say this: Shape your bet to the situation. Hard and fast rules just make things hard, fast. And think about it, if you've been making full preflop raises and you suddenly trim your sails, the big stack behind you might very well think that you're semi-dragging a big pocket pair. Stay flexible, remembering also that if your stack size is medium or better, you always have the option of laying out and waiting for a better place to bet.

Getting Stuck and Giving Up

A funny thing happens to a certain sort of player when he suffers reversals and finds himself in a tough spot. Instead of trying to get back in the match, he actually gives up and pees away his broken stack on goofball calls and desperation raises. "Well, now I have to lose," he tells himself as he pushes and prays at the next opportunity, not really caring, frankly, whether his prayer is answered or not. Has this state of mind ever swamped you? It has certainly swamped me, and that's why I keep a little card on my desk. Corny it is, I know (and sound like Yoda I do), but these words have helped me right my tournament ship more times than I can count. Here they are, in all their locker room rah-rah sentimentality. Copy, clip and save if you're so inclined.

**REFUSE
TO LOSE**

Never give up. Most of the time, yes, when you're grazing the virtual felt, you'll fail to come back. The sharks will circle and you'll be lunch. Most of the time, yes, but not all the time. And the one comeback you successfully stage will pay for all the other crashes-and-burns. Furthermore, if you are in the habit of making the best of a bad situation, you'll find yourself, well, doing better in bad situations. Tempered by adversity and proud of the grit you show in hard times, you'll develop the confidence, the patience, and the cool head you need to make your last tournament shot a meaningful one. And at the end of the day, wouldn't you like to see yourself as the sort of person who *never gives up*? Not for nothing, but you get to like yourself a lot better if you do.

Contrast this with the player who *suffers* his setbacks. We're familiar with what motivates such a player: anguish. Having experienced a horrendous beat or implosive bad outcome, he just wants to *make the hurt go away*. That's why he stops caring, or acts rashly, or both. It's not a strategy for getting back into the tournament; it's a palliative to pain. Can you remember experiencing such pain? Can you recall how you responded?

>>

Someone who has gone from a strong chip position to a terribly weak one is at definite risk for overplaying the next half-decent hand he sees. Be alert to bad plays after bad beats, and be ready to get involved with good pairs and good aces. Avoid playing hands like K-T or Q-J, however. Frantic though your foe may be, he's much more likely to move with a bad ace or a little pair than with, say, a Q-9 or J-8, and if he has even A-6 offsuit, he's a favorite over any non-pair, non-ace wheelhouse hand you could hold. Though you know he's acting rashly, don't you act rashly in return. If applied luck is running your way, you'll be in a position to pick him off with A-J or T-T. If not, no big deal. The bottom line is that this is one poor, sick bastard, and it's *not your job* to get him well.

Underestimating the Enemy

Because your online foe is invisible to you, and because you cannot look him in the eye, it's easy to assign to him the characteristics you want him to have or hope him to have, rather than the ones you believe him to have or know him to have. We frequently see this mistake being made at the river, where players interpret real bets as steal bets—not because they think the other guy is stealing, but just because they want to win the pot, and so let desire color reality. WSOP bracelet winner Antonio "the Magician" Esfandiari has this to say about calling bets on the river: "If you were to fold, versus call, every single river bet for the rest of your life, I guarantee you'll be up. Why? Because most river bets are real."

Think about your own experience of this. Are you a mad river bluffer? Or do you figure, sensibly, that the only hand that can call you can beat you? It stands to reason, then, that most river bets are real. Yet, people make this call all the time, and it's just one example of a very common class of error, the *I don't want you to have the hand you're representing, so therefore you must be a lying sack of sushi* flaw. Obviously, you don't want to sink into this pit of subjective reality yourself, so pause before you act and ask yourself if you're acting on knowledge, supposition, or mere hope. Only you can know your heart, but it's up to you to know it and not fall prey to self-induced lies. Remember:

DECEPTION IS WHAT YOU DO TO OTHERS. DELUSION IS WHAT YOU DO TO YOURSELF.

You're in the middle stage of a tournament when someone raises from early position. You have A-9 suited and plenty of chips, so you decide to take a flier on the hand. The flop comes 9-6-2 and your foe checks. You're golden, right? You bet—but he raises. How do you like your chances now? You're in great shape if he's on overcards, but *terrible* shape if he has a big pair. In reviewing the play (and letting subjective reality creep in), you conclude that overcards is his likeliest holding, not because you *believe* it but because you *desire* it. So you reraise all in. *Take that!* But he has pocket queens, calls easily, and knocks you out of the game. Erp.

To take another example . . . no, I tell you what, *you* take another example. Recall and record a time in a tournament (or even any poker game) (or even any life circumstance) when, to the detriment of your goals, you let hope trump common sense and lead you down a wrong path. If it's never ever happened to you—God bless you—make something up.

>>

Such situations abound. In certain of them, unfortunately, those who err can actually hurt you more than themselves. If they view you as a lying sack of sushi, and it happens to be that you are, they'll call you down when you would much prefer they'd fold. So note the players who seem to be letting their emotions guide their play. You can't count on them to play correctly, or in their own obvious (to you) self-interest, so you should bluff less and value bet more when you're in a pot against them.

By the way, if this seems to conflict with my earlier assertion that mistake prone foes, along with other forms of dead money, will have been eliminated by the time the tournament reaches the middle, well it does and it doesn't. At the outset, every player is (presumably) playing his best, according to his understanding of the game. A flawed player playing his best will do less well, and not last less long, than a skilled one, but here's the thing: As the hours drag by, almost everyone stops playing their best. Fatigue creeps in. All those folds, calls, checks, and raises blur into a passing parade. Even someone playing perfect poker for the first few hours (even you) may become prone to wrong moves or, as in the cases described here, errors in evaluation. Sooner or later, every tournament player discovers what it's like to play flawlessly for *almost* a whole tournament, only to be bounced out by that one tragic, critical misstep.

Squandering Your Stack with Inferior Values

As you guard against underestimating the strength of your foes' holdings, guard also against overestimating the strength of your own hand, either its current value or its potential for later improvement. While this error is somewhat costly in cash games, it's death in tournaments because if you make an overly optimistic call or raise and it doesn't work out, you can't reload and must instead try to rebuild with a crippled stack. No fun, yet it happens all the time. You've seen it happen. You probably saw it the last time you played.

There you are: Having folded your rags, you watch intently as two hands like K-T and Q-9 go to war. What are these slackjaws thinking? Well, they're probably thinking they have better hands than they have. Or they may be thinking that the Balvenie single malt really does have a peaty, smoky finish with just a hint of vanilla in the nose. It's possible, to give them the benefit of the doubt, that one or both is short stacked and desperate, but it's much more likely that they just lost the plot. You couldn't even call it an error in judgment, because there doesn't seem to be much of anything like judgment involved.

Perhaps it's oxygen-debt stupidity. It may be impatience. In any case, in a typical squander scenario you start by getting seduced into the hand by the harmonic convergence of an unraised pot, late position, and cards of indifferent quality like K♦-8♦. The flop comes 8-J-5, and there's a bet and a call before it gets to you. Now is the moment to pause, reflect, and *take your time.* If you rush . . . if you're rash . . . you'll decide that your middle pair good kicker is a rockin' fine hand. Allowing for the possibility that someone might actually be betting top pair, though, you decide to just call, figuring that any eight or king on the turn will turn you to gold, pure gold. But the next card off is an ace, and when there's *another* bet and *another* call in front of you, you conclude that you're beat, as in *beat a hasty retreat,* which you do.

"Now where did my chips go? They were just here a minute ago."

To avoid this class of error, make it your habit to think your way all the way through the hand in advance. What happens if you *don't* get the card you need on the turn? Will you have odds to call a big bet then? Are you willing to put your tournament life on the line with the hand you have right now? If not, then save yourself some grief, some chips, and some chance in the tournament by just not getting involved in the first place.

This circumstance, by the way, this overvaluing of one's prospects, is an unfortunate spawning ground for bad beats. Though *you* wouldn't stay in the hand on the dim promise of a five-outer, there are plenty of players who will, and sooner or later their mistakes will snare you in an unexpected net. Driving top pair top kicker, say, you'll get a bad call from someone holding bottom pair, which you love, who then makes trips on the turn, which you hate. If you're lucky, you'll see the train before it wrecks you; if not, oh well, there's another tournament starting later.

Bad beats happen. This we know. This is not news. Bad beats happen to everyone, though they happen more to players like us because we more often get our money in with the best of it, and less frequently need a miracle card to catch up. To quote Paul Simon, "Breakdowns come and breakdowns go. What are you gonna do about it, that's what I'd like to know." If you whine and moan and go on tilt, you can kiss your tournament chances goodbye. If, however, you still have a (virtual) chip and a (virtual) chair, you still have a chance. Take a deep breath, make the best of the situation you're in right now, and remind yourself:

THERE ARE NO BAD BEATS, ONLY TEMPORARY SETBACKS.

Keep this idea in mind and you'll be able to keep your mind right through the tournament's critical middle stages and on into the promised land of the end game.

11

♣♠♦♥

FULL FIELD TOURNAMENTS—
LATE

♣♠♦♥

We talked about avoiding and exploiting the common mistakes of middle-round tournament play. Let's bring this baby home on a more positive note by talking about some good things you can do to hasten your journey past the money bubble to the final table and, one would hope, a first place finish.

First let's figure out where we're at. In the example we've been using, the money bubble will pop somewhere around the tenth level or so, but this number will vary from site to site, depending on the amount of starting chips, blind structure, the size of the field, and the length of the rounds. In all events, if you're approaching the money, you're certainly at least into your third hour of play, which means you're probably starting to feel at least a little weary. Hopped up on poker, you might not notice it but it's there, and it will affect the crispness of your decision making. So here's one positive thing you can do: Take breaks when they're offered! Get up and stretch your legs. Grab a cup of coffee. Throw some water on your face. Scratch your dog behind the ears. Talk to another human being (or your dog). Of course, you'll be hitting the john. Try not to be putting in a load of laundry, grabbing a meal, checking on your fantasy football team, and paying your bills online. That might be asking a bit much of one five-minute break.

Back from the break, let's say we're resuming play just shy of the money. Pause at this point to review your goal for the tournament. Did you come just to have fun? Recover your buy in? Or are you in it to win it? This is just me, but I'd rather play strongly and bubble off than back into a low money finish. As much as I love my online poker, there *has* to be a better use of my time and skull sweat than earning a paltry $126 return on a $100 (+ $9!) investment. Many of my foes, I know, will be of a contrary opinion, and attacking them is now my priority—and yours. The rising blinds are putting pressure on everyone. If you can put added pressure on those benighted souls who fear to bubble off, maybe you can steal enough chips to make the final table.

After that, anything can happen.

If we just do a few things right.

FINAL STAGES: THINGS TO DO RIGHT

Take Stock

Constantly assess and update your situation vis-à-vis the other players at your table, the blinds and antes, the bubble, and the tournament state as a whole. Know the cost of a lap. Know whether your stack is strong, adequate, or imperiled. Know how it compares to the rest of the field.

Some players don't sign on to this idea. They'd rather not concern themselves with who has big stacks, who's on life support, and how many places remain till the money or the final table. I have no problem with this preference. If you find such data distracting, then by all means keep it at arm's length. Me, though, I find nothing wrong with being informed, and my stack size relative to the mean is by no means irrelevant. Sometimes, when the tables have been reduced to few, I open up several on my desktop, just to start getting a line on the players I (hope to) have to face at the final table. Among other things, this keeps my wandering mind leashed and helps me stay patient.

Patience is key. If you're not short stacked and imperiled, you should be really picking your spots right now. While it's great to be aggressive, you don't have to go nuts. Remember that every move you make in the context of prohibitively high blinds invites the possibility of an all in confrontation. Not to put too fine a point on it . . .

IF YOU CAN AFFORD TO WAIT, WAIT.

This doesn't mean you should go into a shell. If you sit on your stack too long, the rising blinds will reduce it from a tower to a tuffet. Open up your starting requirements a little and look to open lots of pots for a raise. Of course, you'll want to make sure first that the stacks behind you are the right sort of stacks. Even if your own chip position is strong, avoid confrontations with chip leaders because these players will be looking to amass prohibitively large stacks and they're not afraid to go to war with anyone. Small stacks, on the contrary, at this point are usually so small as to be no credible threat. Pick them off . . . or lay out and let others pick them off. You're bobbing and weaving, dancing and ducking, mindful of what Shakespeare said (through Falstaff) about discretion and the better part of valor. Especially be wary of an unexpected lead bet or reraise from an otherwise quiet player. If he has any sort of stack at all, he's not likely to be completely out of line. Like you, he's been trying to pick his spots, and clearly he's found one here. So think before you act. I'm going to repeat that, because it's so crucially important to your end stage success:

THINK BEFORE YOU ACT!

Take it as read that you're tired. You might not think you're tired, but you are. You've been looking at *two cards, two cards, two cards* for several hours now, which puts you in the throes of NTCS, Next Two Card Syndrome, the gradual grinding down of your sharpness and toughness by the little jolt of stimulation you get every time your next two cards are dealt. Waiting for a hold'em hand is like opening a Christmas present—the exact same buzz. Even if most presents turn out to be lumps of coal, all that anticipation fries the brain cells and depletes our mental reserves. I'm not saying you can no longer think effectively; I'm just saying think things through.

Stay Humble

Don't get cocky. Remember that it's easy to objectify opponents you can't see. If you're running well and steaming toward the final table or a high money finish, you will certainly feel an endorphin rush, and it's easy for your biochemical brain to confuse this rush with confidence, arrogance, or a feeling of entitlement. *Not only am I doing well,* your inner voice will say, *I* deserve *to do well. I'm a crafty poker player, a cool tournament head, and a snappy dresser to boot.* Furthermore, if you're having success controlling the table, you can start to consider such control to be yours by right. Remember that part of what gives you control is *selective* use of your offensive weapons. Start using them indiscriminately, just because you think they'll always work, and you're asking for trouble. What's that thing that pride goeth before? Oh yeah, a fall.

Situations do develop in the late stages of a tournament where you can stride forward, raise with anything, and absolutely get away with it. Maybe you're boss stack. Maybe your image is favorable. Maybe you've got such a firm read on the table that you know no one will play back. Maybe they're all just asleep at the keyboard. For whatever reason, it is possible to get on one of these raising jags and feel like no one is ever going to slow you down. Eventually they will, of course. Someone will wake up with a real hand. Someone will play a crap hand that turns into a trap hand. Someone will get short stacked and desperate. Like the sign says . . .

THE TROUBLE WITH TOO FAR IS YOU NEVER KNOW YOU'RE GOING TILL YOU'VE GONE.

With this in mind, think about changing gears even if you don't have to. Suppose you've been having success raising with Q-9 preflop because no one's in the mood to call. That doesn't mean you have to play *every* Q-9 that comes along. Let the others have a turn. It will lend your bets more credence when you resume your thieving ways.

You know, in rereading that last paragraph I'm suddenly self-conscious, because I seem to be implying that Q-9 is some sort of raiseworthy hand in the late stages of a tournament, and it seems as though the motivation to raise arises from the very hubris I'm cautioning you against. Taken out of context, that could be *very* dangerous information. Someone could make that raise, run into A-Q or Q-Q, get hammered, bust out, and wind up cursing my name and ruing the day he bought my book. As I would hate for that to happen, all the cursing and the ruing, let me state for the record that I am *not advocating junk raises!*

Except that I am.

If the circumstances are right, if your reads, table image, stack size, and position are all in proper alignment, there's *no* hand that's not a raising hand. Selective aggression wins in poker, this we know. It's just that sometimes the word *selective* exists on a loosely sliding scale. I think you'll be more successful in tournament poker if you're more aggressive than you probably are right now. But this is a skill of some subtlety. It takes a while to learn, and it's not without its bumps in the road (the kind that blow your tires right off their rims). Still, if you held a gun to my head, I'd have to say be humble, but also be bold.

Adjust the Size of Your Raise

While a bet of exactly the blinds and antes will be generally effective, you might have to raise more than that amount to telegraph the seriousness of your intent. This is especially true if there's a tricky or frisky player behind you, for if you price him into the pot, you give him the chance to mess with you and your junk holdings. Not good.

Let's say you're on the button and a particularly difficult foe is two seats to your left, in the big blind. You'd certainly like to snack on the blinds when it's your turn, only this guy doesn't seem to want to give his up without a fight. The blinds just now are 1,000 and 2,000 with a 100 ante. That puts 4,000 in the pot preflop and argues for a raise from you of 4,000, which you make. The small blind obligingly clears out, but the big blind recognizes that he's getting 4-1 odds on his call, an attractive prospect to a wide variety of hands. Granted, he's out of position, but remember, you know him to be frisky, which means he could bet at the flop with anything or nothing, and unless you hit it big, you won't know where you're at in the hand. You are effectively underbetting the pot and letting your intelligent foe tap dance on your head.

At this point, it seems to me, you have two choices. The safest path is to surrender your button without a fight, unless you have a hand that will play well after the flop, such as big pairs or big paint. Alternatively, you can bring it in for more than your standard 4,000. Suppose you come in for 6,000. Now your foe needs to call 4,000 into a 10,000 chip pot, and instead of getting 4-1, he's only getting 2.5-1; much worse. Worse still, from his point of view, you've made a big enough raise to signal that you're not interested in getting away from this hand cheaply. This will narrow the range of hands he'll feel comfortable calling you with and give you a clearer picture of his potential holding if he does call.

Further to this, remember that the bet you make is a code you send. You obviously want it to be interpreted a certain way, and there's only so much spin you can put on it. Apart from betting more quickly or more slowly by way of sending a false tell, the only truly effective information you can convey is through the size of the bet itself. So whenever you're contemplating a bet or a raise, especially when it's a thick slice of your stack, take a moment—there's our theme again—and ask yourself how the size of the bet is likely to be interpreted by your foe. Sometimes the most threatening bet is one large enough to suggest that you have a hand you're willing to take to the wall. Other times, it's one so small that it looks like it's looking for a call. This slender bet has the dual advantage of looking suspicious, and therefore scary, but also giving you a cheap escape if your foe comes over the top. Use your judgment, use your reads, but above all, use your allotted time.

Drive the Bus

Inside the money bubble, and especially at the final table, players fall into two distinct philosophical camps. One group contends that if their stack is large enough, they could do worse than to snug up completely, get involved only with premium hands, and, basically, back their way up the pay table. "Let's you and him fight," they say, as every bust out increases the size of their prize, virtually risk free. The other school of thought says, "Screw that, Jack, I want the *big* money." I can't tell you which school to join, but I can tell you this: While you can fall upward through several money places, you *can't* back into first place. At some point, you're going to have to put your money in. Even if you sit on a big stack long enough to bust all but one other player, how are you ever going to get that fellow's chips unless you go to war?

And why not go to war? Haven't you been battling all along?

Maybe you've been playing very selectively, but you *have* been getting involved. Had you not, the blinds and antes would have slain you long ago. Now is no time to turn turtle. For what? So that you can snag 3 percent of the prize pool instead of 2 percent? When you have a chance to get the top prize? *Do not look off that chance!* You've worked long and hard to get this shot, and it's not a shot you get every day. Don't settle for a grand or two (in our example), not when twenty-five grand could be yours. A certain conservatism takes over when we make the money. We figure, hey, we overcame maybe 500-1 odds to get here, and we want to squeeze all the benefit we can out of that longshot. Yeah, but now that you're at the final table, you're only a 9-1 shot to reap better than 100-1 on your original $200 investment. You've *earned* that overlay. Now go exploit it.

If you think about it, you really have no choice. The blinds and antes are now so jinormous that it's just not possible to wait. Let's say you're one of five left, holding exactly an average stack: 20 percent of the original 750,000 chips in play, or 150,000. Not a bad stack, except that the blinds are 10,000 and 20,000 and the antes are 1,000, so it's costing you 35,000 per lap. Your average stack is in peril. *All* stacks are in peril. To wait, in a very real sense, is to surrender and die. It's up to you, of course, but I would reiterate: Making the final table of a full field internet tournament is hard. You don't get there often, and you don't get there without a lot of good luck and a lot of good play. Why not make the most of the chance you have? It might be a while before you get one again.

An exception to this "in it to win it" stance—one we considered before—is a destination satellite where a number of identical top prizes are awarded, regardless of order of finish. If you have a stack large enough to coast into the homogenized prize pool without playing a hand, for heaven's sake *don't play a hand!* Not even pocket aces. There's just no upside. Go grab a snack. Lock yourself in the bathroom. Rip your modem from the wall if you have to, but *don't get involved.* I wouldn't harp on this point if I hadn't seen it happen so many times. Someone who's a lock for a trip plays hands he doesn't have to. Why? Pride, maybe. Lost consciousness, perhaps. He takes an unexpected bad beat, then panics, gets desperate, gets reckless, and busts out. Someone else wins the trip instead. Sad. Unnecessary. That's one bus you don't drive.

Get Shorty

For hour after hour of full field play, you'll never have been at a table with fewer than eight, or very occasionally seven players. Now, suddenly, you find yourself at the final table, playing six, five, four handed . . . all the way down to heads up. If you didn't have a lot of experience in this arena, you'd be surrendering considerable edge to those who do, so be sure to shore up your short handed playing ability through liberal application of six handed sitngos and match play. To be fair, the circumstances are not exactly analogous. The blinds put much more pressure on you heads up at the end of a full field tournament than in match play. Also, you might find some dead money in a six way sitngo, which you won't at a full field final table. Nevertheless, short handed skills are indispensable for "closing the deal" in a big online tournament and often spell the difference between first place and a mere high finish. So work on that part of your game.

As the number of players decreases, two complementary forces are at work: speedy orbits and sinking hand values. The shorter the field gets, the more frequently everyone takes the blinds and the more frantically they look for hands to play. At the same time, with increasingly fewer players involved, premium hands become progressively scarcer and a certain subjective reality creeps in, such that the hand you folded an hour ago is a hand you'll raise with now. Strive to strike a balance between stealing your share of the blinds and not getting caught raising with pure cheese. Be constantly adjusting your bet size so that your raises are big enough to sweep the field, but not so big that you can't escape if someone wakes up with a real hand. It's hard to pick your targets with precision and to have them all to yourself, since everyone has a pressing need to get involved. Still, by now you should have good, solid book on everyone at the table. You should know who's capable of making a big bluff and who prefers to raise or reraise with solid values. Above all, you should be prepared to wield your stack while you can. You don't want to let your foes whittle away at your chips until your only choice is push and pray. From four handed on down, pretty much any ace is a raising hand. Any pair. Any two wheelhouse cards. There's such value in stealing blinds that some players consider any two cards to be raiseworthy if there's a reasonable chance the blinds will lay down. This isn't a bad thought, though it does take knowing your foes.

What if you go card dead at the wrong time? You can't be slinging (too many) raises in there with 9-3 offsuit, nor would you like to defend your blinds with such a hand. But the pressure is mounting and the cost of inaction is high. Looking over your shoulder, you can see the blinds bearing down. Should you go all in now with 9♥-8♥ or wait for the next hand, which could be pocket aces? It's a delicate dance and I can't tell you how it's going to break, but bear in mind that the next hand is not likely to be pocket aces, so don't invest more hope in the unknown than the unknown deserves. Remember also that when your total stack dwindles to twice or three times the big blind, there's no way you won't get called. So try to get your case money in the middle while there's still a chance to win without a fight.

Be not afraid! At some point your money *will* go in the middle. You hope that you're a favorite at that time, but you may be no better than the right side of a coin flip. And even if you're a huge favorite, well, bad flops happen to good people. You've done everything you could to put yourself in a position to get lucky. If Dame Fortune smiles upon you, then . . . *score!* If not, then . . . smaller score.

Do a Post-Mortem

No matter how deep into the tournament you go, look back when you're done and identify what you did right and where you need to improve. This can be a tricky business, because we're more apt to pitch our analysis in terms of how we feel than in terms of what we can learn. It's a natural inclination. If you played well, you want to feel really good about what you accomplished, and you're entitled to shine. What's the point of the exercise, after all (money aside) if you can't relish your triumph? But I put it to you that you'll relish it all the more if you take a moment to break it down. You know you did well; you wouldn't have won otherwise. *Where* did you do well? *How* did you do well? What did you do right this time? It's worth noting . . . *so* worth noting . . . so that you can do the same darn thing next time, too.

The downside is a little more harsh. If you bombed out of the tournament, and especially if you know it was some mad blunder on your part that brought you low, it's understandably difficult to face this fact without, you know, feeling like a schmuck. Relax! It's not the end of the world; it's not even the end of the week. The point of analyzing your mistakes is not to make yourself feel like a schmuck, but to flag the traps so they *don't trap you again.* Accept that you're going to feel a little bad this time, so you can get to feel a little less bad (maybe a whole lot less bad) next time.

Better still, don't get caught up at all in the question of how you feel. Feeling good and feeling bad are entirely beside the point. All that matters is improving your play. In that sense, every error you make can be viewed as an opportunity to improve, so long as you're courageous enough to acknowledge your actions, evaluate them honestly, and form a more effective plan. There's no shame in losing. Most everyone who enters the tournament does that. The only shame, it seems to me, is in not telling the truth about you to you. There's no improvement there, and no enhancing your chances to win.

I invite you, then, to play your next online tournament with the following chart by your side. Mark it up as you go along (make a photocopy, maybe) and then when you're done, go back and think about or write about or talk about your many right moves and wrong moves with equal tranquility. To reduce the emotional sting, we'll put nice, non-threatening tags on the categories. We'll call 'em *DG*, for *Done Good*, and *CBB*, for *Could've Been Better*.

DG	CBB

Lest you think you walk through this wasteland alone, let me share with you my notes from the last tournament I played. As you can see, I suck, too, though not all the time— and not nearly as bad as I used to suck before I started paying attention to specifically where, how and why my truck went off the track.

"I have not failed," said Thomas Alva Edison, "I've just found 10,000 ways that won't work." While I wouldn't wish on you the tribulation of finding 10,000 ways to not win a tournament, I can promise you that your failures will far, far outnumber your successes in this realm. The beauty of online poker is you don't have to wait very long to try again. The other beauty is that one success pays for all of those failures,

DG	CBB
folded pocket queens that time	called off a bunch of chips with a bad ace
adopted orphans	didn't see that flush
no reckless adventures	answered the damn phone!
kept track of stacks, blinds & antes	ate a candy bar— sugar shock!
heroic gutsy call; trusted my read & was right	semi-tilt after bad beat
stayed patient, stayed present	weak, cally shit
made book and used it	suicide bluff
attacked a buttload of blinds	cowered out
reraise bluff—fun!	lost heart and pissed away the last of my chips

and then some. The other *other* beauty, if you choose to view it as such, is that every tournament is a journey into our higher capability. We *can* improve. Every single time. All we have to do is want to. If we have that going for us, then the financial rewards are of secondary importance.

But also a lot more likely to come.

12

♣ ♠ ♦ ♥

THE ROAD TO REALWORLD GLORY

♣ ♠ ♦ ♥

Many players see online poker as merely a means to an end—the specific end of satelliting into major realworld poker tournaments like the World Series of Poker and the events of the World Poker Tour, winning one of those, and establishing themselves as working poker pros. These hard-nosed individuals are not interested in the social aspects of gatherings in distant lands. They could care less about convening in the tropics with people they previously knew only by screen name. All they want is the chance to play a certain longshot wager, the satellite parlay, and hope that it will take them where they dream to go.

We know this system works. We've all seen evidence of it. Some punter puts up forty bucks or ten bucks, or even no bucks (using player points, say, or jumping into a promotional freeroll), and wins a satellite-into-a-satellite-into-a-satellite. Two or three elimination rounds later, he has climbed a certain pyramid and booked his ticket to the Show. Should he be fortunate enough and skilled enough to "cop a Moneymaker," and win or finish very high, he earns his piece of poker glory, plus enough money to, well, keep on doing what he was pretty much doing all along—playing poker.

Here's the thing about pyramids, though: They're tall and

pointy at the summit, but vastly broad across the base. For every online player who reaches the top of these towers, there are thousands who fail. For every online player who becomes a glory story, there are thousands who silently and anonymously build the pyramid with their buy ins. And even that "overnight sensation" who makes the parlay pay off probably tried many, many times before a harmonic convergence of hard work, skill, and no small amount of luck brought him to the top. Though tales are famously told of online players who turn the proverbial toothpick into a lumber yard, you never hear about how many toothpicks they went through first.

The satellite structure is ideally suited to this "try, try again" approach. There are buy ins for every budget, which means that anyone who wants to walk the satellite path can do so at a price that will cause him no real pain. This is the key consideration. No matter what your gulp limit, whether it's ten bucks, a hundred, or a thousand, if you can spend that sum over and over again without materially impacting your bankroll or your lifestyle, then the satellite system makes you a seductive offer. Especially in huge field online satellites to big ticket tournaments, the prize pool is amortized over so vast a playing population that it can cost each individual effectively nothing (relative to their bankroll) to play. In a sense, it's like buying a lottery ticket. Sure, your chances of winning are scant, but if you do win it'll change your life forever and anyway you'll never miss the buck you pay to play. And if you don't win and choose to take another whack? You'll never miss that buck either.

Poker is of course different from the lottery because you can affect the outcome of a tournament with the effectiveness of your play, whereas you can't affect the outcome of the lottery by picking your numbers according to your kids' birthdays, alignments of stars, or instructions from voices in your head. Still, the analogy is not entirely off base, particularly in the "why the hell not?" attitude that informs the player in both cases. With the price of each individual tournament so low (again, remembering that you can pick a satellite or a satellite-into-a-satellite for whatever you deem chump change to be) and the potential payoff so great, players come back to satellites over and over again, trying to catch that proverbial lightning in a bottle.

Since you'd rather be the one at the top of the pyramid than the one lugging blocks of stone to the base, let's consider some ways to enhance your chances of winning through from the online realm to realworld poker glory.

KNOW YOUR BUDGET

Truly, it's difficult to go broke a dime at a time, but those dimes do add up. If you find yourself entering six or seven satellites a week with nothing to show for your pains, you'll soon find yourself with a bankroll that can no longer sustain the effort. Work out in advance the number of shots you can afford to take in an attempt to win entry to any given real-world event. For example, if there are seats in a $10,000 buy in WSOP tournament up for grabs, how many $100 online satellites will you play? You might get lucky and snatch the brass ring on the first attempt, but what if you don't? Will you try five times? Ten? Fifty? Obviously, you don't want to get upside down in this, entering so many satellites that you'd have been better off skipping the satellites and buying into the big event directly.

Further to this, be honest with yourself about the real cost of walking the satellite road. Ultimately, just $100 will get you that seat in the $10,000 buy in prestige event, but how many $100 buy ins fell by the wayside en route? Do you know? I think it's kind of irresponsible not to know—irresponsible to yourself and to anyone who cares about your financial and mental well-being. Any given satellite is a bargain, in the sense that it can lead to inconceivably big money at the cost of inconsequentially small money. The real cost, though, isn't of any given satellite, but of all satellites taken as a whole. It's fundamental to the poker experience: You have to keep score; and if keeping score shows that you can't show a profit, you need to fix your game or find a different one to play. Insanity, it is said, is doing the same thing over and over again expecting a different outcome. Many online players become so besotted by the dream of internet poker as launching pad to realworld poker glory that they lose track of, or actively deny, the authentic price they've paid.

MARK YOUR TIME

There's a tradeoff involved in satelliting into major realworld tournaments, especially if you're going the multiple-tier route of satellites into satellites. What you're trading is time for money. Instead of just walking up to the cashier's cage and plunking down your ten grand, at the cost of thirty seconds of your life, you're investing a heavy number of hours, hours that could profitably or productively be spent doing something else. Let's do the math.

SuperJoe has to fight his way through just two tiers of satellites, a $20 buy in qualifier and a $200 buy in direct entry super. If both tournaments together would take a total of fifteen hours to complete, his hourly rate would be pretty handsome: $10,000/15 or $667/hour. But just as he has to account for all his buy ins in calculating his real satellite costs, he also has to account for his time. Unfortunately, he played in ten $20 qualifiers before he caught enough traction to win his first one. The dollar cost wasn't so bad—just $200 (plus fees)—but his average time investment was two hours per qualifier. Now he's up to thirty-five hours, and his hourly wage has dropped to $286/hour. Still not too shabby; you'd have to be a high-end lawyer, consultant, or poker coach to do much better. But, oops, he didn't win his first super and had to go back to the square one of $20 qualifiers and start over. And, oops, he didn't win his second super either. Or, oops, his third. Counting all the failed supers and all the $20 square ones, he actually invested 137 hours in winning his $10,000 realworld tournament buy in. Now he's earning just $73 an hour, and while that's still more than fry cooks make, it's not beyond the reach of an educated, professional type like *SuperJoe*. So I guess all he has to do is work 137 hours at his regular well-paying job, save every dime, enter the big tournament directly, and skip the satellites altogether, right?

Of course not right. Ten grand is a serious chunk of change; a chunk so serious that most of us don't have it just lying around, and most of us couldn't wantonly part with it at any cashier's cage, even if we earned it by the sweat of our own dedicated brows. In practical terms, the satellite path may be the only realistic means we have of entering a top tier realworld tournament. We trade time for money because we simply have no choice. Time is the only currency we have in sufficient abundance.

But time spent playing poker—at least if you're doing it right—multitasks productively. Ideally, of course, it earns you money or moves you closer to your realworld tournament goal. Also, it gives you experience playing poker and—again, if you're doing it right—improves the quality of your play. Finally, as we know, it's fun; for most of us, it's fun, not work, and even if we can earn sufficient money in our jobs to bankroll our poker, isn't it sweeter when our *poker* bankrolls our poker? The underlying logic of investing time in the satellite path, then, is not just that it's the most financially feasible path, it's also the one that lets us do what we really want to do with our time anyhow: play poker for money.

But time is a nonrenewable resource. We each have only so much of it, and then it runs out (so far as we know—let's not take a metaphysical detour here). So you really do have to ask yourself the question and keep asking it as time goes by, "Is this, in fact, how I want to be spending my time?" Just as our money budget can run away from us, we can easily lose track of the time spent, the raw hours behind the closed door of our office or den, trying—*this time, swear to God,* this *time*—to win that big time tournament seat we crave. I'm not saying don't spend the time, for it's your nonrenewable resource, not mine. I'm just saying mark your time, spend it as you see fit, but spend it realistically. Just as it's possible to throw good money after bad, it's possible to throw good time after bad as well.

PICK YOUR SPOTS

I had an enlightening conversation not too long ago with a successful internet poker player. In his short career, he has satellited into big buy in tournaments in Las Vegas, Curacao, Paris, all over the world. His online poker is, in a very real sense, funding his real life adventure. I happened to ask him if he had qualified for a certain upcoming realworld event, and he said, "I haven't tried yet. I won't try till just before the event." All the good players, he reckoned, would enter the early big satellites, win their seats, and drop out of competition. By the time he jumped into the fray, only the stragglers, obsessives, and perennial losers would be left, and the field would be much less difficult to beat.

You could, of course, argue the other side of this logic. It may be that abundant tough players are likewise hanging back and that the supposedly soft field will become the hardest of all. It may also be that there's more dead money in the early satellites, brought in by those players of indifferent skill who will take just a few shots at satelliting in and then give up. Then again, he might be totally right. It could be that the last satellite before the big event is filled with the desperate and the dregs; easy, as it were, pickings. You can't totally know.

You can investigate, though. You can check on the leader board that most sites feature and match the top names there against those who have already qualified for the signature realworld events. You can check out the sign up list just before the start of the tournament and see if it's to your liking. You can count the numbers: a large field means more seats awarded; a smaller field might be easier to get through. You can also hunt for overlays, for very occasionally a site will offer a guarantee that the size of the field won't cover, and the house will have to make up the difference. Wherever your investigation takes you, though, it should always lead you back to this: What are your particular strengths? At the end of the day, you want to enter the satellites that give you the best chance of winning based on how well you think you can do, not on who you're up against.

To cite just one example, here were some of the options available to you if you wanted to go to UltimateBet's 2005 Ultimate Poker Classic in Aruba, and you didn't want to pay full freight.

- $3 + 0 rebuy qualifier
- $3 + 0 turbo rebuy qualifier
- $5 + .50 rebuy qualifier
- $5 + .50 turbo rebuy qualifier
- $10 + 1 qualifier
- $10 + 1 turbo qualifier
- $10 + 1 ultra turbo qualifier
- $20 +1 rebuy direct entry
- $100 + 9 direct entry
- $200 + 15 direct entry
- $300 + 20 direct entry

And that's just one site, one realworld event, one qualifying weekend. Dig a little deeper and you can find, depending on the site and the realworld event, six ways, shootouts, super ultra high speed heads up blowouts . . . anything your tournament heart desires. So then it comes down to this: Where do you excel? If short handed matches are your specialty, look for six way qualifiers. If you have a knack for keeping your buy in while those about you are losing theirs, happily join the rebuy events. If you can marathon through large events, enter the largest ones you can find and settle in for the long haul. Take a moment now and reflect on what are the best tournament conditions for you, and why?

>>

A word about rebuy tournaments. The same logic we discussed in terms of not overspending for satellites definitely pertains here. A $20 rebuy tournament is no bargain if you get six, seven, or eight rebuys deep into the match. Talk about throwing good money after bad! If you find that you've put three or four rebuys into a tournament and still can't gain any traction, contemplate that it's just not your day. Sure, you may owe your losses to nothing more than horrible beats, but even so, *how do those beats affect your head?* Unless you're 100 percent confident that you're still 100 percent on your game, save your buy ins for another day. Don't be desperate, and don't get upside down in the tournament. Remember that your ultimate goal is just to qualify for a certain realworld event. Tomorrow's just as good as today. Don't beat your head against a wall that has a door in it.

KNOW THE PRIZE STRUCTURE

Remember that your endgame tournament strategy is heavily dependent on how the prizes are paid out. If ten or twenty players all receive the same prize package or the same tournament buy in, don't bother playing to win first place; just play to win your seat. You should also know whether prizes are transferable. What happens if you can't go to the realworld event? Will you have nothing to show for your satellite triumph or can you sell off your seat to someone else?

Some sites offer prize structures that include realworld tournament seats to the first few spots and cash to the rest of the top finishers. Do they allow deals? If so, and if you have no interest in playing in the realworld event (or have already qualified), you have the option of playing for a high money finish and dealing off your seat equity to someone else. This can be a tricky business, though, as it often involves players making, and sticking to, good faith agreements to transfer appropriate sums to and from various players' accounts. Even sites that tacitly condone deals will generally wash their hands of enforcement, so if you're on the wrong end of a welsh out, you're pretty much on your own.

WORK ON YOUR REALWORLD CHOPS

Remember that your goal in walking the satellite path is not just to *get to* the World Series of Poker but to win the darn thing. If your poker playing experience is all online, or even heavily weighted toward online play, you'll want to give yourself as much realworld practice as possible between the time you get your ticket stamped and the time the big tournament starts. I realize that this can be problematic for people who don't have easy access to cardrooms, but don't let such hurdles stand in your way. If you were serious enough about the satellite path to go after a major online satellite win, you should be sufficiently serious to give yourself every advantage in the realworld match. Plan a scouting trip to your realworld destination, or to some other public poker venue, and enter a lot of inexpensive tournaments, just to give yourself a feel for realworld play. If that's not possible, at least get together with some poker playing friends and, insofar as possible, simulate tournament conditions. Have your friends probe you for weaknesses and tells, and make them be blunt in their appraisal of your play, for the more flaws they turn up now the better off you'll be later when it counts.

It's a given that if you don't have much (or any) realworld playing experience, there will be issues for you to deal with in live play, all of which require attention and practice. Among these will be:

- *Handling Chips.* If all you know of betting is slider bars and *bet max* buttons, the mere act of moving your chips into the pot will give you grief. Teach your hands how to handle chips so that you can bet what you want when you want, without making mistakes.

- *Measuring Stacks.* You know how important it is to know how many chips the other tournament players have. This information will not be handed to you in live play as it is online. Practice counting or guesstimating other players' chip stacks.

- *Acting in Turn.* Many online players rely on internet poker's *check and fold in turn* button, so that when they get into a realworld game they broadly telegraph their intentions in advance. The simplest way to avoid this devastating tell is simply to never look at your cards until it's your turn to act.

- *Preventing Tells.* Apart from acting in turn, there's a whole host of physical tells that unwary players give off. Enlist the aid of a poker buddy who can watch you play and (brutally honestly) catalog your tells. Control of the physical body is a must for success in realworld tournaments.

- *Detecting Tells.* By the same token, online players are not used to gleaning information from the words and actions of others. Nor do they have long experience with the endless variety of false tells that savvy realworld competitors broadcast like jamming radar. There's simply no substitute for sitting in a game and watching other players play.

- *Being There.* Sitting down in a realworld poker tournament can affect your mind and body in strange ways. Adrenaline may give you the sweats or the shakes. You'll probably be nervous, and your nerves may make you uncharacteristically talky or careless. Don't let your first experience of these things be the one that matters most. Get a lot of practice just being there.

Wherever you are in your tournament journey, whether playing in your first five buck pre-qualifier or sitting at the final table of the WSOP, the single most useful thing you can do is *play right now*. The only tournament decision that ultimately matters is the one you're making in this moment. Insofar as possible, cast aside all thoughts of the past and the future. Don't dwell on any of your false starts. Don't obsess on the end of the rainbow. As smart players say, "Let the game come to you." Let it come to you hand by hand, bet by bet, choice by choice, and with the proper application of time, money, sweat equity, and the ever-necessary luck, you may find your dreams of realworld glory coming true.

PART IV

♣♠♦♥

CASH GAMES

♧♤♢♡

13

♣ ♠ ♦ ♥

TAKE THE CASH (GAMES)

♧ ♤ ◇ ♡

After all this talk of tournaments, it's almost a relief to contemplate the good ol' come-when-you-like, quit-when-you-want internet cash game. As heretofore, we'll be focusing on no limit Texas hold'em, though of course if your taste runs to other games, such as limit hold'em, Omaha, or seven-card stud, with a little hunting you can find what you're looking for online. In fact, with NLHE swamping all other forms of poker in realworld cardrooms, it may be that these other games will eventually *only* be found online, along with razz, pineapple, old school draw poker, and other artifacts of a simpler time. Be that as it may, no limit hold'em is here now, big now, and, given the ongoing torrent of rookies yet flooding into the game, it continues to present a choice profit opportunity for the savvy Killer Poker player.

BANKROLLS AND BUY INS

When we speak of cash games, we're speaking of everything from micro-limit (literally one and two penny blinds) all the way up to massive attacks with $50 and $100 blinds, and buy ins in the multiple thousands. The first question for most players, then, is: *How big should I play?* The answer lies in another question: *How big is my bankroll?* Whether it's $50 or $5,000, protecting it should be among your primary concerns when you play online. After all, apart from the blessed few who draw down a working wage from online poker, the goal for most players is, realistically, to win enough to just *stay in action*. There's nothing wrong with this modest goal; I always say that online poker works best as a recreation, and a low-impact one at that. You never want to go broke if you can avoid it, so just never put all or most of your bankroll at risk at once. While this is rarely a problem for fixed-risk players of tournaments or sitngos, it's the cash player's biggest vex.

The real consideration in no limit cash games, then, is not the size of the blinds, but the amount of money you need to put into a game to play it effectively. This number, in turn, must be measured against your bankroll, to ensure that you're not imperiling your stash of online cash. Let's say you have a bankroll of $500 and you're contemplating putting $400 of it into play in an NLHE game with $2 and $4 blinds. To do so would be to put 80 percent of your bankroll at risk. If you're new to poker, especially online poker, you might not think that's so great a hazard. You can always quit if you start to lose, right? Well, technically, yes, but as everyone with any experience of online cash games knows, leaving when you're losing is a *lot* easier said than done. So much so, in fact, that it's codified as physical law, the First Law of Chair Glue:

**AN OBJECT IN A CASH GAME
TENDS TO STAY IN A CASH GAME
UNTIL ACTED UPON BY AN OUTSIDE FORCE.**

Like being broke.

Plus, as this is no limit hold'em, losses can be sudden, explosive, and significant—the result of being on the wrong side of an all in confrontation. A sadly-too-likely scenario is that you'll start running bad, become desperate to get even, go all in on a reckless adventure, lose your $400, put your other $100 into the game, tilt that off, too, and find yourself out of action until you can drum up enthusiasm (and possibly spousal support) for moving more money from your credit card or Neteller account into your favorite online poker site. Feh, right? Who needs it?

I know what you're thinking—I've thought it myself on many occasions—*But I might win, though! I might double up!* Yeah, you might, if you're skilled, smart, lucky, and fearless. Skilled, smart, and lucky you may even be, but I guarantee that you won't be fearless, not with your case money on the line. As a consequence, you won't optimize your opportunities, or even, necessarily, play correctly. Plus, even if you're skilled, smart, and fearless, you might not be lucky. You might be profoundly unlucky, or even just garden-variety unlucky and wipe yourself out. It's just not worth the risk.

Nurse your bankroll! Grow it. Find a level you can afford and a game you can beat, and keep beating it until you're sufficiently well heeled to step up. As with all aspects of your poker game, be patient. The good games aren't going away. You have all the time in the world.

Some players think they need to play at a certain minimum level to enjoy the game. They claim they can't get excited about playing in $25 or $50 buy in games: The buzz they're looking for just isn't there. They're better off risking their bankroll, they argue, at higher limits where the money is sufficiently meaningful to make them play well. I find this argument specious. If they can't meet the challenge of playing perfect poker at $.50 and $1 blinds, how will upping the stakes really help? Could the hidden issue be pride? Or if not pride, what?

>>

On the subject of specious arguments for playing above one's bankroll, here's one I love: *I can't beat the low buy in games. They play too badly. I need to play higher where people respect my moves.* Folks, bad players are where your profit comes from. Bad players play small. They can't afford to play big. Why? Because they're *bad!* So drop down, and keep dropping down, until you find a game where the buy in fits your bankroll.

And where, exactly, will you find that fit? How much of your bankroll should you be prepared to risk in any given game? Other people have other ideas, but here's mine: 10 percent, max. That may seem overly cautious to you, but I figure if only 10 percent of my bankroll goes into play then I'll have to really suck or get really unlucky ten times in a row before I'm busted. I've had hellacious losing streaks. We all have. I've seen buy ins melt like May snow. If I happen to be running bad, I'd rather not run so bad that I run out altogether. But that's just me.

Here's something else that may be "just me." I can play poker at any level—even nickel-dime, even for play money— still be mentally engaged, still catch a buzz, and still take great satisfaction in beating the game. Perhaps this is because I look at poker first as an intellectual exercise, second as a test of my capability, third as a recreation, and fourth, a distant fourth, as a way to make money. Can you take this idea on board? If you can, you'll find it much easier to play within your bankroll and not feel the need to scratch a prohibitively expensive itch.

If you've been playing poker for a long time, and whether you've been playing profitably or not, you may have forgotten what brought you into the game in the first place. As an exercise in discipline and a test of your pure poker prowess, why not jump over to the free play side for a session and challenge yourself to play as perfectly as you can? See if you can impose rigor on yourself and your decisions even when there's nothing at stake. You'll find it harder than you think, I think. And you'll find it worthwhile to report on your findings, too.

>>

TO MAX OR NOT TO MAX

Most no limit hold'em games on most online poker sites have minimum and maximum allowable buy ins, with the number pegged to the size of the blinds. A typical spread is a minimum of 20 times the big blind and a maximum of 100 times the big blind, but these numbers do vary. The logic for imposing a minimum is to keep cheap chip weevils from trying to parlay a micro buy in into a sizeable stack at the expense of other players who put more money into the game and therefore accept more risk. The reason for slapping a cap on is to keep deep pockets from simply swamping a game through sheer force of bankroll. Suppose somebody came along and plunked $10,000 into a game with $1 and $2 blinds. The rest of the players on stacks measured in the hundreds wouldn't have a chance, not when the bully could simply go all in, all in, all in, all in, and wait for the cards to break his way one time. Sooner or later the big stack would gobble up everybody's dough and the game would end.

There's another reason for imposed maximums. It has to do with the modern state of no limit hold'em, where most of the playing population is new to poker. It's easy for new no limit players to lose fantastic sums of money in short order; buy in constraints have the effect of putting the brakes on a game that would otherwise play so fast as to bust the worst players and, again, kill the game. In realworld cardrooms, though less so online, you'll find NLHE games with exactly mandated buy ins, such as $100 in a game with $1 and $2 blinds, for the stated sake of keeping a level playing field and giving the newbies a chance to find their legs. I suspect that over time no limit hold'em will return to its roots, and the caps will come off even the smallest-structured games. For now, though, most online hold'em games have min and max buy ins.

The question arises, then, how much should we buy in for? There are arguments to be made for both minimum and maximum buy ins, and also for something somewhere in between. Before I run these down, I wonder if you can carve out plausible rationales for each on your own.

>>

Those who favor buying in for the maximum see big stacks as big clubs and seek to swing the mightiest cudgel they can. This outlook has merit, for if you have a whole lot more chips than the other guy, the other guy may think twice before messing with you. In addition, a big stack allows you some options that a small stack precludes. You can, for example, make bets big enough to deny your opponents favorable odds for their draws. You can also attack orphans and ragged flops more liberally, knowing that your foe will be less willing to go up against a stack that can bust him, just on the off chance that you're bluffing. A short stack's strategy is often reduced to looking for a place to push all in; a big stack has room to move.

However, a big stack equals big risk. The more money you have on the table, the more you could potentially lose, which is why some people favor buying in at or near the minimum for the game they're playing. They like the idea of growing a short buy in into a big profit, and it's hard to find fault with that thinking. In exchange for some lost flexibility and lost potential for bully behavior, they get the benefit of limited downside exposure. But there's a tacit decision implied in this rationale, and it's one that must be understood overtly: Someone buying in on the cheap is saying, basically, *This is my one shot. If I lose this money, I won't rebuy.* If he has the discipline to stick to this plan then fine. But if one short buy in is going to lead to another and another and another, he's just fooling himself. In that "short money is scared money," he'd be better off adding up all his budgeted buy ins and getting them on the table at once.

As a matter of personal preference, I don't buy in for the minimum or the maximum, but somewhere in between, say

$200 in a game with $2 and $4 blinds and an $80 to $400 buy in spread. My thinking is this: Unless the money is terribly deep at the table (in which case I'll likely be scouting for a different game anyhow), my $200 gives me necessary and sufficient muscle. I won't feel cramped, scared, or desperate. I'll have enough money to take my time and play my game. Then again, if I run badly or go on tilt (oh, you think it doesn't happen to me?) I'll only have lost $200, *and I'll be done for the day.* It's this last point that's most germane. Whatever logic informs your buy in decisions, make sure that it's *logic* and not *compulsion* that guides your hand. No matter how big or small your buy in—in fact, no matter how big or small your bankroll—you could do far worse than to adopt this caveat for cash games:

IF YOU LOSE YOUR BUY IN, QUIT.

If you lose your initial buy in, don't rebuy. Just don't. If you haven't sufficiently scratched your poker itch, go find yourself a nice cheap sitngo in which to pass the time. Be *very reluctant* to put another buy in into any cash game that has recently defeated you. I understand that there will be times when "the game is still good." I recognize that you may have just been the victim of bad luck, bad beats, or (others') bad play. I know that you can lose your whole buy in (large or small) thanks to some nearly inconceivable circumstance that was *not your fault.* All of this may be true. Then again, it may not. One thing's for sure: In the moment of catastrophic chip loss, psychic pain will make it hard for you to measure objectively your future prospects for profit in the game. Don't give yourself a chance to guess wrong. On most sites, whenever you stack off, a seductive little window pops up. *Buy more chips?* it asks. It's so easy to just click *yes* and jump back into the game. Can you honestly say that your state of mind is conducive to perfect poker in the moment when you've been felted? If yes, okay, reload. But if no—*or even if maybe*—decline to be seduced. Like I said, go jump into a nice, cheap sitngo. You can cool off there. Don't worry, there'll always be another juicy cash game waiting for you once your ire has waned.

CASH GAMES ARE TRAPPY AFFAIRS

Recall our discussion about the psychological difference between trapping and bluffing, how trappers trap with confidence, knowing that their deception is backed by good cards, but bluffers bluff with trepidation, knowing that they can get caught stealing and perhaps lose a lot of chips that they needn't have risked at all. This psychology permeates online cash game play. Since the money is real, and often quite large, players would much rather get their money in with a lock or near lock. It's simple human nature. We poker players are not opposed to risk; if we were, we'd be playing Sorry with the kids. Nevertheless, we don't like to lose, and rare is the online cash player who can move a ton of chips in on a stone bluff. So rare, in fact, that I discount almost entirely the possibility that when I'm facing a big bet I'm facing a big bluff. Consider this situation:

In a $5 and $10 blind NLHE game, our two players of interest are *gumpshun* in the big blind and *KittnKaboodle* on the button. *Gumpshun* starts the hand with $110 and *Kittn* has $500. It's folded to *Kittn*, who makes it $30 to go. The small blind folds and *gumpshun* calls, bringing the pot to $65. The flop comes K♣-3♦-6♥. *Gumpshun* checks. *Kittn* bets $40. *Gumpshun* raises all in, putting his last $80 into a pot now worth $185.

What do you think *gumpshun* has, and why?

>>

I'm pretty sure he has a good king and not just because I'm writing the scenario. I'd be shocked to find him putting in his case money on a naked bluff, especially knowing that *Kittn* has enough money to call, no sweat, and that at better than 4 to 1 pot odds, *Kittn* is getting the right price for any decent draw he has. With all this in mind, is it not the likeliest case that *gumpshun* was looking for a way to get maximum return on his last $80, and so set a check-raise trap?

Remember your man Occam, and his famous Razor that states, "The simplest explanation is usually the best," a principle that's often also expressed, "When you hear hoof beats, think horses, not zebras." In this example, you'd really have to be thinking zebras to conclude that *gumpshun* is trying for the super-deluxe-double-reverse-psych-out bluff. It's simpler, and therefore more likely to be correct, that *gumpshun* is trapping, not bluffing.

What does this mean for our cash game play? For one thing, be very reluctant to call big bets. Keep a weather eye out for bluffers, of course. It's unrealistic to think that *nobody* ever bluffs. The bluffers you do spot should be noted and booked, for if they're inveterate liars, you may be able to catch them at it and make them pay. But when someone comes flying out of nowhere with an extraordinarily large bet, credit him with a hand. I promise that you won't lose money in the long run by folding to big bets that might be bluffs but probably aren't.

Also, recognize that while trapping is the lie of choice for most online cash game players, there are other sorts of deception as well. Good players will routinely take stabs at pots that nobody wants, even though they have nothing at all. They'll drive at draws (semi-bluff). They'll raise and check-raise, not to trap, but just to see where you're at. These functional falsehoods are not big bluffs. They are small attempts to steal pots, send misinformation, or define hands. But when the hammer falls and a player makes a big all in move, he has defined his hand as *better than yours*. Unless you're sure he's wrong, give him the benefit of the doubt. Making big calls against big hands in the hope that they're big bluffs is a big leak no cash game player can afford.

This raises a certain question. If it's true that big bets are more likely to be traps than bluffs, and thus more likely to be read as real hands, does this not mean that you and I should be in there bluffing like crazy, knowing that our intelligent foes will lay down rather than pay us off? There's a little bit of "I know that he knows that I know that *he* knows" double-think in here, but the real answer to the question is this: Most of your opponents won't be that intelligent—not if you've done your job right. And I presume you have. I presume that you've chosen your table appropriately, using all the benchmarks outlined in *Killer Poker Online,* clues and cues from your sniffers, and just your native sense of whether or not you're in a game you can beat. You know that there is always a good game out there somewhere, and you've learned not to succumb to the hubris or inertia that would put you or keep you in a game with a bunch of players who are slicker, trickier, more creative, or more unpredictable than you'd like. With all of this in mind, you're (ideally) in a game where your opponents are *not that smart,* and not nearly smart enough to get away from their hands when they're beat. Of course, they're not! That's why you're playing with them, so that they will pay you off. Classic poker wisdom says,

DON'T BLUFF THE UNBLUFFABLE.

I would take this a step further and say,

IF YOU'RE IN A GAME
WHERE BLUFFING WORKS,
YOU'RE IN THE WRONG GAME.

Muse upon this notion for a moment. It's really an interesting idea. For a bluff to work, your opponents need to be alert to the possibility that you have them beaten—so at minimum, they need to be alert. Who wants to play against players like that? Go find the weak, passive, and clueless. You know they're out there. They abound.

14

♣ ♠ ♦ ♥

FULL RING GAMES

♣ ♠ ♦ ♥

Since correct poker play is shaped, among other things, by the number of foes you face, you want to pick a version that suits your style and strengths. On the one hand, if patience is a problem for you, you'll go nuts playing a full ring game, where patience is not just a virtue but vital. On the other hand, if you like to play the waiting game and you're not comfortable frisking it up with the FNL crowd, you should steer clear of short handed games, where the tight, conservative style appropriate to full ring play is a recipe for slow death.

In a perfect world, of course, you'd have the skills, temperament and flexibility to play in both type games. Since we strive for perfection around here, let's look at some realities peculiar to, respectively, full ring games and short handed tables. While some sites offer nine handed and five handed variants, for the sake of these next two chapters, we'll assume that a full game is ten handed and the short game goes six way.

In hold'em, one starting hand in five will contain an ace or a pair, so in a full ring game, an average of two players per deal will have a decent hand. With such a high likelihood of quality starts (quality here being defined as something better than the unpaired, unaced hands we're most frequently dealt), we should be generally unwilling to put money in the pot if we don't have to. Those who lack this discipline have a big leak in their game. In no limit cash games online, this leak becomes a gaping hole that gushes money. If you just play tight in most full ring games, waiting for strong hands and betting them strongly, you'll make money from the multitudes who can't seem to master this art. Your A-K will get paid off by A-T or A-J, and your T-T will get paid off by A-8 when the flop comes 8-3-2. These are common outcomes in full ring games online. Please be sure you're on the right side of them. In short, have the A-K, not the A-T.

The beauty of online play is its speed. The hands come quickly enough that you can afford to throw away bad ones and wait for your inevitable share of good ones. Yet, the very pace of online play creates its own accelerating "need for speed." We get so used to seeing hands *now,* that we become impatient to wait even a few short moments from now. Having folded under the gun with J-9, we might be out of action for the next thirty seconds or *even a full minute.* That can seem like a lifetime online, so much so that we might rationalize calling with that J-9, just so we don't have to sit there and wait. You know what? Just say no. Just say no to playing bad hands out of position. Say no to self-indulgent calls. Take up knitting between deals if you have to. Don't let impatience move you off your sound basic strategy of selective-aggressive poker.

JUNKING IN

That said, do look for opportunities to take cheap flops with speculative holdings, for much of your profit in online no limit will come from the (granted, infrequent) monster flop that creates big action and lets you take some unsuspecting slackjaw off his stack. Make no mistake, these junk calls can be hazardous to your health, but if you're in the right kind of game, one with lots of callers and few raisers, they can be profitably played. In such games, if a couple of people limp into the pot from early position they often start a limp stampede, or *limpede* if you like, a cascade of callers yielding correct odds for a wide variety of hands such as unpaired picture cards, small suited connectors, and pairs of any size. Warning: Only join the limpede if you're confident that the blinds won't make a play for the pot with a big sweeping raise. Most often, the blinds will just call, too, though, because the sheer number of pot participants discourages frisky raises. Nevertheless, some players love to raise into big fields of limpers, and you should know if you've got one of these guys in the blind before you decide to junk in.

Once you've junked in, you're looking for one thing and one thing only: the perfect flop. Not an okay flop. Not a draw. You want the nuts. And not just the nuts but the nuts disguised so well that your unwary foes will hand you their stacks and never know what hit them. True, this occurrence is rare, but it does happen, and it's the *only* thing you should be looking for with your junk calls.

Suppose you joined a limpede with 5♥-6♥. If the flop were to come 4-3-2 rainbow, you'd get action from A-4, certainly A-5, overpairs, maybe even naked overcards. You'd slightly fear involvement from someone holding a set, for he'd be drawing to seven outs, plus runner-runner, but you can't worry about that. Your goal is to bet big and get paid off by someone drawing dead with a good hand because he can't conceive that you'd be in there with 5-6. Of course he can't conceive it. That's why you're there in the first place!

I'm having another one of those moments of self-doubt where I fear I might be leading you very far astray. I can't recall seeing any hold'em book anywhere that says getting involved with 5-6 is a good idea. I myself have described such a hand as little poison and warned mightily against its toxic properties. But online no limit full ring games are a different breed of cat. If the game is sufficiently weak and loose (and boy, those games abound online), your junk holdings have incredibly high implied odds. Just make sure to save this play for when the situation is exactly right: late position; many limpers; slim chance of a raise behind; and most important, Wallies who will pay you off when you hit.

And whatever you do, don't confuse flopping perfect with flopping dangerously almost perfect. Suppose you junk in with 5♥-6♥ and the flop comes 9♥-8♥-7♠. Yes, you've flopped a straight, but it's the idiot end, vulnerable to J-T holdings, and also to naked tens or jacks looking to improve. And yes, you're drawing to a flush, but if there's another flush draw out there, it's almost certainly better than yours. As in the previous example, you'll have sets drawing to full houses to worry about, but in this instance that's just one of the many threats you face. The only card off the deck you can really love is the 7♥ for a straight flush—and God forbid someone has the J♥-T♥. Having achieved the rarity of flopping a made hand, you'll nevertheless have to fold if you face significant heat. Can you do it? I'm not sure I can.

Let us say, then, that junking in is a dangerous game. There's tremendous reward when it works, but if you don't know how to run scared when you miss—or often even hit—you're better off sticking to your standard tight-aggressive formula. It's not flashy. There aren't a lot of fireworks. But you know it works, even if you never get to read the deliciously tilted chatbox rant, OMG, how could U play that f***ing s**t?

NON-PREMIUM PAIRS

In a loose weak ring game, where people will call with any two cards higher than an eight (and, again, these abound) I almost never raise with small or medium pocket pairs. Having raised preflop, I'd be expected to make a continuation bet, but what sort of flops can I bet at? Highly coordinated flops are scary. Flops with aces are scary. Flops with wheelhouse cards are scary. About the only flop that's not scary is, well, the one I hit. Unless I'm naked bluffing (in which case, again, it doesn't matter what I have), I'm going to have to shut it down, which means that I not only wasted my raise but also some image equity. I exposed myself to unnecessary risk, and I *hate* that.

There's another approach to the play of non-premium pocket pairs, one that works particularly well online where so many hands transpire in so short a space of time. It's predicated on the math of flopping a set. As we know, we'll pick up a pocket pair once every seventeen hands, on average. Having started with a pair, the odds against flopping a set are 7.5 to 1. By my math, then (never my strong suit, but what the hell) we'll flop a set about one time in 145 hands. To play 145 hands in a realworld cardroom will take you all night, but online you can whip through that many hands in a couple of hours or so. Since this is well within the timeframe of most of our online sessions, we can realistically expect to flop a set at least once before we're done for the day.

So here's the thought. Suppose you play squeaky tight. Suppose you make standard raises with standard big hands, but also throw your pocket pairs into the mix as calls, not raises. As with junking in, this is a highly speculative endeavor, and it requires that you not get caught up in nonsense when you don't connect. But if you have the discipline to play "hit or git," you might put yourself in a position to trap a foe for his whole stack, which is really the whole point of the move.

IN BOSS COMMAND

Of course, there are other ways to make money in no limit besides swiping stacks. You can also chip away at them by simply being more aggressive and more fearless than the rest of the table. Now you're in there raising with Q♠-9♠; with small pairs, and with middle suited connectors. Since you're raising with good hands and bad hands alike, your foes won't know from one hand to the next whether or not you've got the goods. If they're obligingly weak-loose, they'll call your pre-flop raises and fold to your postflop bets. If they're not obligingly weak-loose, simply don't use this approach.

If you *do* use this approach, expect to have a lot more volatility in your game than that of your tighter compadres. You'll win and lose bigger pots with greater frequency, and this is not the sort of roller coaster ride for which everyone has the stomach. It's okay if you don't; I want to stress again that most online poker games are so good that straightforward selective-aggressive poker is really the only tool you need. Should you care to get frisky, though, recognize that your goal is not just to win money but to *confound the crap out of everyone.* You want people shaking their (virtual) heads at you in either disbelief or plain annoyance. Sure, you will get caught speeding from time to time, but in the meantime you can take the entire table for a ride.

Know how to get away from your hand. Recognize that when people play back at you it *might* be out of sheer pique, but it's more likely to be that they've been waiting to trap. How frustrating it will be to them when you come driving through the hand, run into legitimate resistance, and stomp on the brakes without paying them off. Your notes and your reads will help you with this, so even as you're taking over the game, pay attention to the different individual reactions around you. If someone you know to be strong and tight plays back at you, you've got a problem on your hands. But if someone peeved and tilty reraises out of spite, then it's *damn the torpedoes and full speed ahead!*

Full speed ahead is not a modus operandi that comes naturally or easily to every player. If you're one of those who has trouble being hyper aggressive, may I suggest the following exercise? Find a game where the money doesn't matter to you (one with a $10 buy in, say) and do your level best to *just go nuts.* Find out how others react, and, crucially, how you react,

when you're the straw that stirs the drink. Record those feelings here.

    >>

    Yeah, you might lose $10. But the experience of seeing
yourself as someone who at least *tries* to play like a maniac
will be more than worth the sawbuck, I predict.

15

♣ ♠ ♦ ♥

SHORT HANDED PLAY

♧ ♤ ◇ ♡

Since it requires patience to play a full ring game properly, and since many, many players know they lack that patience, short handed poker has become intensely popular online. It's sure popular with me; I'd much rather play six handed than ten handed, for I know about me and that patience thing. I love that the hands play so fast. I love that the blinds force me into action fully a third of the time. I love that if I have to fold a hand, the next one is just seconds away. I love having only a handful of slackjaws to iron out, instead of the unruly mob you find in full ring games. I love that I get to force other players to tough decisions that much more frequently.

And mostly I love that I don't have to wait for good hands. In fact I can't. *Kewl!*

Where full ring games are about patience and waiting for quality starts, this must necessarily not be the case short handed. Fewer hands are dealt, so fewer hands are good. While there will be about two paired or aced hands every deal at a full table, there'll be only one, on average, in a short handed game. This means that a lot of less-than-good hands must be played and makes the game much less about knowing your cards than about knowing your foes.

PASSIVE/AGGRESSIVE POKER

In short handed no limit hold'em, the pots can get big in a hurry. All it takes is a pot size preflop raise and call, a two-thirds pot CB and a call on the flop and, whoa Nelly, there's a serious chunk of chips in play. If you're involved in these situations, it will be either as the bettor or the caller, and as you know, "It's better the bettor to be." To make sure that you're driving most of the hands you're involved in, loosen up your raising requirements and, at the same time, tighten up your calling requirements. This will ensure that, on balance, if you're in the pot, you got there first and you got there biggest.

Let me not mince words: It's bad to be just calling. You surrender initiative. You're back on your heels. That's a bad place to be with inferior cards, though not so bad if your hand is strong. Therefore, let the quality of your cards make up the loss of command in the hand. In other words, it's okay not to be driving if you've got hidden strength. It's a disaster not to be driving and also not to have good cards.

This boils down, weirdly, to a "passive/aggressive" strategy for short handed no limit play. You're passive about getting involved when someone else wants you to, but extremely aggressive about inviting them to tangle with you.

THREE TYPES OF FOES

To make this strategy work, you have to know your foes. There aren't so many of them at a short table that you can't get a great sense of the tendencies of everyone arrayed against you. Critically, you want to know what they feel they need to hold to get involved in a hand. Some short handed players are "any two will do" types. Others want to have at least a little something-something before they feel comfortable either to attack or defend. Draw a distinction between the two groups, update your reads constantly, and then do this:

- Against hyper-aggressive types fold crap hands, call to trap (not to chase) with good hands, and reraise with your best hands.
- Against those who only play at least modestly good starting cards, be more aggressive in your steal attempts, but prepared to back off if they show a willingness to get involved. These are CRR or RRR types, who can be trusted to let you know when they're strong.
- Very occasionally you'll find short handed players playing according to full ring strategy; that is, sitting tight and waiting for premium hands. This can be problematic for them, for the increased frequency of the blinds and the decreased frequency of quality starts conspire to drain their stacks while, at the same time, their tightness makes them predictable and easy to read. Any time you detect someone playing too snug for short handed play, you should *really* turn up the heat. They'll fold almost all their hands, and when they do get involved, you can reliably put them on quality cards.

Players will adjust, of course. No one likes their blinds or limp calls to be attacked with such relentless aggression. Eventually, they'll rise up and reraise, either with a real hand or without. On the one hand, this can be a tricky moment for you. If you've been playing at a level of aggressiveness appropriate to short handed play, you don't want to start looking all weak by folding to reraises. On the other hand, you don't want to get all cally when your foes could have strong cards. On the other *other* hand, you don't want to be reraising just to show 'em who's boss. On the other other *other* hand . . . no, that's enough hands. Just do this: Fold the first time you take serious reraise heat. (Remember: kosher until proven tricky.) Lay out for a few hands and give the impression that you've been sufficiently chastened to have given up your thieving ways. Then . . . *resume your thieving ways*. If your opponents are giving up their hands too easily, you'll make more money in the long run by grabbing (more than) your fair share of steals and simply yielding to their infrequent reraise power grabs. If they stop giving up their hands so easily, then they're no longer the tight, cautious players that you perceived them to be or that they used to be, and you can default back to your passive/aggressive standard of raising with good to great hands and folding to raises with good to poor ones.

FLOP MOVES

If you do find yourself calling raises, be sure that you're calling either to trap or to outplay your foe on subsequent streets. Be wary of calling with draws because, given the shortness of the game, you'll only rarely get proper pot odds to call, and then only from foes who don't know to price you off your draw. So if you call a raise with something like K-T, you're looking to hit a king or a ten, not a queen and a jack. If you hit your flop, you can either bet it, or let the other guys bet it for you. Short handed players *love* to steal, as the economic incentive for attacking unwanted flops is not insignificant. If your opponents are the sort of players who routinely try to steal and therefore get out ahead of their hands, you can trap them for a lot of money.

If *you* are the sort of player who routinely gets out ahead of your hand, you can get killed. Say you're on the button in a five handed game, and you have something very indifferent, like Q-8. When it's folded to you, you go ahead and raise, as part of your standard passive/aggressive strategy, hoping for a routine blind steal. Both blinds call, though, which you don't love. The flop comes K-J-8 and it's checked around to you. What do you think? Should you check or bet?

>>

It's a toughie. You have bottom pair, and your hand is only good if both of your foes either whiffed or nearly whiffed (pairing an 8 with a worse kicker). You could bet here to find out where you're at, but if you're raised you're probably beaten. If you bet, get called, and don't improve on the turn, you really have to shut it down, even if this means surrendering the pot to a bet on the river. The problem is that either of them might have a hand that's not good enough to bet out with (a bad king, say, or Q-J) but plenty good enough to call you down if they think you're just being a bully. Again, we see the need to know how to change speeds. To fold a winner is bad, but to blow your whole stack on a reckless adventure is catastrophic.

DELAYED CB

In the name of not getting out ahead of your hand, then, you don't make your normal continuation bet. You know it's expected of you, but you figure there's too good a chance that a better hand is laying for you, so you decline to do the obvious. Where does that leave you on the turn? Well, that depends on what the turn card is. Remember, in this example, all you have is bottom pair. Obviously, you'd welcome an eight or a queen, but these outcomes are unlikely. As for the rest of the deck, it's either above your eight or below it. If the turn card comes high and they check to you, go ahead and check again. Remember, they both called from the blind, which suggests that they had high cards. If they didn't hit the flop, they may have hit the turn or picked up (or completed) some kind of draw. Yes, you let them get there for free, but you got there for free, too, and if that turn card comes high you're done with the hand anyhow, so they can't make money off you.

If the turn card comes lower than an eight, though, you're probably in good shape, at least good enough shape to bet if it's checked to you. Why? Because it's unlikely that anyone, either with or without a piece of the flop, can get too excited about a turn card lower than the board. The only exceptions are underpairs that hit trips and weak kickers that connect. Occasionally, an undercard will create a straight or a flush draw, but those draws rarely have correct odds to call and so can be discounted. Likewise, a hand that whiffed the flop but connects with an undercard on the turn now has only bottom pair and can't be too enthusiastic about calling a bet.

What we're talking about, then, is a *delayed* continuation bet, which you use when you have reasons not to want to bet the flop, but can bet the turn if the turn card serves your purpose. Reinforce the veracity of this move by using it from time to time on flops you've actually hit; if they know you to be a slow playing son of a gun, they may just dump their hands when you bet the turn.

This move is also useful against certain opponents when the flop comes scary straight or scary flush, and you opt to go for a steal on the turn rather than get heavily involved. Let's take a look at that scenario.

You raise preflop with K-J offsuit and get two callers. The flop comes 7♣-6♣-2♥, creating both a straight draw and a flush draw on board. They check to you, presenting you with a CB opportunity. Yes, you could bet at this flop, and often you will, but if (in the worst case) one opponent has a pair and the other has a draw, you won't like the calls you get, and you won't feel too warm and fuzzy about betting again on the turn when, unless you hit, you'll be bluffing at the pot a second time. If you check instead, you're essentially surrendering the pot to any coordinated card on the turn. That's not a terrible surrender, given that your investment in the pot is minimal up to now. However, you're prepared to bet if the turn card comes brick or—better still—scary to the other players' perspective. A scary card for them would be any unsuited overcard. Obviously, the ones that hit your hand are good for you, but a card like the A♠ is not only not helpful to straight and flush draws, it also looks very much like a card you were hoping to hit, given that you opened preflop for a raise, but declined to CB on the flop. (This would be a good time to re-member that raises look like aces to most players.) Now if you bet roughly the size of the pot, no draw has correct odds to call. Moreover, someone who made a pair on the flop may fear the ace enough to yield. Yes, occasionally you'll run into someone who called with A-7 or A-6, but hey, that's poker. The combination of their actions and your book on them will tell you how to proceed if they don't lay down for you like you'd like.

To make this strategy work best, then, don't always make continuation bets when you hit the flop, and don't always re-frain from making them when you miss. Give your foes rea-son to believe that you're capable of leaving the flop alone and then betting the turn, just for the sake of trapping their sorry aspects. Always be guided by the texture of the flop and let your guidance boil down to this:

- If the flop is ragged, bet the flop.
- If the flop is coordinated, check the flop.
- If the turn hits the flop, check and fold.
- If the turn misses the flop, bet it to get it.

SUCCESS IN SHORT HANDED PLAY

The situations described above are ones you see over and over again in short handed play, since those who favor this game know that they have to (get to) be involved in a lot of hands, which means that there's a lot of tricky postflop play to con-sider. Your success in this realm depends to a great degree on how well you grab pots that nobody wants and how well you avoid stepping into traps set by others. Remember that every time you make a move, your foes' responses will give you use-ful information. Even if your move doesn't pay off this time, that information will refine your approach to subsequent confrontations. You may discover, for instance, that *grimsly* will never fight for a flop he doesn't hit, but *Sloping Forehead* will bet any piece any time, and poor *OkraChef* constantly gets stuck on his draws. Go forth and prosper, for short handed play is an action player's paradise, and if you can control the action, most of the profit can be yours.

PART V

♣♠♦♥

PART V

♧♤◇♡

16

♣ ♠ ♦ ♥

THE DAY OF LIVING
DERANGEROUSLY

♧ ♤ ♢ ♡

DATE: AUGUST 6, 2005

TIME: 3:26 AM
GAME: NONE
MUSIC: NONE
MENTAL STATE: NOT AWAKE

This may be the stupidest idea ever.

Twenty-four hours of internet poker, chronicled all the way in diary form.

Yep, stupidest idea ever.

But it's one I've had in mind since I first started writing this book, and with my deadline just weeks away now I can put off no longer the so-called "day of living derangerously." So what's the plan? Just me, Microsoft Word, music, DSL, my choice of online cash games and tournaments, and lots and lots and lots of coffee. When I cooked up this scheme, I thought it would be enlightening, or at least a lark. Now that it is upon me, I think it must be insane.

I mean, seriously, what is to be proved by this? That I

have the endurance and dumb stubbornness to sit at my desk till my ass goes numb? That I can get far enough into sleep debt and poker overload to piss away my entire online bankroll? That I have enough Visine to keep my eyes from dying of screen burn? That I'll do anything to generate a few thousand words of text? That I really know how to throw a solo poker party? I don't know. I don't know what's to be proved. I just know that I told myself I'd do it, and I won't cower out—not on so meaningless and grandstand a challenge as this. So when I awoke just now in the middle of the night, instead of doing the sensible thing and rolling over and going back to sleep, I thrust myself to my feet, forced myself across the hall into my office, and hit the *power up* button on my computer.

Okay. My eyes have adjusted to the glare of my monitor. My fingers are warmed up, and as soon as the coffee kicks in my mind will be, too. Let's get some tunes going (quietly, for the civilized world is still well asleep) and get this demented party started!

TIME: 3:38 AM
GAME: TEN HANDED NO LIMIT HOLD'EM
MUSIC: THE CLASH, *LONDON CALLING* (ON HEADPHONES)
MENTAL STATE: GIDDY WITH ANTICIPATION

I'm thinking it's a good idea to start slow, so I've signed myself up for a ten handed single table sitngo. There aren't enough other maniacs online at this ungodly hour (ungodly, at least, across the face of North America) to fill the table immediately, but I'm sure I won't have too long to wait. Online poker favors the insomniac maniac; I set the over/under at ten minutes. Meanwhile, I didn't get up at this ungodly hour to sit on my hands, so let's jump into a cash game. I find a tasty looking NLHE game and buy myself in.

First hand: pocket queens. Oh, it's gonna be a good day. I go to tune a raise—and realize that I can't. I have accidentally signed up for a *limit* game. Oh, man, I haven't even played a hand and already I've made my first mistake.

Okay, let's try this again.

I leave that table and go to the main lobby to find the no limit game I'm looking for, when suddenly I'm called to my sitngo. Not the ten handed regular speed tourney I thought I'd signed up for, but a six way turbo that I apparently accidentally signed up for instead. Cripes, I am definitely not awake yet. Nor can I leave the tournament now; it's bought and paid for.

Sigh.

Onward.

TIME: 3:53 AM
GAME: SIX HANDED TURBO SITNGO ($50 BUY IN)
MUSIC: CLASH, CONTINUING
MENTAL STATE: DEMI-DAUNTED

I need to play this thing *very* slowly. Give my brain a chance to catch up. Think I'll just sit here and fold a lot and listen to the Clash.

So I sit around for twenty or twenty-five hands and do nothing. I play one hand, A-T on the button, and win the blinds. By the time I play my second hand, my image is so tight that of course they all fold, right? Right?

As if.

I raise from the small blind with some egregious cheese. The big blind calls with 9-9. He's not frightened by my bet into a flop of A-Q-x, so I deem it prudent to shut it down, check it down, and minimize my loss. Did I do it right? Would he have folded if I had bet the turn? Doyle Brunson says that sometimes you've got to fire that second shot. Well, I held my fire and now my stack has taken a hit. Plus I've lost a lot of bluff equity. My next hand will need to be a real one.

And so it is. A♥-K♥. With the blinds already at 50 and 100, I don't have time to get cute. There's a small raise from a frisky player in front of me. I reraise all in and he calls with A-7. Can you guess where this story goes? Folks, I am *not* the type to gripe about bad beats, but seriously . . . a seven on the flop . . . I pick up a flush draw on the turn . . . no help on the river.

I played three hands in that sitngo.

Time of death: 4:14 AM.

TIME: 4:26 AM
GAME: NLHE, TEN HANDED
MUSIC: CLASH, CONTINUING
MENTAL STATE: ADRENALATED

Yikes! A reckless adventure! I pick up 2♥-3♥ in the small blind. There are six calls and no raises when it gets back around to me, so of course I complete. I've got implied odds for anything, right? The flop comes 9♥-7♥-4♥. I'm not thrilled to bet my flush, for fear of a better flush or at least a draw to one. But I'm damned if I'm going to check. I bet the pot. Big blind calls. It's folded around to late position, who raises all in, covering me. I call. Big blind calls. Turn is a heart and I'm sure I'm dead, but no! Big blind has 9-9. He flopped a set. Small blind has 9-7. He flopped two pair. I almost triple through.

In the chatbox I read, **nice all in moron.** I write back, **what do you want? I flopped a flush.** He writes back, **not u, the other moron.** Seems to me the moron may have been the guy who didn't raise with top set. Not that it would have moved me off my hand. Anyway, he seems upset. A moment later, he leaves the game, trailing a stream of profanity in his wake.

Internet players are nice.

TIME: 4:51 AM
GAME: TEN WAY SITNGO (NORMAL SPEED)
MUSIC: BECK, *GUERO* (ON HEADPHONES)
MENTAL STATE: GUARDEDLY OPTIMISTIC

Let's try to play this one better than the last, shall we?

Well, we all try to play right all the time, don't we? Don't we? I don't know . . . maybe you do. Me, I know I'm prone to loose calls when I get bored. One thing about being in this for the twenty-four-hour haul, though: I have no need for loose calls. There will be plenty of time for calls of all types. Loose, tight, collect, local, long distance, and cattle. What I mostly have need for is patience and pacing. Maybe one of the problems we face with this online poker business is we try to cram too much vitamin p into the small corners of our otherwise busy lives. If we just gave ourselves *nice, long sessions* to play, perhaps we could play more correctly, knowing how long a haul we were in for.

Or maybe longer sessions would just make everyone more insane: This sitngo isn't five minutes old and already a chat war has broken out. It's a nasty one.

You're the worst dumb azz I have seen on thi site yet.

f agggggggggg!

can u be my bich?

All quotes in this diary, by the way, are guaranteed 100 percent verbatim; you can't make this shit up. As a writer, I pride myself on the precision of my prose. I don't mind the chat wars so much. I find them amusing, in fact, because people can get so earnest in their insults and macho posturing. What I mind is the heartless mutilation of the written word. Tom Robbins said, "Intelligent speech is under pressure in our fair land and needs all the support it can get." It's sure not getting much support here, **u no whut i meen?**

Not that I'm above wading into a chat war from time to time. If I think that a few well chosen words will push a tilter past the tipping point, I'll certainly throw them at him. I just spell my barbs correctly, that's all.

Or no, you know what? I don't. When I'm chatboxing, I try to be as unlike me as possible. Bad grammar, bad syntax, bad attitude . . . they all seem to go hand in hand. Hey, maybe that's what everyone else is doing. Maybe they're all actually brilliantly literate writers and thinkers, but for the sake of disguising their true selves, they put themselves across as **f***ing morons.** Nah, probably just they are.

I think that keeping this diary is helping my discipline, though. It definitely gives me something to do between hands and gives me incentive to fold. (I've got to fix that typo now!) Then again, it also definitely drags my attention away from the game. Apart from the ongoing chat war, I just know I'm missing valuable information about my foes. It's a tradeoff, I suppose. If I keep my head in the game, I get antsy and want to get involved with inferior hands, just for the sheer hell of it. If I divert myself with words, I play with much greater selectivity, but much less awareness. Well, if it's true, as Graham Parker says, that "nobody hurts you harder than yourself," I'm better off playing with patience, even at the cost of awareness. If I could just master the trick of both . . .

Forty hands into this sitngo, having played virtually nothing up till now, I reraise all in with A-K and get called by A-Q. This nightmare again? Nope. This time the hand holds up.

Confirmation bias says we always get the bad beat, but confirmation bias is horseshit. My luck . . . your luck . . . everyone's luck . . . it's no better or worse than anyone else's.

On hand sixty-two, already down to three handed, I raise again with A-K. This time no caller. Amazing when you think about it: Aside from trying to slide into a couple of unraised pots (with no success; I folded to raises), the only two hands I played between the start of this sitngo and the bubble were A-K and A-K. Only got action on one, but that action was good enough to back me to the money. Interesting application of the principle, "less is more." Think I'll try it again. But first, more coffee.

TIME: 5:57 AM
GAME: NLHE, TEN HANDED
MUSIC: GRATEFUL DEAD, LIVE AT FILLMORE EAST,
        APRIL 29, 1971
MENTAL STATE: TRUCKIN'

I decided not to play another sitngo right away. I noticed that the same damn yammerheads had already signed up for it, and I just couldn't subject myself so immediately to another noisy chat war. I shouldn't use this criterion, I know; these are bad players, and I should be eager to mix it up with them. But there are other bad players out there, maybe ones less noisy, so I think I'll play a cash game and catch up with a different sitngo later. Not for nothing, but if I can't at minimum enjoy my online playing experience, I don't see much point in even having it.

As soon as I finish this cup of coffee I'm going to go walk the dog anyhow.

Meanwhile, what I'm doing in this particular $3 and $6 blind NLHE game is pretty much completely not playing. I've been at it almost half an hour now and haven't done anything but dump my blinds. Even for a preternaturally frisky player like myself, I can't find a hand to play. Though in fairness this is a ten way game, as opposed to my standard six way (action junkie that I am) and I know that patience is a pearl of great price in so crowded a field. Maybe I'm just folding playable hands because I'd rather write than bet. Nah. I'd play aces if I had 'em.

It's getting light outside. The sun will be up soon, and we'll have another toasty Southern California summer day on our hands. I will spend the whole entire day inside playing poker on the internet. I won't be at the beach, or brunching in street cafés with friends, or hiking in the hills. Seriously, what kind of fool am I?

On the button I get K-9 offsuit. There's one limper, *deucemoose*, in the cutoff. I raise. The blinds fold, and *deucemoose* folds. In my note box on *deucemoose*, I record the observation that he'll LF—limp fold. I may not play against him ever again in life, but so long as we're together at this table, and so long as I have position over him, I'm going to look to sweep every limpet he lets me.

Dumb: I'm in the big blind, unraised pot, five players. I've got 7-4 offsuit. Flop comes A-Q-7 rainbow. I check. It's checked around. The turn is a 3. As it's lower than the board, I take it into my head to take a shot at the pot. Dumb. Too many players. Too great a chance that someone is unwilling to bet a bad ace or a good queen, but happy to call with one. Or just plain dragging a monster. I get one caller. That's one too many. I check the river and fold to a big bet. Wrong time, wrong position, wrong flop to try to steal. Dumb.

Time to walk the dog.

TIME: 7:50 AM
GAME: FULL FIELD TOURNAMENT
MUSIC: DEAD (CONTINUING)
MENTAL STATE: CHIPPER

We're off headphones now. If the neighbors don't like it, screw 'em. Meanwhile, I've registered for a full field tournament that starts in ten minutes. I'll probably open a second window and play a cash game, too. I shouldn't, but I will. What can I tell you? I don't do everything right.

But I did do something right by walking the pooch just now. I had made a dumb play and was berating myself for it. I know from long experience that dumb plays followed by a stern self-rebuke do not normally eventuate a renaissance of strong, solid play. In fact, the opposite is usually true. It's as if the dumb part of me wants to prove that dumb isn't dumb by *being* dumb, but getting away with it. Getting away *from* it is a much better idea, so that's what I did. Now I'm back, and the derangement continues, with this tournament that's just getting underway . . .

Press **PAUSE**

Press **PLAY**

I pick up a couple of strong hands early that I'm able to play strongly and show down. This puts me in the uncharacteristic tournament position of playing many hands in the early rounds. I'm usually content to lay back, go to school on my foes, and wait for prime opportunities. But my image is such right now that no one wants to mix it up with me, which gives me an unusual degree of early-round latitude. Provided I don't overuse this club, I should be able to smack the table around with it for a while now.

And oh yeah, I decided not to play a cash game at the same time, at least not now. I know that some people swear by multi-tabling, either to maximize their hourly win rate or just to fill the empty spaces in their heads. If it works for them (for you), fine. As for me, I've tried it enough times to know that it's not likely to enhance either my win rate or my online playing experience. I'm not saying that way lies madness. I'm just saying, "Concentrate on the task at hand," or maybe, more direly, "Self-indulgence equals self-destruction."

Speaking of self destruction, I just saw somebody reraise all in with K♣-3♣. Of course, his hand didn't hold up. In the name of all that is right and holy, there's no way it should. I just want to know how he got himself into such a mess in the first place. He wasn't short on chips. Just short on brains, I guess.

Meanwhile, I got myself into a tight little bind just now, but was able to bet my way out of it. *Nobodyhome* made a small raise in front of me. I had pocket queens, so I came over the top with a pot-size reraise. The flop came A♥-J♥-3♦ and I kicked myself for not going all in preflop, for if *nobodyhome* has an ace here, I'm toast. He checked to me. I wasn't all that keen to bet, but I couldn't just check behind him, not unless I was prepared to surrender without a fight. As "surrender" is not my current table image, I decided to take a stab at it. I bet 250, about a quarter of the pot, in hopes that *nobodyhome* would interpret this as a hoover bet. Get this: Not only did he fold, he folded and *showed* pocket kings. Wow. **Good laydown,** I type as I wipe the sweat from my brow. Kids, never show your good laydowns. What does it avail you, except to make you feel boastfully good about yourself?

Like this other guy in another hand who just now chat-boxed, **almost tried to bet you out, but not worth it.** This is not the sort of thing someone says for deception; he is speaking his mind. And I can't figure out why he would do that. His opponent, who won the uncontested pot with bottom pair, said, **ida probably folded.** This at least has a *chance* of being a lie. But that other? Pure information giveaway. I just don't see the point.

Just got Q-Q again. Bet pot preflop, got three callers. Bet pot postflop, got three folders. Next case.

Happened to have a squiz at the pay table for this tournament just now. It pays 20 places, but on a $50 + $5 buy in, the bottom ten money winners get $62.50. Hardly seems worth the time and effort. Guess that's why so many double or done types reckon if they can't put themselves in position to win big, they'd just as soon not play. I buy that as an argument for taking appropriate risks, but—especially early on—it just seems like a rationalization for kamikaze plays or unprofitable bully behavior. Still, "the ocean is blue but it's also wet." There's more than one right answer and more than one right way to play these tournaments. Even within my own mind I find myself bouncing back and forth between naked aggression and canny trapping. I know that with poker everything is "it depends," but, with the exception of folding crap hands and raising with A-A, I rarely have the feeling that I know 100 percent correctly what to do.

Yet again they chat, and yet again I can't see the logic of it. I'm in the small blind, stealing with K-4 offsuit. The big blind, *ubfree,* says, **lol, stealin my bb.** Well, he certainly has me read right, but then he adds, **i want to call,** so of course I know he's not going to. More to the point, though, I now know that he's alert to blind steals. Not everyone is, you know. A lot of people, when you raise from the small blind, being out of position and all, they'll credit you with a real hand. Well, I've got this character on my left until the table breaks, so I can plan my moves against his blinds now with a certain enhanced knowledge. Based on what he's told me, I can rate him as more likely to defend (by reraising) with crap or semi-crap, and much more likely to trap himself if I should happen to catch a real hand one time.

Our next blind versus blind confrontation, however, makes me rethink this a little . . . that maybe there is an argument for his line of chat. He has gotten me wanting to probe him, to find out if his talk was just talk, so I raise from the small blind with Q♦-J♦. He slaps me back by raising all in, forcing me to fold. Then shows A-5 offsuit. Well. He certainly has me thinking about his defense of blinds now. In a sense, he has taken control of our little battle. All it took was a little chat, followed up by a pretty bold "walk the walk" reraise. Apparently, I'm going to need a real hand to come after him again, and if I credit him with being a thoughtful player and not just a yammerhead, I've definitely lost some edge here. Interesting.

Then again, maybe fixating on blind confrontations isn't that good an idea. *Ubfree* just made his own steal raise in the small blind and ran spang blam into pocket aces in the big blind. The aces flopped quads, not that they needed to, *ubfree* lost a big pot. Uhm, "Live by the blind, die by the blind?" Or something.

But our friend *ubfree* is not eliminated quite yet. A lap later, he's got less than a thousand in chips, and he's in the small blind. I've got A-J offsuit, and I reraise him all in, knowing that he'll call with any two high, or even highish, cards. Sure enough, he jumps in with K-8 offsuit. Hits a runner-runner straight, and now I'm short stacked and imperiled. Gee, this is an interesting way to spend a Saturday.

If by interesting I mean suicidally maddening, that is.

A few hands later, *ubfree* goes overboard when his pocket tens lose to an ace on the river. "Live by the . . ." oh, never mind.

As for me, my time of death is 9:57 AM. I finish two places off the money.

Good.

I didn't want the lousy ten bucks profit anyhow.

TIME: 10:00 AM
GAME: TBD
MUSIC: STILL DEAD
MENTAL STATE: DETACHED

It's not altogether surprising, but I've been playing for more than six hours now and I find I'm starting to not care about outcomes. So I lost that tournament? So what? Did I play it correctly? Well, more or less, but I don't even care about that so much. Like I said, this is not altogether unexpected. We know all about passing the point of pain, losing so much that you stop caring how much more you lose. I'm not losing—yet—thanks to that lucky 2♥-3♥ big win at about 5 AM. But the mere passage of time is cutting into my usually urgent need to play correctly and to win. This might be good in a way, for I certainly feel a sense of calm tranquility (or fatigue, you decide). Then again, it could be a recipe for disaster, especially if my equanimity inspires me to jump into a really big game looking for a big, quick score. Let's call it acute what-the-hellism and hope that something other than coffee will inoculate against it.

And it occurs to me to wonder: If I'm already this cognitively displaced at 10 AM, how will I be twelve hours from now?

Okay, I've decided to do two things: play a heads up sit-ngo, which I frequently do, and play under my own name, which I almost never do. I feel kind of naked, exposed, not cloaked behind my secret identity. Anyway, it will be interesting to see if "the real John Vorhaus" comes off as a playah, or just another slackjaw. As it's heads up, I won't have time for commentary. I trust you'll understand.

Press **PAUSE**

Press **PLAY**

Well, that was fun. Got into a heads up match with a guy who knows me and totally disrespects my work, while someone who likes my books and claims they've made him money sweated me from the sidelines. I won two out of three matches, but that's not really the thing. Here's the thing: It took everything in my power to focus on the game and not on the chat—and there was a ton of it. I've been in this situation before, where I get all caught up in being "that Killer Poker guy" and forget to just play good poker. I find that my best defense in such circumstances is false humility. I chat actively about how badly I play but how lucky I am. It's a page borrowed from two outstanding sources: Mike Caro and Annie Duke. Mike is *always* promoting his "just having fun and just getting lucky" image, and—the proof is in the long historical pudding—it works. People like to lose to Mike, and they honestly don't know how he wins. I know how: He plays well and talks up the luck. As for Annie, many is the time I've seen her smile and say of her (seemingly bad, but good according to a different idea) play, "What can I tell you? I'm a donkey." She made that word household, at least in poker households, and uses it to—well, how shall I put this?—lull her foes into a false sense of stupidity. Of course she's not a donkey, and of course everyone knows it. But when she talks down her own play, she creates a disconnect between what she says and how she acts. Even if you're aware of the disconnect, it can be very unsettling . . . and very hard to play against. Are you battling the image? The skill set? Neither? Both? It's enough to make your head spin.

But anyway, that was fun, so I think I'll go do it again. Play under my own name, I mean. It seems to spark a fire, though it's an open question as to who, exactly, will get burned.

TIME: 12:01 PM
GAME: TURBO SIX WAY SITNGO
MUSIC: PAUL SIMON, *GRACELAND*
MENTAL STATE: *TRANQUILO*

Not for nothing, but you should definitely give this a whirl. Not the sensory overload part. Not the sleep debt part. Not the twenty-four-hours part, God knows; *These men are professionals, kids. Don't try this at home!* No, the diary part. That part you should try: playing poker and writing madly about what you play and how you play while you play. That's a useful exercise. Much will be made clear to you about you.

Seriously. Consider it homework.

Okay, what we have going on now is a turbo six way sitngo. These things play fast—by definition—so I need to be prepared to play a variety of hands, push small edges, and try to build a big stack if I can. At the same time, I don't want the need for speed to rush me into rash action. *You have time, JV. Not a lot of time, but time.*

Eleven hands in, we already have one player overboard, *Spizz Energy*. I'll bet he's already signed up for another sitngo, too, and he's not even playing "day of living derangerously." For him it's just, you know, Saturday. I suppose the dialogue could go like this.

SPIZZ: Fricka-frackin' slackjaws, how come they always suck out on me?

MRS. SPIZZ: Honey, you said you'd mow the lawn.
SPIZZ: I'm in a sitngo. It just started.
MRS SPIZZ: That's what you said an hour ago.
SPIZZ: I'll do it when I'm done.
MRS. SPIZZ: That's what you said an hour ago.

See, this is why I hire a gardener.

The deeper issue here, of course, is getting your spouse or other loved ones to recognize that your depraved hobby is a serious depraved hobby, and when you're doing it you can't be bothered about mowing the lawn or not mowing the lawn. It helps if your hobby can show a profit (or win the odd trip to wherever) or at least not bust the family cookie jar. But it mostly requires that we (I, you, they, everyone) be able to impose limits, so that someone else doesn't forcibly impose them for us. To borrow from the booze advertisers, "Know when to say when." Seriously, there's a time to play poker online and a time to mow the lawn. If you don't respect the lawn, they won't respect the poker.

This sounds comical, I guess, coming from someone in the midst of a *twenty-four-hour online poker jag*. The difference is (ha!) this is my job. Experimenting, I mean, and reporting my findings in print. God help me if I had to just play poker for a living. I'm quite confident that I wouldn't have to worry about any lawns, except, perhaps, the one in the park where I slept at night. Nor would I want it to be my job. I'm happiest with poker as my unhinged avocation, and a convenient scratching post for my writer's itch.

Press **PAUSE**

Press **PLAY**

Oh, man! That's another reason I wouldn't want to have to do this for a living. I just got all the money in with A-J versus A-T and lost to a ten on the river. **The universe hates me!** I don't really believe that's true, of course, but I'm certain I could come to believe it if I had to take beats like that all day every day for work.

Ah, well. Right back on that horse.

Or rather "those horses." I know I said I have a rule against double dipping, but what can I tell you? Rules are made to be broken. So: A six seater full field tournament (paid for with player points) on one side, heads up sitngo on the other. Don't tell me I'm insane. I figured that out before dawn.

Press **PAUSE**

Press **PLAY**

I wonder if there's such a thing as playing a tournament out of the corner of your eye. I do seem to be more bold, unpredictable, and intuitively correct when I'm fitting my tournament decisions into the spaces between my match play choices and my word carving. Or is that just the causally unconnected coincidence of a couple of happy flops? The latter, I hazard to guess.

Weird. I'm starting to see trails, little pixilated afterimages, as the cards are dealt and folded and otherwise flashed across the screen. I wonder if that's normal . . .

And my right wrist is starting to throb just a little. I wonder how many mouse clicks it's been so far . . .

And I don't seem to be making such crystalline decisions right now. I wonder why that is . . .

And I *know* it's just confirmation bias, but it's sure starting to feel like the Day of a Thousand Suckouts to me. And not, needless to say, in my favor . . .

Ah, finally, a foe I can beat in match play! He's lost his internet connection, and he'll be blinded off until he gets his connection back. If he just stays away long enough, I'll . . . rats, he's back. Guess I'll just have to beat him by guile and good looks. A card or two wouldn't hurt, though, swear to God.

Or maybe a little nap . . .

TIME: 2:35 PM
GAME: SIX WAY NLHE CASH GAME
MUSIC: BLESSED SILENCE
MENTAL STATE: SLIGHTLY FRAYED

Yeah, I knew that wasn't gonna work. Considering that my blood composition is now three parts adrenaline and two parts caffeine, trying to nap was a joke. I just lay there, staring at the ceiling watching flops dance before my eyes. I wouldn't let me operate heavy machinery right now, yet here I am, back playing poker. Does anyone like my chances? Good thing I got a reasonable advance for this book—though as I recall (and I've looked) nowhere in my contract does it say that I have to dondo off my money as a human guinea pig in some diabolical, self-imposed poker overdose experiment.

But I've staged a modest comeback here, in my post non-nap hours. It's amazing how quickly you can win a lot (okay, or lose a lot) in no limit cash games online. I'm glad I'm a responsible adult, or was anyhow before this exercise began. I'm quite sure I wouldn't trust me with internet poker if I were a testosterone fueled twenty-something with too much disposable income and not enough respect for money. I don't want to be your mother about this. That's not my job and it's not my inclination. But do go to school on my experience here today. I'm deliberately bingeing on online poker, just to see what it feels like. And you want to hear something funny, not funny ha-ha but funny sort of sad and pathetic? Right now, I can't stop. In about two hours I'm going to get a break because some friends have invited me over for a swim, and I'd be depraved (and have to admit to it) to decline the invitation, just so I could do ... more ... of ... this. Which doesn't change the fact that chair glue, and I mean serious chair glue, has me by the ass right now. I'm not surprised. I knew it was coming. I've hit exactly the fugue state of poker I was aiming for. Of course, just because I've achieved my goal doesn't make it any less moronic.

And I'm only twelve hours in.

On the plus side, my wrist doesn't seem to hurt anymore. I have literally passed the point of pain. Now's the time to try four simultaneous sitngos, oh yeah ...

Press **PAUSE**

Press **PLAY**

Yeah, no, I didn't do that. I stayed here in this tranquil little cash game, building my stack bit by bit and bet by bet. I seem to have entered a new phase where I'm playing correctly once again. Steady on my feet. Making good, crisp decisions, aggressive bets, shrewd laydowns. It's probably just an artifact of poker poisoning, like nitrogen narcosis. No doubt I'll start to hallucinate in earnest soon, probably see a mermaid. They say sailors do that just before they drown. Still and all, I am having fun. Sure beats mowing the lawn, right, *Spizz*?

I just won two monster pots back to back, first by sucking out and then by victimizing my foe's insta-tilt. Two points worth noting. First, no, the luck doesn't always go against me (you, anyone). Second, if you hang around long enough, without digging yourself too deep a hole, the luck will show up and it will be meaningful. Third (okay, that's three points, I'm having some trouble counting now), if you ever make a tilt raise into me and I reraise you all in, chatting, **give you a chance to get well,** probably don't call, because I probably have big slick. That's applied luck—the A-K sure arrived at the right time—along with the judicious application of needle.

You know, I'm just replaying that suckout hand in my mind, and I'm not sure it was all that much of a suckout. Let me lay it out for you, and you judge. I had red pocket jacks in middle position. The guy on my immediate left had a habit of raising all in to steal the blinds, and I flat called, hoping he'd do that here. Not obliging me, he folded. But the guy to his left (we'll call him *insta-tilt*) made a minimum reraise. I thought about coming over the top, but *insta-tilt* had shown a tendency to soft play big pairs, and I wanted to know where I was at before I made my move. So I just called. The flop came Q-x-x with two spades. I bet two-thirds pot to see how he felt about that queen and those spades. He just called, so I guess he wasn't all that enamored. The turn was an offsuit eight. Again I bet, and again he just called. At that point I started smelling trap, and thought I might have to shut down on the river. But the river came a jack, so I felted myself and got an immediate call from *insta-tilt* . . . who had pocket eights. Now you tell me, did I put a bad beat on him, or did he kind of do it to himself by not reraising me on the turn when he made his hand? I grant you that I got lucky, but he gave me the chance to. Protect your hands, campers. I think it's better to win a sure thing big pot than to get cute in the name of grabbing the other guy's last dime. Remember, you don't have to get lucky (or not get unlucky) if they fold.

It's what happened next that I really want to point out, though, because it's a textbook example of the price of psychic pain. Here I'd just put this beat on this guy (though he was an unindicted co-conspirator in the crime), and so what does he do on the very next hand? Puts $20 of his last $100 into the pot. There I am with my A-K and my **give you a chance to get well.** There was no doubt in my mind that he would call, and call with a substantially worse hand. He was so suddenly and completely out of control, there was no way he could *not* call. If the poker gods had been kind, they'd have given him a truly trash hand there, just to keep him out of trouble, but it was not to be. He called with K-T and my hand held up.

ty, I type sweetly, **fu** he replies as he leaves the table.

internet players are nice.

So my whole history in this particular cash game has been fold, fold, fold, fold, fold, try to see some cheap flops, stay out of trouble, and try to get lucky. It's not a very interesting strategy, and not at all my typical reckless/aggressive modus in six way action, but like I said, there's more than one right answer, and waiting for guys to fall apart is another way to do the job.

Well, that was a mighty successful session. I did many things right and no things particularly wrong. I changed gears, made good reads, bluffed and semi-bluffed, bet for value, all that good stuff. Also got lucky, let's not forget. Now I get to go for a swim. That'll be nice. My friends don't play poker, though, but maybe I can teach them.

TIME: 8:47 PM
GAME: THIS OR THAT; WELL, THIS *AND* THAT
MUSIC: BOB MARLEY, KAYA
MENTAL STATE: BEST NOT TO ASK

That was a fine few hours off. Nice dip in the pool. Good chow. Spirited persiflage with intelligent friends. I told them about my grand experiment, and of course they all agreed that I was six different kind of nuts. Won't get much argument from me right now, but, "Anything that's worth doing is worth overdoing," so let's get back to the game.

More poker. Oh, goody.

I feel a little like a kid whose father caught him smoking a cigarette and, to prove a point, made the kid smoke a whole pack. "If that doesn't teach him a lesson," barks dad, "I don't know what will!" It has been pointed out to me that this "lesson" is self-imposed and, truly, I can quit any time I want. But I've come this far. I kind of want to see it through. I hate to glorify this depravity by likening it to exercise, but it's as if I were running a marathon and somewhere up ahead I'm about to hit the wall.

What happens next is anybody's guess.

I'll tell you one thing: I am way too old for this shit. I understand there are kids (and by kids of course I mean adults of legal age) who can do twenty-four hours of online poker standing on one leg. Me, I'm pushing fifty. By the time you read this, I will have pushed it clear into the next half-century. I just don't have that kind of stamina. Oh, I'll make it past midnight and into the beckoning arms of the new day, I'm sure of that. I'm no quitter. I'm just hoping I get a second wind before I hit that wall. Otherwise, things could get ugly.

Well, running provides a second wind in the form of endorphins. Poker provides its second wind in adrenalin. I just knocked off a sprightly heads up match and that made my heart beat a little and my head clear a little. But the real hand of note was over on the full field tournament side. It's one worth talking about, too, for it illustrates a vital "don't" of no limit hold'em: *Don't price them into the pot!*

I'm in an unraised big blind. Three of us see a flop containing two clubs. There's about 250 in the pot, and I have the

K-x of clubs. Small blind checks, I check. Button bets 30. *Thirty!* Small blind calls. I'm delighted to call, for I'm getting better than 10-1 pot odds on my draw. The turn is a brick, and the pattern repeats: check, check, min bet, call, call. The river is my club. Small blind checks, I check. Button bets 200 or so. Small blind raises to 600. I come over the top for all my chips. Yes, I know there's a possibility that I'm up against the nut flush but what is life if not risk? Well, sleep debt plus risk, but whatever. The min raiser folds, and the small blind goes broke with Q-x of clubs. I don't know what the min raiser had, but if he had any piece of the flop, he did an execrable job of protecting it and if he was bluffing, he did too weak a job of that, too. How many times do we need to be reminded? Don't give 'em proper odds for their draws. This is one of those no limit basics. If you don't feel strongly enough about your hand to bet it, then check it down and fold if they bet. But if you're going to bet, *bet*. Otherwise, it's just like handing them a big bat to beat you with.

Anyway, now I've got some chips in the tournament and now I've got a little jolt of artificial energy. It won't last long. I can't see myself making quality decisions for much longer (if, indeed, I'm still making them now). I'm about as far from sharp as I can get and I know it. So why am I still playing? Because I'm stupid and stubborn and I glorify these things by calling them "dauntless." At least I'm protecting myself by playing in cheap tournaments and sitngos. The point of this experience is just to have it, after all, not to set money records. Reminds me of a time I participated in a three day novel contest, where the object was to take a long holiday weekend and write as much novel as seventy-two hours allowed. Mine was crap. I like to think "inspired crap," but probably just crap. I did spend seventy-two hours whacking away at it, though, and I learned something important about myself as a writer: that I could do what a writer does, plant his ass in a chair and write. In that sense, the experiment was a success because, at minimum, I did what I set out to do. Folks, sometimes your goals are odd ones, off-kilter maybe, flat wrong maybe. Still, they're your goals, and fulfilling them, for better or for worse (maybe even for better *and* for worse) must necessarily make your life rise, because you get to see yourself as someone who did what you set out to do.

Take professional poker. We all know that for most of us a viable playing career is a crazy longshot, something on the order of making it big as a movie star. The job requires so many things—smarts, heart, strength, social support, math, memory, intense dedication, oh that list goes on and on. Most of us are bound to come up short in one crucial area or another. Does this mean we shouldn't try? Does it mean *you* shouldn't try? Of course not. If you have a passion for it, and if your life circumstances allow you the freedom to roll those dice even once, I think you'd be crazy not to. To wax philosophical for a moment, I believe that in this life it's not the doing but the trying that counts. You don't want to look back and say you never tried. And if it's a fabulous failure, all you've lost is money, mere money. But what you'll gain, in terms of defining your character and testing yourself against a formidable challenge, well, to me those things are worth money, and quite a lot of money at that. Not to mention that you might succeed if you try, but certainly won't succeed if you don't.

Oh, man, listen to me. I'm getting all Oprah Winfrey on your ass. That's the sleep debt talking. You'll have to forgive me. Look, do what you're going to do. It'll either work out or it won't, but as long as you're alive and walking around on the planet, still breathing in and breathing out, you're so far ahead of the game that the rest of the game doesn't even

count.
TIME: AFTER MIDNIGHT
GAME: WHO KNOWS?
MUSIC: JAZZ RADIO
MENTAL STATE: DETERIORATING

Where am I now? How did I get here? Whose dumb idea was this in the first place? I have been up for more than twenty-one hours, and have spent a good eighteen of them doing nothing but playing poker and writing. I've won and lost in some cash games. I've won and lost in some sitngos. I made the final table in my last full fielder of the night, but I really couldn't even tell you how. It's like it happened when I wasn't even looking. I don't know, I guess my mind was elsewhere. It's been untethered these last few hours. I suspect you're not surprised. I suspect you wrote me off as daft a half a day ago anyhow. So be it. I feel daft. But good. Good and daft. Like I've left something behind. Need, I think, is the thing, the thing I left behind.

At my worst, when I play online I can get so unspeakably cranky. Bad play or bad luck or a toxic cocktail of the two can leave me muttering to myself in a dark, cancerous glower. All my negative prophecies start to self fulfill, so that no bad beat surprises me. After a while I come to expect them and I'm actually surprised when a hand holds up. This is a common self protective cynicism, I know; it's not unique to me. But what informs this darkness? Why do I get so down? Looking deep within myself, I see a certain thwarted need. It's not a need to win money, for I'm never, ever playing for need money. No, it's just a pure need to win, to see myself as someone who wins. When that need isn't met, or is explosively disappointed, my world turns black. I guess what I've gotten tonight—well, last night, this morning, this afternoon, and tonight—is a mainline poker fix so big as to blow all that need away. I've experienced so many outcomes—good and bad hands, lucky and unlucky board cards, clever plays and boneheaded lapses of reason—that they all blur together into one. Suddenly, I see what I've known all along: Individual outcomes don't matter. They don't. They never did.

I don't get this sensation in a short session. All the outcomes matter because my need is so palpable. Tonight, I have shed the need, or rather seen it swamped and swept away by the sheer volume of play. How could I possibly care about any one outcome when there are so many outcomes out there? How can one matter? Answer: It cannot. Not if I don't let it.

This feeling may pass. An artifact of my weary and bleary mind, it may fade by tomorrow and be kicked aside by the usual grumps next time I play and things don't go my way. Tonight, though, I'm in touch with the oldest idea, the Buddhist idea, *detach from outcome*. If I can just hold onto that one idea, if I can just get that one thing right . . .

I played poker with Orel Hershiser once, at Bellagio in Las Vegas. At that time the former Dodger pitching great was the Texas Rangers' pitching coach, and as our conversation turned to coaching he taught me the difference between a bad coach, a good coach, and a great coach. A bad coach, he said, can tell you what you're doing wrong. A good coach can tell you how to fix it. A great coach can tell you one thing that will fix five things. I feel like *detach from outcome* is that one thing. If I marry that thought, everything else falls into place.

And if that happens, my day of living derangerously will have been worth every minute of sleep I lost, every twinge in my wrist, every swollen blood vessel in my eye (every swollen blood vessel in my ass), every crick in my neck, every ache in my back. It will have been worth all the words typed (8,000) and all the money won ($800). It will have made me a much more complete and comported poker player. It will have taken my spirit, if not my game, to the next level. And that's not bad for one day's work.

DATE: AUGUST 7, 2005

TIME: 3:26 AM
GAME: NONE
MUSIC: NONE
MENTAL STATE: COMA

Press **PAUSE**

♣ ♠ ♦ ♥

OUTRODUCTION

♧ ♤ ◇ ♡

God grant me the serenity
to fold the flops I don't hit,
courage to bet the flops I do hit,
and wisdom to know the difference.

It's been six months since I began this book by recounting my painful and costly misadventure involving sleep debt, strong ale, and online poker at London's Heathrow Airport. Now, some 85,000 words later, I find myself, hey, right back in Heathrow, waiting for a plane to Zurich. I'm off to teach comedy to the Swiss. And yes, you can teach comedy to the Swiss. Though they doubt their own aptitude for it, I always begin my workshops there with these inspiring words: "If you work hard and dare to dream, some day I can make you as funny as the Germans."

Yep, I'm back at Heathrow, a hellhole of gate holds, canceled flights, lost luggage, security logjams, and air traffic control flubs that makes LAX on its worst day look like a grassy landing strip in the Australian outback. Once again I'm in the departure lounge pub, sipping a cask-conditioned red ale, and thanking God for British brewers. They can't make airports in this country, but they can sure make beer. As before, I'm wasted after an exhausting overnight flight from LA. I'm so tired that these words blur before my eyes as I type them, and I must trust able copy editors to catch all the typos because I sure can't trust to catch them myslef.

Weakened though my mental state may be, I have resisted the temptation to repeat last trip's mistake of booting up, logging on, and playing internet poker. Having spent half a year on this book I've at least learned not to play online for real money under the debilitating influence of sleep debt and strong ale. That much at least I've learned.

Six months isn't a long time, but it's a lifetime for the hothouse flower that is internet poker. In just these six months, we've seen the game take another quantum leap in public impact, growing from a haven for enthusiastic hobbyists into a genuine pop phenomenon, so that none of us is terribly surprised to hear our mechanic or pastor or parent say, "I was in this sitngo on Party last night . . ." We've seen internet players swamp the fields of realworld tournaments, swelling their numbers to record after record after record. We've seen internet qualifiers snag prize money in the tens of millions at the World Series of Poker. We've seen internet poker talked about, tutted over, championed, or lamented in every communication medium from television newsmagazines and radio talk shows to cereal boxes and fortune cookies.

I, of course, have been an ardent fanner of this flame. I've blogged major poker tournaments. I did color commentary for Fox Sports Net's broadcasts of the first ever televised tournament of internet-only players. I've written for every poker magazine I can lay my bylines on. And I've written this book, which, if all goes according to hope, will help thousands of people around the country (maybe even around the world) (maybe even in Zurich) do better what they like so much to do: play poker online.

Everyone who plays internet poker carries within himself a certain fantasy of wealth, and why not? What could be more wonderful than to make your fortune, or even just your living, in your living room, *playing a game?* The well adjusted among us recognize that this fantasy becomes actual, factual reality for very few. We know that poker is "a hard way to make an easy living," and that's true whether you ply your trade in your local cardroom, you follow the tournament circuit around the world, or your ass never leaves your desk chair or divan. Most of us are simply not gifted enough or smart enough or fearless enough to make poker our profession, and that's okay; most of us can't hit a major league fastball, either. Yet we try. We never stop trying. My experience of internet poker is that we all dream of the secret winning formula.

For some, it's that mythical website, some SevenCitiesofGold .com, where the fish always bite and the sharks never show. Others take the prosaic approach of working the system. They jump on every bonus offer, participate in every rakeback scheme, and aggressively recruit their friends in the name of scoring signup windfalls. For some this method works, just as some slot machine or table game players find that they can turn their Las Vegas voyages into (marginally) profitable trips by working the casinos' comp policies for all they're worth. For others, no amount of signup bonuses or rake reductions can compensate for the fact that, well, they just don't play too well.

Some in their search for online poker's magic bullet put great stock in the almighty win rate. They chart their results with a fervor bordering on the religious, and whenever they find an edge they think they can exploit—six handed sitngos at six in the morning or heads up matches against players with numbers in their screen names—they jump all over it, playing two, four, six, eight games at once, all in the name of leveraging that win rate into a bona fide living wage. Again, a few find success with this method; many others crash on the rocks of that one terrible losing streak that wipes out their lovingly crafted win rate and leaves them wondering where the hell they went wrong.

Then you have your numbers geeks who wouldn't think of essaying even a single online poker session without the ample support of sniffer software and tens of thousands of banked hands revealing their foes' preflop calling rates, defense of blinds, aggressiveness quotients, and so on. They try to reduce poker to a mathematical certainty, a set-and-forget playing platform that uses automated responses based on known probabilities to suck the luck out of the game. Those who follow this plan without fail—who never, for example, deviate from the numbers' dictates in the name of a hunch or greed or tilt—may find that it turns online poker into a net-plus play. Others get so hooked on the numbers that they lose the forest among the trees: *How could that guy flop quads in that situation? He hasn't played a little pair out of position in 2,000 hands!*

What about you? Where do you invest your conviction? What cherished fantasy of online poker carries you forward from day to day? What system of online poker do you swear by, convinced that it would work for you every time if only it, you know, sometimes didn't?

>>

Me, I have tremendous faith in the heads up sitngo. I passionately believe that when I reduce poker to single combat there's no way I'm not smarter, stauncher, more patient, more able than the other guy. I'm convinced that match play reduces luck in poker to its absolute minimum. And you know what? It does. But luck at its minimum works pretty much the same way as luck at its maximum: Sometimes you get lucky; sometimes you don't. More to the point, sometimes you go off the rails and play online poker in foreign airports. So let's take a moment and review a few—admittedly hard—truths about online poker.

- Online poker works better as a hobby than a career.
- People should be very careful about how much money they put into the game.
- The pace of play turns most players' leaks into floods.
- Fantasies of wealth through online poker are just that— fantasies—for all but the tiniest minority.
- In online poker, as in life, there's no such thing as a free lunch.

What other—possibly hard—truths of online poker have you gleaned from your own experience?

>>

Then there's this: Whatever else online poker may be, it sure is *fun*. Even after the thousands of hours I've played (perhaps because of the thousands of hours I've played) I can't think of anything I'd rather do with a few idle minutes than boot up, log on, and try to iron out those slackjaws again. As a challenge and an intellectual exercise, as a chance to add a few numbers to the net-plus side of the ledger, I find online poker to be an intriguing exercise, a compelling mind sport, a gripping puzzle to be solved. One might call it spellbinding. One might even call it . . . addictive.

Oh dear, now I've done it. I've gone and used the "a" word. I've acknowledged the elephant in the living room. Well, as long as we all see it, let's note it and observe it and stroke its leathery skin. In doing so, I know I risk biting, as it were, the hand that signs my royalty checks. It's a subject, though, that I feel I have to raise. After all, the purpose of this book is to help you play online poker to the best of your ability, and if yielding to your atavistic urges (as I have certainly yielded to mine, at Heathrow and elsewhere) cuts into your proficiency, then that's something we need to discuss.

Well, then, what is it about online poker that makes us want to play it to the point of needing to play it? It's not the money. It can't be the money. If it were, the sensible majority of us would long ago have turned to more reliable revenue streams like insurance fraud or selling the contents of our closets on eBay. It may be the sense of community. Or, it might just be a matter of competition. Winning is a rush, this we know.

But no, I don't think so. I think the buzz of online poker, the buzz of all poker, in fact, lies in the cards to come. While we're waiting to receive them, our heads fill with questions.

*Will I get a playable hand? Will I pick up a monster? Will I face a
tough decision? Will I maybe make some money? Do I get to be involved?* If the answer to these questions is yes, then the
promise of poker's baseline buzz is fulfilled. If the answer is
no, then we must fold (if we're disciplined and smart) and
wait patiently for the next hand.

But here's the thing. If you're playing poker in a cardroom,
you get the baseline buzz of those next two cards maybe
twenty times an hour. Revisiting our old friend context density, we find that the buzz is broadly diluted over time. Online,
you get that buzz much more frequently. Maybe a hundred
times an hour. If you're playing heads up, the buzz comes at
you almost constantly. This, I believe, is why online poker is so
addictive. It delivers a such a highly concentrated version of the
poker buzz. Those next two cards keep coming and coming
and coming until we're saturated, stimulated, and ultimately
overstimulated by all the decisions we get to make. I hesitate to
use a cocaine analogy because it's really kind of ugly and negative, but I've tried to tell the truth so far and why stop now?
Online poker is to realworld poker as crack is to blow. It's the
same stuff, only more so. Much, much more so.

The observant or culturally aware among you will recognize the quote at the top of this chapter as a bastardization of
the Serenity Prayer of Alcoholics Anonymous. I ran across it
during a Google search not long ago and, as is my wont, scav-
enged it and rewrote it to my own ends. But that was just a
byproduct of the search, whose real goal you'll see below: a list
of the warning signs of alcohol addiction, repurposed to online poker. (I've removed a few from the list; I don't believe
anyone has ever awakened from a night of online poker and
not known where he was.) Look, I'm not trying to harsh your
mellow with this, and I'm not trying to invent a problem
where there is none. I'm just saying if there's an elephant in
any of our living rooms, the one thing we must do is note it,
observe it, and stroke its leathery skin.

Of course, I took the test myself, to see if there was an

addictive streak running through my own relationship to on-line play. Not that I'd be surprised to find one, for I'm com-pulsive by nature, and online poker is a compulsive person's paradise. Still, I tried to answer as truthfully as possible, and here were my responses.

- Do you lose time from work due to online poker?

No. It is my work. Or at least writing about it is. Okay, then, yeah.

- Is playing online making your home life unhappy?

No. Not unless you count how I rant and glower when I lose.

- Is online poker affecting your reputation?

Enhancing it, weirdly.

- Do you hide or disguise the amount of online poker you play?

Well, yeah.

- Have you ever felt remorse after playing online?

Yes, when I play stupidly or without self-discipline. And of course when I lose.

- Have you gotten into financial difficulties as a result of your online play?

No. But that's only because I'm cautious to play with just recre-ational sums.

- Has your ambition decreased since you started playing online?

No. And my ambition to beat stupid IKallYerBluff *has increased a lot.*

- Do you crave online poker at a definite time daily?

Yes. At the end of the work day—if I wait that long.

- Do you want to play again the next morning?

Yes, win or lose, I'm always ready for more.

- Does online poker cause you to have difficulty in sleep-ing?

Only if I stay up too late playing. Or lie awake wondering how that nimrod IKallYerBluff *could MAKE THAT CALL!!*

- Has your efficiency decreased since you started playing online?

Yes. I constantly interrupt the flow of my writing to "take a breather" with some online play. My output of words has dropped considerably. Though in fairness if it weren't poker, it'd be Lemmings, sudoku, or something. A man needs his breathers.

• Is online poker jeopardizing your job or business?
No. If anything, it's abetting my business. But I have an odd business.

• Do you play to escape from worries or troubles?
Oh, yeah.

• Do you promise yourself or anyone that you'll cut back?
When I feel like I'm overdoing it, I remove all the online shortcut icons from my desktop. That, at least, forces me to make a little effort to open the program files. Slows me down. Makes me think.

• Do you binge on online poker?
What, you mean like playing twenty-four hours nonstop? Who would do a crazy thing like that?

You and I have come a long way together in this book, and I hope by now you trust me not to lead you too far astray. So just one last time, I would ask you to do an exercise. Contemplate the questions above and answer them truthfully for yourself.

>>

I'd be surprised to find that you found yourself with a serious problem on your hands. If you were really that far gone in the gamble, you'd probably want nothing to do with a book like this in the first place, one that places such a premium on unblinking self-honesty. However, I'd also be surprised if you didn't find yourself answering "yes" to a couple of the more problematic questions—those having to do with productivity or sleep patterns, say. This doesn't mean you're hopelessly hooked, but online poker does make a powerful argument for itself, and if you find that the argument is costing you too much money or too much time, you might want to take a step back.

I know plenty of people who have. I run across them in cardrooms all the time. "I used to play online," they say with a certain contempt, "but I quit. You just can't beat the game." I think what they really mean is that they just can't beat their own atavistic urges, or the holes in their game that online play so magnifies, or the damnable 24/7/365 availability of it all, so they've decided just to hold the whole thing at arm's length. They play in cardrooms because cardrooms take some effort to get to, and because the buzz is defrayed by time.

Internet poker, then, is proving to be much more compelling and much more involving, than even its founding fathers (lo these scant years ago) could have imagined. If you've been with online play since the early days, then you know that it started out as an unsatisfactory simulacrum of real-world play. Over time, as technology has improved, the experience of playing online has become much more like its realworld counterpart. With the huge size of internet tournament fields, in fact, and with the dizzying pace of play, it has become in some senses even more real than "the real thing." Will this trend continue? It takes no Nostradamus to guess yes. All we have to do is look at the massive market for internet poker, the intense competition for customers, and the evolution of ever more supple interfaces that make the game playing experience that much more compelling and "real." In a few years, I imagine, we'll look back on internet poker as we now know it and say, "What a flat and unsatisfying experience *that* was."

We'll also see a continued blurring of the lines between what we think of as fake and real. Considering how quickly the in-table shuffle machine has replaced hand shuffled decks, why won't cardrooms do away with dealers altogether if they can? Give each player his own terminal and let the computer deal the game. Especially for today's young players, weaned on internet poker, that would be the best of both worlds. They'd get to manipulate their cards and chips in the way they know best, with a mouse, and yet still be able to look their opponents in the eye. It'll happen. Call me *Not*stradamus if it doesn't.

Another place where the lines will get nice and fuzzy is in the area of "technical assist." Already, thousands of players are using sniffers to inform their decisions. Others are writing computer programs to make those decisions for them. At what point does one leave off and the other begin? Once your poker tracking software has an *always follow my advice* toggle, man has given way to machine. People decry this. Bots, they say, are a scourge and must be destroyed. Yeah, to me not so much. No more than internet poker itself, or the internet itself, or any other technological advancement is a scourge that must be destroyed. Technology advances. That's what technology does. This isn't a good thing, and it's not a bad thing. It's just a thing that is.

Eventually, I think we'll see a split in the online poker market. Some sites will tout themselves as "pure poker," where the use of sniffers is banned by caveat, controls, or consent. Other sites will be the wild blue yonder of external playing aids where the whole point of the exercise will be to pit your skills at software data management against the similar skills of others. Neither version of the game is inherently better or worse than the other. One version is bare-knuckles boxing while the other is Battlebots, that's all. There's a place in the world for both, plus countless enhancements and variations we can't even conceive of yet.

And so, as I write these words in a pub in Heathrow, my layover having been extended and extended again by one of those delays-for-no-apparent-reason for which this airport is famous, I'm prepared to state without fear of contradiction that if you have a passion for internet poker, you'll be able to indulge it in a variety of new and interesting ways for many years to come. You'll be able to play on your cell phone (you already can). You'll be able to set up intranet "home games" with just your friends (you already can). You'll be able to shape your online poker experience to suit your taste and style, with or without attendant whistles and bells (you already can; you'll just get much more interesting choices as time goes by). Yep, no doubt about it. From PokerSpot to UltimateBet to WhatComesNext.com, internet poker is here to stay.

And that's a good thing, too, because you know what? Screw it. They're never gonna call my flight. I think I'll play a sitngo.

London Heathrow
September 2005

Appendix A
RANDOM ACCESS

Those who know my books know that as I write them, random topics accumulate in the back of my notebook and then make their way to the back of the book. These are those from this one.

PROP GOES THE WEASEL

I got an email from a guy asking, *What about online propping, JV? Do you think it's a career path or what?* This brought to mind my own experience as a proposition player at the now defunct Regency Casino in good ol' Bell Gardens, California. I thought it was just super that they'd pay me eight bucks an hour to play poker and figured that with that kind of cushion there was no way I could lose. Well, I filled out a succession of short handed games, lost $300 on day one, lost $500 on day two, called in sick on day three, and gave up the pretense on day four. With a win rate of minus $50 an hour, I decided that this was a job I could not afford to keep.

Online propping is a slightly different, well, proposition. For one thing, getting stuck in a short handed game is much less of a problem for online players than it is for realworld players, since short handed games in casinos are generally quite tough, but online even the short games tend to be filled with a homogenous mix of good, bad, and really bad players. Also, we online players have much experience with and no particular fear of short handed play. Many of us prefer it. So getting stuck in a short, and therefore allegedly bad, game is not that big a burden for the online prop.

You can work at home, so that's good. You don't have any of the attendant realworld prop expenses such as transportation, meals, tips (and taxes—did I say that out loud?). Granted, you still have the rake to deal with, though since the anchor of most prop deals is a rakeback scheme, this can be less of a problem for the online prop, too.

Still, to be a successful online proposition player, you have to be a winning online poker player, and many people are drawn to propping precisely because they can't show a profit on their own merit and hope that the monetary support of their prop deal, whatever it may be, will push them from the red to the black. Maybe. But you still have to put in your hours—lots of them if you intend to be the sort of prop who gets work. And if your game has leaks, even eensy-weensy tiny little ones, all those hours will drain your bankroll far faster than propping can prop it up. Not only that, if you lose your bankroll entirely, *you can't quit.* Not unless you want to stop being a prop altogether and, you know, go flip burgers or something.

Bottom line, then: If playing poker is a hard way to make an easy living, then propping is a hard way to make a hard living. Should you be one of the few who can regularly and consistently (and demonstrably over a span of years) beat online poker for good money, then you might be able to show a profit as a prop. But I put it to you that if you're really that good to begin with, you don't need propping. You can probably make more money with canny site selection and game selection, thereby exploiting the sort of options and opportunities that being a prop precludes.

YOUR KNOW YOU'RE AN ONLINE POKER PLAYER WHEN . . .

Online poker is a cultural phenomenon, this we know. It has been the subject of much press and no small wringing of hands in every media outlet from ABC's *Nightline* to, probably, *Cat Fancy* magazine. "Internet poker is a cultural phenomenon," pronounce the pundits.

Yeah? "Sun sets in west. Film at eleven."

But no cultural phenomenon has truly arrived until it has its own *you know you're a . . .* list, such as *you know you're a redneck, you know you're a reality TV star,* or *you know you're an Enron executive.* Never one to shirk from the responsibility of bending pop culture to my own snarky vision, I happily present *you know you're an online poker player when . . .*

- You think "sitngo" is a real word.
- Your fingers are calloused from clicking *bet pot.*
- You come home from playing poker and immediately play more poker.
- You've played poker for years but have never actually seen a deck of cards.
- You know most of your best friends by their screen name only.
- The first time you played in a realworld cardroom, you looked for the *bet all/raise all* button.
- You stay up till three in the morning because "there's this bitchin' freeroll on Party."
- You miss your mother's birthday because "there's this bitchin' freeroll on Full Tilt."
- You wear a catheter for no medical reason.
- You haven't seen the sun in three days.
- Your idea and your girlfriend's idea of "all in protection" are two very different things.
- You won't play in your local cardroom because there's no refer-a-friend bonus.

- Your entire wardrobe consists of online player's hats and shirts.
- GL, NH, NB, GG, and TY all make sense to you.
- You stop reading this list in the middle of reading this list to play a little online poker.
- You stop writing this list in the middle of writing this list to play a little online poker.
- Though you can't walk and chew gum at the same time, playing four simultaneous sitngos is no problem.
- You don't remember your own phone number, but know your Neteller details by heart.
- You upgraded to DSL and a high resolution twenty-inch monitor "for no particular reason."
- You can cram a four-course meal into a five-minute tournament break.
- The first question you ask of any vacation spot is, "Do they have internet?"
- You haven't seen your spouse/lover/significant other in weeks, but you see *RustyNail23* every damn day.
- Sleep? Who needs sleep?
- You've taken every bad beat known to man—except the next one.

INSTANT HAND HISTORIES

Imagine this moment in a realworld cardroom: You make a river bet, get called, and turn over your hand. Your opponent mucks his cards without showing, but curiosity gets the best of you, so you reach into the muck and peek at his hand. How many times do you think you could do this before they threw your sorry angle-shooting ass out of the casino?

Yet online you can do this very thing all day, every day, and if you're not aware of it you should be. Every online poker site has a handy little feature called *instant hand histories*. At the click of a button, a little text box pops up or, on some sites, a graphic clone of the hand just played. There, much to your delight, you will see the cards of everyone who called the final bet, whether they voluntarily showed their hands or not. Likewise, if everyone checked on the river, everyone's cards will be laid naked to the world in the instant hand history.

This tool is so massively useful that it's sometimes worth not betting on the river, just to see what the other guy had. Suppose you make a raise up front with pocket eights. You get reraised from 'round back and call, but the flop comes so scary, say three to a royal flush, that both you and your foe are frozen into inaction. By the time you get to the river, you're pretty sure that if you bet he'll fold, and if the pot's big enough to be worth winning, of course you'll bet. But suppose both your and your foe's money is very deep (or you're in the early rounds of a sitngo, when chips are cheap). If you check, and he checks behind you, your hand will be revealed first and if you have him beat his will go in the muck. But it'll still be there in the hand history, and a click of a button will reveal it to you. *Why that lying sack of sushi! He reraised with 7-8 suited! Well!* Well, indeed. That's a thing worth knowing.

I find that instant hand histories are indispensable in match play, where I'm concerned with the betting patterns of just a single opponent, and it's vital to know whether he considers A-x a raising hand, whether he likes to drag his monsters, and, most crucially, whether he'll call with cheese. Instant hand histories give me access to this information and, as noted, it's sometimes worthwhile just to check it down at the river for the sake of seeing what he's got. It's amazing how quickly the picture comes clear.

Think about all the times you've said to yourself, "Damn, I wish I knew what that guy had." Thanks to instant hand histories, a lot of times you can know. All it takes is remembering to peek.

BIG BET HOLE

In realworld poker when you make a sizeable bet or raise, you have to count out the chips and push all those chips, maybe even stacks, into the pot. The visceral act of placing the bet makes you think—and sometimes makes you think twice— about whether you really want to be taking so big a risk. Online, though, the act of betting big is the same as that of betting small: You click the mouse. Oh sure, you could argue that big bets require a more vigorous push on the betting slider, but I think you'd be splitting hairs and would have none of that. No, the fact is that making a big bet takes no more effort than, and really feels no different from, making a small bet. This is true whether you're calling, raising, or reraising, and it can lead to sudden and unexpected disaster if you don't stay alert to the risk.

Consider: You're holding A-T and you're up against one opponent—let's say it's someone you know to be frisky, tricky, and capable of raising with anything or nothing at all. The two of you see a flop of A-6-3. When he checks, you figure you're golden, so you go ahead and click *bet pot*. Mr. Frisky suddenly wakes up and responds in kind. He clicks *bet pot* back. *Oh yeah?* you think. *What kind of naked steal attempt is that? Thinks he can run me over, does he? Take that!* And before you even know you've done it, you hit the *bet pot* button again, and now the pot is huge, much bigger than you'll want it to be if it turns out that Mr. Frisky's on a better ace than you. And it's a damn sight bigger than you'd let it get if you'd paused, really paused, to consider whether his raise was a steal attempt or, you know, betting with the best hand. This is the problem with mouse-click betting: It's just too easy to make rash, rushed bets without thinking things through.

Want a piece of advice? Take your hand off the mouse after every bet you make. That way, it will be required of you at least to move your hand back to the mouse before you go madly clicking your money away. If that doesn't work, write yourself a little note that reads *take a breath before you bet,* and put it in your line of sight. Over time, you may not need such artificial aids, but if you think they're silly or unnecessary, just consider that if they save you from even one bad bet, they will have more than earned their keep. Big bets should be thoughtful bets. The faster you act, the greater your chance to act wrong.

SMALL BET HOLE

We know how important it is in no limit hold'em to deny our foes proper odds for their draws. If there's $200 in the pot and you bet just $10, you're inviting every Tom, Dick, and Susie with an open ended straight draw (or even an inside straight draw) to jump in and swim in a pool of your cash. This is a ridiculous example, of course; however, less ridiculous though no less incorrect examples abound in online poker, and the culprit for this ridiculousness has a name: the *bet minimum* button.

On virtually every internet poker site, bettors have the option to click *bet minimum,* and so make the smallest allowable bet, one equivalent to the size of the big blind. Some players do this because they're just cowering cowards and don't want to risk a lot of money. Others do it under the shaky reasoning that any bet, no matter how small, will drive out players who whiffed. Mostly, though, it's a matter of dumb convenience. The *min bet* button is there; let's hit it and move on.

Very occasionally there's a good reason to make a min bet. Sometimes, when you don't want to check and surrender all initiative, it can be used as a blocking bet, one that inspires your foe to just call instead of raise. It may also be a hoover bet, if you have your opponent drawing dead, but know that he'll call if, and only if, you make the price low enough. Generally, though, min bets are incorrect in no limit hold'em for the specific reason that they allow your foes a cheap opportunity to catch the card they need to kill you. Yet players make this bet all the time.

Not only that, they carry the habit over into realworld cardrooms. It's a tell of a certain sort, and certainly one you don't want to fall prey to. Police your betting practices, both online and in the realworld. Make sure that every bet has a clear strategic purpose and that the size of the bet is tuned to that purpose.

"I HATE YOU, I HOPE YOU DIE"

It is a fact of internet poker that players can be far more offensive, objectionable, rude, annoying, or profane online than they'd ever get away with in a realworld game. Say, "You played that hand like a moron, moron," to somebody's face in a cardroom and you're likely to get a second opinion from his fist. Online, the most anyone can do is mute your chat or, in extreme cases, rat you out to member services. Big whoop. Likewise, if you spent a lot of time in a realworld game yowling about how you never catch a break, or nattering that "realworld poker is fixed," the looks of scorn you got would shut you up in a hurry. Yet, some people spend hours online typing the vilest, crudest, or whiniest chatbox twaddle imaginable. Have you ever done this? Won't you please promise never to do it again?

Aside from degrading the discourse in an online poker game (none too high to begin with), this form of chat is wildly counterproductive to your poker goals. If you show anger, you peg yourself as an angerbot. Do you think this will make others want to go easy on you? You know that can't possibly be true. Likewise, if you bitch about your bad luck, you simply define yourself as a loser and, again, how can that make it easier dominate and crush your foes? In short, all displays of chatbox negativity are self-defeating drivel.

I recognize that some people think they're faking when the let anger leak into their chat. Someone puts a beat on them and they type, nice call dickweed, hoping to present themselves as someone who can't take a bad beat in stride but really can. I suppose they think that by faking anger they can fake tilt and get some calls they wouldn't otherwise get. But you know what? Someone faking anger is at least a little bit angry, and some of that fake tilt is at least a little bit real.

Now, I have to admit that from time to time I've given the needle to angerbots and chatbox whiners. I figure that anyone who generates so much black noise deserves all the tilt-inducing backchat I can spew. Sometimes this tactic works too well; I try to get someone to tilt, but instead just get him to leave. That's no victory. That's a loss.

So let's be clear. Anything you type into the chatbox should have a strategic purpose. Are you trying to appear clueless? Friendly? Hostile? Tilty? Any of that stuff is fine, so long as it's done for a reason you can name, and *so long as it's just not true.* If you're chatting your true feelings, beliefs, opinions, fears, analysis, anything, you're giving away information just as surely as if you were flashing your cards. If you can't chat with iron discipline, just don't chat at all.

By the way, I have had someone chat exactly those words at me, i hate you, i hope you die. I was well on my way to cleaning him out, and his intemperate chat just inspired me to finish the job, so that's that with that.

THE MOOKS AMONG US

I've never lent a poker player money in my life. I've almost never been asked. Maybe I don't look like a soft touch, or maybe I just don't travel in those degenerate circles. For whatever reason, the poker mook has been blissfully missing from my life. But not online, though. He's there. He's there in spades. There I am, minding my own business, playing my little heads up sitngo, when all of a sudden an observer starts pleading away in the chat window, trying to wheedle five bucks out of my account and into his.

It's spam of a sort, filling the chatbox with chaff: pathetic panhandling, tragically innocent of the rules of spelling, syntax, or grammar (id b so greatful for 5$). Now, you know and I know that it's a simple matter to turn off the chat and make the mook go away (in the sense, at least, that Schrödinger's Cat went away when Schrödinger shut the door). But I can't help wondering, what is going on in the mind of this mook? How did he get where he is?

By losing, of course. Losing so frequently and relentlessly that now he's broke, lost, and adrift, a Flying Dutchman of internet poker, doomed to log on over and over again into his empty account and wander from table to table, looking for a soft touch. He imagines, no doubt, that he's just one handout away from running up a significant stake. If he can only get his hands on five bucks, he'll put that fiver into a cheap sit-ngo, double through, then double through again, and again, and again, and again. With just a little bit of luck (and isn't he about due for some luck?) he'll be back on his feet in no time.

Sad, pathetic mook. His plan can't work. It just can't. Even if he could mook ten bucks or twenty or even fifty out of you, he'd still be playing with short money, case money, and therefore scared money. He's not likely to be any kind of skilled player in the first place, but even if he were, he can't be expected to play effectively that close to the felt. Five dollars isn't going to get him out of any kind of hole. It's not going to satisfy his poker jones. It's not going to bring him peace. It's only going to make him suffer more, because when it's gone he'll just have to torment and humiliate himself by going out looking for more. Sad guy. That is one sad guy.

You know what? I used to make fun of the mook. I used to tease the ones that crossed my path. Not any more. Knowing what a powerful jones the poker jones can be, I have nothing but sympathy for these guys, plus a certain "there but for the grace of God go I" relief. So I don't tease or taunt. But I sure as hell don't give them money. And I don't think you should either.

Appendix B

INFORMATION OVERLORD

From the moment I started this book, I wasn't at all keen to tackle the subject of sniffers—poker tracking software—and their role in online poker. It's not just because I'm lazy, and getting to the bottom of a decent sniffer, figuring out what it can do and how to get the most out of it, is dauntingly hard work.

Nor is it because I'm arrogant. I recognize that the online poker world is full of sniffer-abetted and sniffer-savvy players who routinely go into battle better armed than their "free-style" opponents. I know that many players dismiss this sort of support as unnecessary and believe that their natural aptitude for poker will overcome puny geekware any day of the week. The deservedly and undeservedly arrogant alike insist that they don't need such crutches, but I'm not one of them. I concede that any time I don't use a sniffer I'm giving away edge to those who do.

And I'm not particularly afraid of having my ignorance revealed. I always figure I'm better off owning what I don't know, confessing to it in advance, rather than running the risk of having someone find out later. As the saying goes, "I like to apologize for my work before I do it." So, no, I don't think I can do the world's best job of explaining sniffers to you, and also, no, I don't think that's a disgrace. With all of this in mind, I've decided to turn the following pages over to someone who knows sniffers inside out and can give you a much defter overview than I could. The logic of this is simple: Have you ever seen me try to fix my car? Some things are best left to those with the knack.

Tony "Mojo" Guerrera is typical of today's young online poker players. He is both serious-minded and single-minded in pursuit of perfect poker, and he eagerly field tests each new sniffer that comes along, knowing that every program has something to teach him and something to add to his game. He impresses me as someone who not only beats the game as he finds it today but also stays out ahead of the curve of change, so that he can continue to beat it in the months and years to come.

Whether you choose to invest your time, money, and mental energy in sniffers is up to you. To be honest, I know players who do quite well playing freestyle, and I know others who'd get crushed, just crushed, without their geekware. At the end of the day, only you know you. I will say this, though: If you've never tried a sniffer, you should. It may not be your cup of tea, but then again it may be exactly the tea you need. You'll never know till you try it, and though many a wayward college student has been introduced to tequila by that same fuzzy logic of *try it, you'll like it,* I think you have more to gain than to lose by taking a sniffer out for a test drive.

Now here's Tony Guerrera, guesting in to give you an overview of sniffers and an answer to the question, "What can sniffers do for you?" Take it away, Mojo.

THE WORLD OF SNIFFERS
by Tony Guerrera

Being a winning poker player is all about awareness of your opponents' tendencies and unbiased, honest evaluation of your own play. These two operations are hopefully happening continuously while you are in the heat of battle. If you really want to improve, then they should happen after your sessions as well. While b&m players only have their memories, online players have some help in the form of sniffers. Sniffers are software packages that import your hand histories into permanent databases and do all sorts of wonderful things with them, making post-game analysis of your play (and your opponents') extremely accurate, unbiased, easy, and efficient. The better ones have the capability to be used for on-the-fly in-game analysis, but we will talk about that later—basics first!

ANALYZING A PLAYER VIA "GENERAL PLAYER PROFILE NUMBERS"

The General Player Profile Numbers (GPPNs) provide a player overview. To make future discussion concise and to accustom you to expressions or acronyms that you may read elsewhere, they are listed here:

- Hands Played: Total Number of Hands Played
- BB/100: **B**ig **B**ets won per **100** hands (a big bet is twice the big blind)
- VPIP or VP$IP: % of hands you **V**oluntarily **P**ut money **I**n the **P**ot
- VPSB or VP$SB: % of hands you **V**oluntarily **P**ut money in the pot from the **S**mall **B**lind
- PFR: **P**reflop **R**aise %
- ASB: % of hands you **A**ttempted to **S**teal **B**linds

The simplest number is self-explanatory, the number of hands you have played. Whether you like it or not, we have entered the world of statistics, and the bottom line is that none of the GPPNs make any sense unless you have played enough hands. The generally accepted guidelines are that anything under 10,000 hands is not a big enough sample size for most of the statistics. For the BB/100 statistic, you actually need at least 50,000 hands, if not more, to get even close to a proper estimate. For most players, playing that many hands will take an unreasonable amount of time. Furthermore, unless you are playing the highest stakes games online, where the playing pool is small and consistent, it is unlikely that you will ever have that large a sample of hands for an opponent. However, these numbers still yield much information. We are more concerned with trends than theoretical absolutes, so you can come up with meaningful analysis of your own play after even just a few thousand hands. Often, these numbers will reveal useful information about your opponents after a few dozen. This is good, because the reality (and the mathematically minded player's philosophical quandary) of poker is that you are forced to make decisions of a statistical nature based on statistically insignificant sample sizes . . . you have to simply work with the data you currently have and refine things as you accumulate more data.

Just keep in mind that the more hands you have, the more meaningful your numbers are. Also, keep in mind that your play will probably evolve over your poker life, so when you analyze your own hands, you will need to decide for yourself whether to include every hand you have ever played or to filter and only view your last 5,000 hands or so. It is probably best to do a combination of both so you can simultaneously get a good feel for your recent trends and for the big picture. Also acknowledge that the maniac you have played with for the past 10,000 hands is capable of becoming the hardest rock ever to have mucked two cards. People do change.

The next important statistic is your BB/100. BB/hand is not used because it is less than one. By multiplying by 100, you get numbers that can be rounded to whole numbers. BB/100 is great because it is independent of stakes, but use caution when combining results from different stakes to calculate a universal BB/100. Different stakes play differently, and your expected BB/100 will probably decrease as you move up the ladder and play theoretically tougher competition. Your sniffer should allow you to filter hands so you can, for example, only view $100NL hands even though you have played $25NL, $50NL, and $200NL. Your sniffer should also allow you to view everything lumped together. However, I highly suggest not doing this for any of the statistics or analysis to be discussed. Simply put, never do it. Treat every limit differently so you can easily figure out where you are most effective and where you need to improve.

It is imperative that you understand that the magnitude of this number is somewhat meaningless until you have played tens of thousands of hands. Assume that you have played 10,000 hands of $200NL ($1-$2 blinds), and you are up $4,000, for a BB/100 of 1000/100 = 10. Now, assume that you have $1,000 in front of you. You get AA, go all in preflop against the other $1,000 stack at your table, and to your delight, he is holding KK. You are an 81.946% favorite to win the pot. What can you expect your new BB/100 to be? If you win, your overall $200NL profit will be $5,000. ($5,000/$4)/ (10,001/100) = 12.50BB/100. If you lose, your overall $200NL profit will be $3,000. ($3,000/$4)/(10,001/100) = 7.50BB/100. Your expectation value for your new BB/100 is (12.50)(.81946) + (7.50)(1-.81946) = 11.60. You have played 10,000 hands, yet your 10,001st hand results in an expected 11.6% change in your BB/100!

If you are the type of player who likes to cash out after obtaining large stacks (3+ buy ins), then your BB/100 will have less volatility; however, if you are playing within your means (and if you're not, then you should seriously re-evaluate your playing habits), and if you are positive EV (expected value) against the other big stacks, you will show much larger profits in the long run if you stay around and butt heads with the other large stacks in restricted buy in games.

Assuming you have 50,000+ hands under your belt, numbers in the 7-10 range are superb. If you are extremely good, play one table at a time, and very carefully select your games, you can probably sneak into the low teens. If you are beating the $200NL at your favorite site for 4 BB/100, then you should be pretty happy with yourself, and remember, that as long as your BB/100 is more than 0, you can call yourself a winner. Also, realize that if you are multi-tabling, your BB/100 will most likely be lower than it would be if you were to focus on only one table. The reason to multi-table is to increase your hourly win rate by squeezing in more hands, but this only works if you are a solid winning player when you focus on one table. The very best players are able to play 4 (or more in rare cases) and maintain BB/100s around 10. This is true even at six handed tables, where the BB/100 for an expert player is slightly higher, though playing four simultaneous six handed tables is not for the faint of heart!

Though the truth can hurt, it is actually really good that sniffers are brutally honest. The reason a lot of poker players are horrendous complainers is that they are hopeless optimists whose positive hopes are dashed in the long run by things working out as statistically expected. You have played 200,000 hands of $200NL, and you think you are the next Phil Ivey. You are ready to quit your job and start pounding the $400NL for an estimated $150/hr; however, your sniffer says your BB/100 is 0. Well, now is not the time to quit your day job. You've played 200,000 hands and only broken even? While you are doing better than average (without the rake, you would be profiting), you were probably hoping to make at least *something* if you have played that much poker. To help your cause, evaluate your BB/100 after only a few thousand hands at a time and combine this with being brutally honest and unbiased in your judgment of your play.

Furthermore, an accurate memory is going to be of paramount importance. You need to remember all the really big hands that could have tipped the scales heavily one way or the other, and to somehow account for those. If your overall profit is $1,000 after 1,000 hands, and you recall the wild $1,000 pot you won when you pushed all in by accident with your 2-7 offsuit and cracked someone's A-A, then your $1,000 profit is not really a true indicator of your expected profit. Your theoretical BB/100 is probably below where your sniffer says it is. Poker is not only about accurately judging your opponents in the absence of statistically significant sample sizes; it is also about accurately judging yourself under the same constraints.

Now, whenever you think about poker, you should be thinking about doing whatever is within poker rules and etiquette to maximize your theoretical BB/100. The first statistic that will be important to a lot of players on the quest of BB/100 optimization is VPIP.

Since the tight-aggressive player is the one about which everyone writes, let us approximate what the VPIP for a typical tight-aggressive player is in a ten handed game. These starting hand requirements will vary depending on the texture of the game and the judgment of the particular player; however, the following is a good approximation of starting hand requirements as a function of position in an unraised pot:

Unraised Pot Starting Requirements for a Typical Tight-Aggressive Player

SB: [AA,22]; [AK,A2]; [KQ,KT]; [K9s,K2s]; [QJ,QT]; [JT,65]; [J9,64]

BB: Any two cards

UTG: [AA,88]; [AK,AJ]; [KQ]

UTG+1: [AA,88]; [AK,AJ]; [KQ]

UTG+2: [AA,88]; [AK,AJ]; [KQ]

UTG+3: [AA,22]; [AK,AJ]; [KQ,KJ]; [QJ]; [JT]

CO-2: [AA,22]; [AK,AJ]; [KQ,KJ]; [QJ]; [JT]

CO-1: [AA,22]; [AK,AJ]; [KQ,KJ]; [QJ]; [JT]

CO: [AA,22]; [AK,AT]; [A9s,A2s]; [KQ,KT]; [K9s,K8s]; [QJ,QT]; [JT,65]; [J9,64]

Button: [AA,22]; [AK,AT]; [A9s,A2s]; [KQ,KT]; [K9s,K8s]; [QJ,QT]; [JT,65]; [J9,64]

The interval notation here works as follows. All you do is count down the first and second hole card separately until you go from the first hand to the last hand. [AK,A2] for example, represents the set of hole cards {AK, AQ, AJ, . . . , A4, A3, A2}, and [JT,87] represents the set of hole cards {JT, T9, 98, 87}. Lower-case letters denote whether the cards are suited or not, and the absence of a lower-case letter means that unsuited and suited combinations are included.

Note that hands like the low pocket pairs will not be played by a tight player in late position if no one else has entered the pot, as he will need pot odds and implied odds to draw for his set, and that he will usually play any pocket pair in early position in a loose-passive game. Arguments can be made for other modifications to this distribution, but at the very least, it will help us get a rough idea of what the VPIP for a tight-aggressive player is.

In a raised pot, the tight-aggressive player will most likely only play [AA,JJ] and [AK,AQ]. Sometimes he may muck A-Q and even A-K. Sometimes he may elect to reraise a loosy-goosy with 9-9. Also, all pocket pairs may be played in large multi-way pots in deep-stacked games. The very best tight-aggressive players can be very tricky at times and are very good at knowing when hands like A-K and 9-9 are good and when they should be mucked; however, since this is an approximation, we will assume the following distribution:

Raised Starting Requirements for the Tight-Aggressive Player
All Positions: [AA,JJ]; [AK,AQ]

To finish this calculation requires some basic combinitorics. Knowing how to do this stuff is by no means necessary. If you would like to learn how to do these types of calculations yourself, then finding a book on probability would be best, though you can probably also find a good tutorial online.

The following list gives us the number of combinations of various holdings.

Any 2 hole cards: 52nCr2* = 1326
Pocket Pair: 4nCr2 = 6
Specific Unsuited Holding (AK for example): (4)(3) = 12
Specific Suited Holding: (4)(1) = 4

*nCr means the number of ways to choose r elements from a group of n elements. 52nCr2, for example, is how many two card combinations can be chosen from a set of fifty-two cards.

The unraised pot distribution, as a function of number of combinations, is as follows:

SB: (13)(6) + (12)(16) + (3)(16) + (8)(4) + (2)(16) + (6)(16) +
    (6)(16) = 574
BB: 1326
UTG: (7)(6) + (3)(16) + (1)(16) = 106
UTG+1: (7)(6) + (3)(16) + (1)(16) = 106
UTG+2: (7)(6) + (3)(16) + (1)(16) = 106
UTG+3: (13)(6) + (3)(16) + (2)(16) + (1)(16) + (1)(16) = 190
CO-2: (13)(6) + (3)(16) + (2)(16) + (1)(16) + (1)(16) = 190
CO-1: (13)(6) + (3)(16) + (2)(16) + (1)(16) + (1)(16) = 190
CO: (13)(6) + (4)(16) + (8)(4) + (3)(16) + (2)(4) + (2)(16) +
    (6)(16) + (6)(16) = 454
Button: (13)(6) + (4)(16) + (8)(4) + (3)(16) + (2)(4) + (2)(16) +
    (6)(16) + (6)(16) = 454

The player is in each position a tenth of the time; thus, the VPIP in unraised pots is the following:

(57.4 + 132.6 + 10.6 + 10.6 + 10.6 + 19.0 + 19.0 + 19.0 + 45.4
+ 45.4)/1326 = .2787

For raised pots, the VPIP for this player is [(4)(6) + (2)(16)]/1326 = .0422

To get the final VPIP, we need a weighted average accounting for how many pots are raised versus unraised. There are so many game types and relative frequencies of each game type that people could debate for days about this and get nowhere. We are going to assume that 35% of pots are raised and 65% of pots are unraised. The final VPIP for this player is $[(.35)(.0422) + (.65)(.2787)] * 100\% = 19.59\%$. If your experience indicates different percentages for raised and unraised pots, by all means plug them in.

Now, if you are a classic tight-aggressive player, should your VPIP be 19.59%? Of course not! A big part of profiting in no limit hold'em is postflop play. Being selective about what you enter pots with makes many subsequent hand decisions easier, which is why tight-aggressive play is so successful; however, a very skilled player can play a wider mix of hands and be quite successful through shrewd, insightful postflop play. It is very important to understand that the distributions suggested here (and elsewhere), while they can be profitable, are really only presented for the sake of calculation. Each poker hand is a unique situation, and your decision on how to play each one is always a function of the particular situation you are in. You ultimately need to use what you have figured out about your table to deduce what hands to play and how to play them.

Having said this, most players' number one flaw is that they are simply too loose. If you are playing ten handed, your BB/100 after 50,000 hands is negative, and your VPIP is above 25%, then you should consider tightening your mix of hands. I mention BB/100 here, because these statistics do not exist independently of each other. It is all the GPPNs combined that tell your story, not just one in particular. If your VPIP is 35% and your BB/100 is 20 (assuming you've played enough hands), then it goes without saying that you probably should not change what you are doing. If your VPIP is down in the low teens, then you are probably playing too tightly. Chances are that your BB/100 is somewhere close to even, and you are going to have to get comfortable playing a wider range of hands to increase your winnings. However, if every game you happen to play in has been a maniac festival, your VPIP will most likely be in this region, or perhaps even lower. Again, if you are profiting, you have nothing to worry about. However, be aware that your BB/100 will have higher variance associated with these loose-aggressive games, so as warned about earlier, you better have a lot of hands under your belt before making any hard and fast conclusions.

A lot of this VPIP talk has been aimed at ten handed players. However, a lot of people like to play at the six handed tables available on most sites. Because of the nature of short handed play, your VPIP should definitely be higher; it is feasible to beat these games with a VPIP in the low 20s. With the nature of short handed play, and the number of heads-up confrontations that occur, though, it is really difficult to pin down a precise VPIP. Six handed play is as much psychological warfare as it is cards. Many different preflop playing styles, from slight modifications to the classic ten handed tight-aggressive, to outright maniacal, can yield significant profits if you keep your head on your shoulders and pay close attention to your opponents. There are people with VPIP's close to 40 who pull in BB/100s in the low teens at the lower limit six handed games. If you find that you are not handling a lot of tricky postflop decisions well, then you will probably want to play a tighter mix of hands and see how your BB/100 changes as a function of your reduced VPIP. Outside of that, there is not really much to say about VPIP relative to your own short handed play. In short handed play, these statistics are really much more important in gauging how to deal with your opponents, since vastly differing styles can be profitable.

VPIP can give you some decent information about your opponents. In the absence of any other statistics, assume that a player with a VPIP below 15% is a rock. If such a player is at your table, then you should be able to steal many pots from him, and if he is to your left, then you are very lucky indeed, for many a blind steal attempt will be successful. When he plays back at you, know that you are probably beaten and run away to fight another day. If, however, you are dealing with players with VPIPs in the 40s (or above—yes, you will run into these, and yes, they are usually gold mines), tighten up a little bit and pick your pots carefully. Against these loose players, fancy bluffs are going to lead to you getting called down with ace high, so it is best to simply wait for your good hands and extract maximum value. It should be noted that some players play differently preflop and postflop, but it is usually correct to assume that this is not the case until you find evidence to the contrary. Also, it is really VPIP combined with other numbers that guides your decisions; however, VPIP is usually a good initial indicator of what type of player you're facing (loose-gambling type versus tight-conservative type).

Related to VPIP is the VPSB statistic. While only 1 out of 10 hands are played from the small blind at a ten handed table, the truth is that a lot of money is lost from players in the small blind. There are some players who defend their small blind, even against an under-the-gun raiser, simply because they put money in the pot (this is more common with big blinds, but there are a stubborn few who protect their small blind like this as well). There are many more players who call an unraised pot from the small blind with any two cards regardless of the number of players in the pot because only having to call for half a big blind seems like a tremendous deal, not to mention all the implied odds they fool themselves into thinking they have. Because your pot odds are better from the small blind, your VPSB statistic should be higher than your VPIP statistic. The tight aggressive player from before would have a VPSB of $(574/1326)(.65) + (56/1326)(.35) = 29.62\%$. While you can perhaps add a few more hands to the distribution, realize that you will be out of position every hand you play from the small blind. Also, the implied odds that people claim they have are usually grossly overestimated. Remember, for money to be tossed in on future betting rounds, not only must you hit your hand but your opponent must also hit a big enough hand simultaneously. Assuming you both hit, you still are not guaranteed that enough money will go in the middle, and furthermore, even if you hit your hand on the flop, there are reverse implied odds associated with you hitting on the flop but eventually losing a big pot when your opponent catches up and beats you at showdown. Simply put, you should not be limping in from the small blind with 7-2 offsuit (and other garbage). However, if it is folded to you, and the big blind is weak tight (VPIP lower than 15%), by all means raise from the SB with it, and if you are just called, toss in a continuation bet on the flop—you will profit with any two cards in this situation in the long run!

Your VPSB will be higher if the games you play are more passive than the 35% preflop raise rate suggested here; however, if your VPSB is higher than 50%, you are very likely throwing many half big-blinds away. Recall from before that making 7 BB/100 is superb. 7BB is equal to twenty-eight small blinds. If you avoid 4 bad calls from the small blind in a 100 hand session (10 orbits meaning 10 small blinds), then you are 1/7 way to having the stats of a highly profitable player. If your BB/100 is -.75, then saving those 4 small blinds will turn you into a profitable player. Remember that the money you save by not making bad calls can equate to money won at the end of the day . . . little things can add up very fast!

While VPIP is widely advocated as the measure of how tight/loose an opponent is, VPSB can in some ways be an even better indicator. Since most people play too loosely from the small blind, what you are really looking for are people who play too tightly from the small blind. If a player is tight from the small blind, then that player is probably really tight from all positions, meaning that you should be wary when this player decides to contest a pot. If he is in past the flop, then you probably need to have the goods to win the pot.

VPIP and VPSB give information about how many hands you and your opponents play. Now, it is time to look at statistics about aggressiveness. PFR, the percentage of times a player raises preflop, is the primary statistic to look at. The tight-aggressive player is where we started off when looking at VPIP and VPSB, and it will be where we begin analyzing PFR as well. The following is a rough estimate of the raising distribution for the tight-aggressive player in a pot that has not been raised:

SB: [AA,TT]; [AK,AJ]; [KQ] = 94 combinations
BB: [AA,TT]; [AK,AJ]; [KQ] = 94 combinations
UTG: [AA,JJ]; [AK] = 40 combinations
UTG+1: [AA,JJ]; [AK] = 40 combinations
UTG+2: [AA,JJ]; [AK] = 40 combinations
UTG+3: [AA,JJ]; [AK,AQ] = 56 combinations
CO-2: [AA,TT]; [AK,AJ] = 78 combinations
CO-1: [AA,TT]; [AK,AJ]; [KQ] = 94 combinations
CO: [AA,TT]; [AK,AJ]; [KQ] = 94 combinations
Button: [AA,TT]; [AK,AJ]; [KQ] = 94 combinations

Thus, the PFR in unraised pots is 5.46% for our tight-aggressive player. There is a lot of room for adjusting this distribution. For example, some tight-aggressive players like to sparingly pull off a play where they raise with virtually any two cards from the big blind after a lot of limpers have come in, knowing that most likely they will pick up all the weak limps without any contest. Some tight-aggressive players will pull off similar plays from late position with the same philosophy and the added benefit that they will have position on all postflop action (there is something to be said for having a first-aggressor advantage for continuation betting on the flop in these situations though). Some players may not like raising with A-J and K-Q in a situation where they will be out of position for the rest of the hand. Also, we could debate about playing A-Q from early position as well as 8-8 and 9-9 in late position. However, the previous distribution is good enough for approximation's sake. This distribution is the distribution of hands where, most of the time, you will be playing with people with hands worse than yours if play proceeds past preflop (including A-J and K-Q out of position), and the whole tight-aggressive philosophy is about getting people to pay maximally when they are behind.

Now, in a pot that has been raised, we are going to assume that our tight-aggressive player only reraises with A-A and K-K. Occasionally, Q-Q and A-K will be reraising hands, but these hands are very delicate to play in the presence of a raiser in a NL game. In general, tight-aggressive players like to be the first aggressor. There are cases where tight-aggressive players will reraise with much worse. These cases are usually when the raiser is notoriously loose. However, in general, when a tight-aggressive player reraises, it is time to run for cover, and thus, I stand by this very narrow distribution. In raised pots, the PFR for our tight-aggressive player is therefore .90%.

Assuming again that 35% of pots are raised, we get a final PFR of $(5.46)(.65)+(.90)(.35) = 3.864\%$. If this number seems low to you, then you are right. To come up with a better estimate, blind steal situations must be considered for the unraised pot distribution.

This is what the ASB statistic is for. A blind steal situation occurs when the CO (cutoff) or button has the option to enter a pot that has been folded to him. Any raise in this situation is considered a blind steal attempt. When presented with such a situation, the tight-aggressive player will open up his raising distribution quite a bit to put pressure on the blinds, who will have to play out of position on all subsequent betting rounds. While stealing the blinds is a very important play in tight games, players can tend to abuse this play and bleed away a lot of chips in bad situations. An aggressive blind stealer will begin to get reraised from the blinds, and he will not know whether his opponents have something legitimate or if they have simply gotten tired of being run over.

The tight-aggressive player will try to steal the blinds with a distribution that looks like the following: [AA,66]; [AK,A2];

[KQ,K8]; [QJ,QT]; [JT,87]. Some of the more adventurous tight-aggressive players may include lower suited connectors, low pocket pairs, and possibly other random holdings, especially if the blinds are tight. If the blinds are loose, then the suggested distribution may be tightened a tad by removing hands like A-2 and 8-7. With the assumed distribution though, our tight-aggressive player will have an ASB of $[(9)(6) + (12)(16) + (5)(16) + (2)(16) + (4)(16)]/1326 = 31.83\%$

Again, it must be stressed that while this is a reasonable distribution of hands to steal blinds with, your playing circumstances may dictate a wider or narrower distribution. The key concepts are that if your ASB is low (say less than 20%), then you probably are not taking advantage of enough opportunities. If you are still new to the game though, it is probably best to be on the low side, since being on the low side ensures that you will have fewer difficult situations as the hand develops. Conversely, if your ASB is over 50%, then it is very likely that your opponents will be playing back at you, putting you to tough tests. If you are showing a profit from these situations, though, then more power to you (we will talk in a bit about how sniffers can show if you are profiting here). Having an ASB of around 30% represents a balanced attack where you are taking advantage of opening in late position while, simultaneously, not exposing yourself to a large number of dangerous, tricky situations.

Now that we know about ASB, we can go back and finish our PFR calculation. Let us assume that for unraised pots, 20% of them are blind steal situations. This means that the raising distributions from the CO and the button are now 80/20 weighted averages:

SB: [AA,TT]; [AK,AJ]; [KQ] = 94 combinations
BB: [AA,TT]; [AK,AJ]; [KQ] = 94 combinations
UTG: [AA,JJ]; [AK] = 40 combinations
UTG+1: [AA,JJ]; [AK] = 40 combinations
UTG+2: [AA,JJ]; [AK] = 40 combinations

UTG+3: [AA,JJ]; [AK,AQ] = 56 combinations
CO-2: [AA,TT]; [AK,AJ] = 78 combinations
CO-1: [AA,TT]; [AK,AJ]; [KQ] = 94 combinations
CO: [AA,TT]; [AK,AJ]; [KQ] = 94 combinations (80%) 422
    combinations (20%)
Button: [AA,TT]; [AK,AJ]; [KQ] = 94 combinations (80%)
    422 combinations (20%)

Our new PFR for unraised pots becomes 6.45%. Putting raised pots into consideration, the PFR for the tight-aggressive player becomes 4.51%. Adding another percent or two for situational raises along the lines of those discussed earlier, the PFR for our hypothesized tight-aggressive player is 5.51-6.51%. If your PFR is on the low side, you may be finding that the lower end of your good hands (e.g., A-J, K-Q, and J-J) are ending up being played unprotected in multi-way pots. If your PFR is too high, then a likely problem is that you are putting a disproportionately high volume of money into pots with the worst of it preflop.

Now, let us apply all of this knowledge to your opponents. When your opponent raises, your task is to figure out the distribution of hands he is raising with. It sounds easier than it is; however, your opponent's PFR combined with the types of calculations we have been doing can allow you to quickly surmise what your opponents are raising with. Keep in mind the raising distribution presented here for the tight-aggressive player, and remember that after factoring some small number of fancy, situational plays, the PFR for our hypothetical player is 5.51%-6.51%. This is the benchmark percentage range that you will use to compare all players against. If you are facing a raise from a player with a PFR of less than 3%, fold all but the best of your premium hands, even if his VPIP is 45%, because it is painfully obvious that even though your player will call his house away, he is only raising with a distribution that looks something like [AA,QQ]; [AK]. This is a very hard adjustment for people to make, because they automatically want to punish the calling station; however, this type of subtle observation will save you quite a few costly all ins over time. If your opponent's PFR is above 10%, then you are going to need to buckle up and start reraising and perhaps limp reraising with hands like [TT,88] and A-Q if the raiser is to your left. You will find that these players will often fold to your reraise because of some of the junk they are raising with. If you, in turn, get reraised again, then you need to hope that you have data from another hand where your opponent was in this betting pattern. You may be badly beaten by an overpair, being in a 20/80 situation with your T-T; you may be a 56/44 favorite against his overcards; or, if he has A-x, then you may be lucky enough to be a 70/30 favorite. He may even have a pocket pair lower than yours, making you an 80/20 favorite to win. If you know all the hands in his re-reraising distribution, then you will know whether to fold, call, or go back over the top. Typically, a table with a player with a high PFR soon becomes a very loose table, where the amount of money put in preflop makes paying the blinds negligible. Everyone loosens up trying to catch the preflop raiser. If your game has become a game of this texture, hold out and wait for your most premium holdings before entering the shootout. The cost of blinds will be insignificant compared to the sizes of the pots you will be contesting.

While this analysis is good for ten handed play, a lot of these numbers become somewhat meaningless when applied to your own six handed play, much in the way that VPIP did. There are players who are very profitable at six handed play seeing the flop almost 40% of the time and raising over half the time they come in, which corresponds to a PFR of 20%. Such maniacal play is highly profitable when executed by players who know when their marginal hands are good and when they should be tossed. In particular, a lot of six handed games are populated by players who will let themselves get run over by preflop raises and continuation bets on the flop, and a six handed player aware of such stats is brutally taking advantage of these games. Conversely, a classic tight aggressive approach also beats a lot of the six handed games currently being played online. On balance, a loose-aggressive approach will likely lead to a higher BB/100 in these games, but it is much more difficult to play successfully. Suffice to say, it is tough to look at your PFR and know whether it is indicative of six handed problems since, again, vastly different styles have proven to be profitable in these games. However, the analysis in the previous paragraph is absolutely vital if you are going to be a successful six handed player (it is pretty darn important if you are playing ten handed as well). It cannot be stressed enough how important tying VPIP and PFR to preflop hand distributions is.

When classifying players, it is customary to simply speak of their VPIP and PFR numbers, because as we see, a lot of information can be derived from them alone. VPIP and PFR allow you to classify players as loose-passive, loose-aggressive, tight-passive, and tight-aggressive, and even the degree to which a player belongs in a category. While these numbers by themselves will not help you fix any major leaks in your game, they may point you in the right direction. However, these numbers are very useful in coming up with reads on your opponents. With proper knowledge of the VPIP and PFR numbers corresponding to various calling and raising distributions, you are well on your way to knowing exactly what your opponents' holdings may be.

Your sniffer will spit out many other statistics relating to preflop and postflop play. A lot of these statistics are much tougher to analyze than those discussed earlier since they are very sensitive to the types of games you are playing in. Just be aware that there are many numbers available to you, and with thoughtful analysis, you can decide how helpful they are in evaluating your own play and in enabling you to dissect your opponents' games until you know your opponents better than their own mothers do.

SITUATIONAL ANALYSIS AND
INSTANT REPLAY

The statistics discussed earlier are intended to give an overall picture; however, poker is not a game of generalities. It is a game that stresses properly handling very specific situations. While sniffers are great for accumulating statistics, their greatest use lies in enabling you to analyze particular situations by letting you filter your data. Combine the ability to filter data according to situations with the ability to graphically replay hands, and you have a very powerful learning tool. When shopping for a sniffer, make sure that your sniffer supports the graphical playback of hands, for anything less is simply unacceptable.

There are so many different ways to organize situations that it will be impossible to cover everything here. Every player is different and will have different things to focus on. However, the following is a check list of items that will serve as a good starting point for your play and your personal quest for BB/100 optimization:

- Look at your stats organized by starting hand. Start with the hands that have the worst BB/100 and figure out what you are doing wrong. Are you playing the hand too much out of position? Are you playing the hand too much in raised pots? By being able to graphically play back all 100 hands you have played for an overall loss with A-J, say, perhaps you can see patterns that develop in the pots that you are losing money in.
- Look at your stats organized by position. You should have the highest profit from the button, and as your position gets earlier your profit should decrease. You will probably be losing money from the blinds; however, if you subtract the cost of the blinds themselves, you should be positive from the small and big blind. If you are nega-

tive, you are calling too much. If you are losing money from early position, you are most likely playing too many hands up front. Your VPIP should increase as you go from early position to late position. If it is constant, you are either playing too much up front or too little from the back.

- Look at your statistics sorted by table session. Study the tables where you performed badly to figure out what went wrong and how to adapt against these types of players in the future. Also, study your successful tables and figure out what made you successful. Positive reinforcement is just as important as studying your mistakes!
- Look at your statistics sorted by time of day and week. This will not necessarily help you develop as a player, but it may help your play/don't play decisions and ultimately your BB/100. Perhaps there are times at which your game of choice is softer (or you play better!) for some unknown reason. Use your sniffer to find these times.
- Look at hands you played in blind steal situations, and then filter further by starting hand. Look at how profitable open raising from late position is for the various starting hands. See where you make mistakes in continuing to play after the blind reraises you.
- Look at your defense of blinds. Are you defending too much? Not enough? Blind defense situations are very tricky, and the way to play them is largely a function of your opponents. By reviewing a lot of these situations, you can hopefully get a better feel for what works for different opponent types.

This list serves as a good starting point. The more conversant with sniffers you become, the more creative and insightful you can get with your individual hand studies. When you replay your hands, evaluate the pot odds you are getting when you call. Evaluate the pot odds you are offering to your opponents when you bet/raise. If you won a big pot, don't just pat yourself on the back; also ask yourself if there was a way you could have extracted more money. If you made a bad call, don't just say "I made a bad call." Find out what led to you losing money in the first place, so you can avoid repeating the costly error in the future. If you analyze everything closely, you should see a dramatic improvement in your results as your poker mind expands. Always be inquisitive!

OVERLAYING GPPNS IN YOUR GAMEPLAY WINDOW

The better sniffers on the market either have built in the ability to display player stats in your gameplay window or have the ability to support additional software that accomplishes this task. If you do a lot of thinking about what different VPIP/PFR combinations mean, then you can do a lot of damage in your games with software that overlays the VPIP and PFR of your opponents right on your playing screen. Some people find the additional display to be too distracting; however, these displays are well worth getting used to if you can prevent yourself from being distracted, and if you know how to properly use the information being revealed to you. Besides displaying the basic VPIP and PFR numbers, you can usually also display ASB along with a few other numbers such as how frequently an opponent defends his blinds!

Do not think that having all these stats means that you can ignore your opponents. The stats will help you optimize your preflop play, especially when considering reraising or folding, and in blind defense situations. If you can do the hand distribution analysis done throughout this chapter, then these stats more or less give away your opponents' preflop hand distributions for calling and raising to the point that it is almost unfair (a big reason I showed those calculations instead of just giving you the results); however, they do not tell much about how your opponents play past the flop. There are a few post-flop statistics such as "went to showdown %" that some players find helpful for knowing which players to bluff and which players to value bet. If you can learn to use those numbers to your advantage, then your technical understanding of the game is very good. However, for postflop play, there is no substitute for raw, human observational power. Do not ever be lazy or complacent at the poker table (live or online)! Also, remember that if you also play live, you will not have available a statistical overlay on your cardroom opponents. Use and love the tool since it is helpful, but don't let it become a crutch.

CLOSING WORDS

In short, sniffers are very powerful tools, provided you understand what all the numbers they spit out are telling you. Taking advantage of their ability to focus your post-session analysis will increase your understanding of the game and lead you to profitable new insights. Using the in-game statistics displays can sharpen your in-game decisions and can possibly make multi-tabling more manageable. These are wonderful pieces of software for any player trying to optimize his BB/100, so try some of them out for yourself!

Glossary

*My words mean exactly
what I want them to mean,
neither more nor less.*
— Lewis Carroll

Angerbot. A player who loses his temper online and lets it show in his chat.

Anyace Line. Demarcation between tight players and loose ones; someone who will play an ace with any kicker is said to dwell below the anyace line.

Applied Luck. A betting sequence leading to one conclusion if the cards fall a certain way, but a different conclusion if they come otherwise.

b&m. Brick and mortar; a casino or cardroom in the realworld.

Bookbot. Someone who follows a very precise style of play as outlined in poker books.

Bubble Off. To bust out of a tournament on the bubble, one place off the money.

Chatbox. Conversation in an online poker site's chat window.

Confirmation Bias. The tendency to remember bad outcomes and therefore overestimate their frequency.

Context Density. Information divided by time; the more information available in a given space of time, the greater the context density.

Continuation Bet. A postflop bet made almost automatically by the preflop raiser.

Cop a Moneymaker. To parlay an online satellite into major realworld poker tournament triumph.

Destination Satellite. An online tournament where the prize for winning is entry into a realworld tournament.

Dondo. Small-minded, stupid, weak, loose, or silly.

Double Dip. To play two games online at the same time.

Drag. To slow play a big hand.

Fakiac. A fake maniac; someone who seems to be out of control but isn't.

Felted. Taken down to the felt, put all in, or busted.

FNL. Fast 'n' loose, an aggressive, tricky style of play.

Fold Equity. The extra value associated with betting draws, given that you sometimes win the pot without a fight.

Gamnesia. A gambler's selective memory that tends to remember wins and forget losses.

Gogglebox. Opinionated and ill-informed.

Gulp Limit. The minimum amount of money you can put into a poker game or tournament such that losing it would cause you psychic pain.

Hit or git. A strategy for playing speculative hands requiring sufficient discipline to fold when you miss the flop.

Hoover. A small bet with a big hand, intended to induce a call.

Image Equity. The contribution that an aggressive stance makes to your image, even if the sum outcome of your preflop raises is break even.

Kosher. Straightforward, predictable play or player.

Limpede. A stampede of limpers, such that even good hands don't feel comfortable raising, for the field is too large.

Limpet. A flat call, especially if one in a series of limps.

Limpfest. A game with lots of callers and few raisers.

Little Poison. Starting cards lower than eight.

Lunken. Like a drunken lunkhead.

Make Book. To record and store information on online players.

Milked. Tempted by a series of small bets into calling off a lot of chips against a made hand.

Min Raise. Minimum raise; the smallest legal bump.

NLHE. Standard acronym for no limit hold'em.

Nous. Intelligence, skill, or capability; deep understanding of the game.

NTCS. Next Two Card Syndrome; the buzz of anticipation that accompanies waiting for the deal.

Orphan Flop. A ragged, low flop just looking to be adopted.

Outs. Outstanding (as in live) cards that will complete one's hand.

Package Hands. Middle suited connectors, added to one's "package of raising hands" for the sake of variety and deception.

Poker Porn. Poker on television; so called because watching it does nothing so much as make you want to do it.

Real Estate Raise. A steal attempt from late position.

ROI. Return on investment, a simple way of expressing pot odds; for example, pot odds of 3 to 1 offer a 3-1 ROI.

RTB. Raise, then bet, another way of expressing *continuation bet*.

QFM. Quick flush mode, the astoundingly swift loss of bankroll characteristic to an online poker losing streak.

Sitngo. "Sit and go"; a tournament that starts as soon as all the seats at the table are filled.

Slackjaw. Pejorative term for opponent or foe.

Sniffers. Poker software programs that track and analyze online play.

Squeeze Raise. An overbet designed to intimidate foes into folding.

Squiz. Quick look or glance.

Stealth Ace. An ace on board that's utterly invisible to someone holding pocket kings.

Test Tube Baby. A poker player with only, or largely, online poker experience.

Timmy. Timid player.

Trouty. Fishlike; weak.

Up-Down. A starting hand that's split high and low, like K-3 or Q-4.

Variation Raise. A raise made with substandard cards for the sake of mixing up one's play; see *package hands*.

Wally. Cally Wally; a loose, passive player.

Wheelhouse. Cards between ten and ace.

Whiff. A flop that completely misses a player's hand.